ENDORSEMENTS

"Gripping! I could not put it down! It is also most disturbing, for Ryken argues that most modern Bible translations sell their readers short. They are not exact enough, and their style is not right for reading aloud or memorization. Everyone considering the choice of a Bible translation for use in private study or public worship should read this book. It will help you distinguish the wheat from the chaff."

—GORDON WENHAM, Professor of Old Testament
University of Gloucestershire, UK

"What is at stake here is huge! Our children and grandchildren will rise up and call Dr. Ryken blessed, if his words (!) will be read and heeded by this generation. How odd to live in a time when biblical scholars labor over the very words of Scripture (in Hebrew, Aramaic, and Greek) to understand Scripture's meaning, and at the same time many of the same biblical scholars endorse a translation theory of the Bible in which the 'ideas' or 'concepts' of Scripture are used for translating Scripture's meaning in another language. Ryken's *Word of God in English* demonstrates clearly and forcefully that the widespread practice of 'dynamic equivalence' in translation takes us away from the path of careful, accurate, faithful rendering of the very words of God for English readers."

—BRUCE A. WARE, Senior Associate Dean
School of Theology
The Southern Baptist Theological Seminary, Louisville, KY

"A masterful and convincing argument for literal, that is to say, transparent translation of the Holy Scriptures."

—DR. J. I. PACKER, Professor of Theology
Regent College, Vancouver, B.C.

"Brilliantly convincing! This book stands alone on the subject of English Bible translation. Dropped into the muddy water of English versions, this tablet brings instant clarity, revealing how anything other than a literal translation undermines the Word of God. That serious charge is carefully established and proven page after page. May our Lord give Dr. Ryken a loud voice, so as to rescue many from versions that diminish the glory of divine revelation by being more concerned with the human reader than the divine author."

—PASTOR JOHN MACARTHUR
Grace Community Church, Sun Valley, CA

"This is a very important book. The persistent, detonating logic of Lee Ryken's pen will educate and convince any fair-minded person that the primary Bible for study and preaching must be an essentially literal translation."

—DR. R. KENT HUGHES, Pastor
College Church, Wheaton, IL

"Ryken's winsome and unanswerable arguments are the best I have ever read. He carries the day for the 'essentially literal' method for translation of God's Word in English."

—DR. NEIL NIELSON, President
Covenant College, Lookout Mountain, GA

"Not all Bible translations are the same, and they are not all equally excellent! In a courageous book that challenges much modern thinking, Professor Ryken draws on decades of experience in teaching literature to college students to show that many modern English translations fail to meet accepted standards of excellence in accuracy, faithfulness to the words of the author, clarity, vividness, concreteness, preservation of metaphor, preservation of ambiguity, preservation of verbal interconnections, respect for the principles of poetry, theological precision, retention of the world of the biblical text, retention of multi-layered meaning, respect for the abilities of the reader, effective rhythm, and beauty of expression.

"Ryken gives us reason for deep concern about the present 'destabilized' text of English Bibles, in which nobody in a Bible study can be sure what a verse says because many modern translations have failed to translate the author's very words and have given us instead their own varied and often watered-down interpretations of the author's thoughts. Ryken calls for a return to the historic principles used by the 'essentially literal' translations that may vary slightly in wording but preserve substantial agreement on the meanings of most of the words.

"I predict that after you read this book your eyes and ears will be opened to read and hear every translation of the Bible with a level of insight and understanding that you never had before."

—DR. WAYNE GRUDEM, Research Professor of Bible
and Theology, Phoenix Seminary, Scottsdale, AZ

"I highly recommend this book. It is my hope that it will convince many that there is scarcely any greater need in the church today than for an essentially literal translation."

—G. I. WILLIAMSON, *New Horizons* Magazine

"An important book—one for which many have long waited. Ryken's central thesis . . . is ably and repeatedly defended, cutting through the fog generated by debates over contemporary Bible translation philosophy. His chapters on 'Common Fallacies of Translation' are worth the price of the book on their own."

—DR. W. BINGHAM HUNTER, Pastor of Adult Ministries
Harvest Bible Chapel, Rolling Meadows, IL

"An ideal guide to choosing a translation of the Word that transcends trendy words. In the process, he implicitly indicts those who settle for less."

—DR. MARVIN OLASKY, Editor-in-Chief, *World* Magazine

"The best single-volume survey of these critical issues, offering a perspective that is both unique and invaluable. I found it so interesting I could not stop reading it."

—REV. PAUL T. MCCAIN, Interim President
Concordia Publishing House, St. Louis, MO

"A sensible and crucial call to count on and relish a Bible translation that stays as close as possible to the original words God inspired. How refreshing to hear this new voice in the translation debate—from a distinguished professor of English literature who is a lover of words and of the inspired words of Scripture."

—DR. KATHLEEN BUSWELL NIELSON
Writer and Bible Study Teacher

". . . my most important read of the century—or, for that matter, of the millennium. . . . [Ryken's book] may do more to change how you view the Bible (and how you read it) than any book, preacher, professor, or other influence you have ever had. . . . Leland Ryken devastates the dynamic-equivalent position. Systematically, comprehensively, repetitively, he argues in such convincing fashion that I predict you will never again be satisfied with a translation of the Bible that is even mildly 'dynamic.' . . . It will increase your wonder for the very words God has used. It will draw you into closer personal fellowship with God Himself."

—JOEL BELZ, Chairman, *World* Magazine

Other Books by Leland Ryken

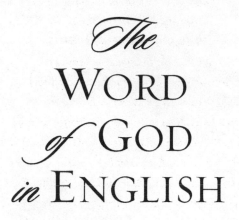

The WORD *of* GOD *in* ENGLISH

CRITERIA *for* EXCELLENCE *in* BIBLE TRANSLATION

LELAND RYKEN

CROSSWAY BOOKS

A DIVISION OF
GOOD NEWS PUBLISHERS
WHEATON, ILLINOIS

For
Lane and Ebeth Dennis

The Word of God in English

Copyright © 2002 by Leland Ryken

Published by Crossway Books
      A division of Good News Publishers
      1300 Crescent Street
      Wheaton, Illinois

Cover design: Josh Dennis

Cover photo: Getty Images

First printing, 2002

Printed in the United States of America

Library of Congress Cataloging-in-Publication Data
Ryken, Leland.
   The Word of God in English : criteria for excellence in Bible translation / Leland Ryken.
      p. cm.
   Includes bibliographical references.
   ISBN 1-58134-464-3 (TPB : alk. paper)
   1. Bible—Translating. 2. Bible. English—Versions—History.
I. Title.
BS449 .R95   2002
220.5'2—dc21   2002013925

BP		13	12	11	10	09	08	07	06	05	04
15	14	13	12	11	10	9	8	7	6	5	4	3

CONTENTS

PART FIVE
CRITERIA FOR EXCELLENCE IN AN ENGLISH BIBLE

ABBREVIATIONS

ASV	American Standard Version
CEV	Contemporary English Version
ESV	English Standard Version
GNB	Good News Bible
Jerusalem	Jerusalem Bible
KJV	King James Version
NASB	New American Standard Bible
NEB	New English Bible
NIV	New International Version
NIVI	Inclusive Language New International Version
NKJV	New King James Version
NLT	New Living Translation
NRSV	New Revised Standard Version
REB	Revised English Bible
RSV	Revised Standard Version
RV	Revised Version
SEB	Simple English Bible
TNIV	Today's New International Version

PREFACE

THIS BOOK HAS AS its purpose to define the translation principles that make for the best English Bible translation. My project began as an assessment of English translations from the perspective of literary criteria. The scope then broadened to include as many of the issues involved in Bible translation as a short book would allow.

My own expertise is as a literary critic, not as an expert in translation theory. Far from disqualifying me from writing on the topic of translation theory, my literary orientation allows light to fall from a new angle. The Bible is a written document that obeys the rules of literary discourse at every turn. A narrowly focused linguistic approach to translation has often lost sight of larger literary principles, and part of my project has been to reintroduce those principles into the discussion of English Bible translation. To anticipate one of the main emphases of this book, any translation theory that consistently violates how we deal with literary texts and the discourses of everyday life cannot be the right theory.

My discussion occurs within a current debate about translation theory, and I will be forthright in positioning myself in the debate. Dynamic equivalent Bibles have had the field to themselves for the past half century. The tenets of dynamic equivalency are so firmly entrenched that I have repeatedly found people to be incredulous that anyone would not accept dynamic equivalency as an axiom. I do not accept it as an axiom, and in fact I have never been favorably impressed by dynamic equivalent translations at the levels of either content or style. Until recently my resistance was based on literary intuitions.

Having served on the translation committee for the English Standard Version, I gradually came to a deeper understanding of why I found most modern translations lacking. This book articulates the understanding that I have reached about a variety of translation issues. I did not set out to defend the essentially literal theory of translation. I began with the question of what principles should govern what we do with written texts. On the basis of that inquiry, I ended with a belief that only an essentially literal translation of the Bible can achieve sufficiently high standards in terms of literary criteria and fidelity to the original text. Concomitantly, I have ended with a deep-seated distrust of how dynamic equivalent translations treat the biblical text.

By an essentially literal translation I do not mean one that renders the original text so literally as to be incomprehensible to English readers. The syntax must be English rather than Hebrew or Greek, and idioms that are incomprehensible to English readers need to be rendered in terms of meaning rather than literal equivalence. But within the parameters of these necessary deviations from the original, an essentially literal translation applies the same rules as we expect from a published text in its original language: The author's own words are reproduced, figurative language is retained instead of explained, and stylistic features and quirks of the author are allowed to stand as the author expressed them.

While my purpose is thus partly polemical, I want to record my respect for people and translators who come down on the other side of the issue. I believe that their translation theory has done damage to the biblical text that English-speaking readers have at their disposal, but at the same time I want to acknowledge that modern translations have been widely used for good. I believe that there is a place for a range of Bible translations, including children's Bibles and Bible paraphrases. My subject in this book is what constitutes the *best* Bible for English-speaking people and serious students of the Bible, and also for the English-speaking church as a body. If at points I record my dismay over modern trends in Bible translation, it is safe to assume that the disagreement that exists between my position and the rival position is mutual, with parties on both sides equally convinced of the rightness of their own position and the wrongness of the alternate position. In this book I have articulated a position that needs to be aired precisely because it is a less visible position in a debate of which the general public is scarcely aware. Indeed, the average reader of the English Bible is ignorant of rival translation theories and of how much has been lost and changed from the original text in most modern translations.

A final clarification that I wish to make is that my topic is English Bible translation for English-speaking readers. I am not qualified to theorize about the difficulties of translating the Bible into foreign languages for members of non-Western cultures. I leave it to others to consider how the principles set forth in this book might affect translation of the Bible into other languages for other cultures.

I wish to record my gratitude to the scholars who critiqued my manuscript and spared me from dozens of follies and infelicities: Jack Collins, Lane Dennis, Philip Ryken, Ray Van Leeuwen, and Dennis Zaderaka.

INTRODUCTION:
THE CURRENT DEBATE ABOUT
BIBLE TRANSLATION

MY AIM IN THIS introduction is to establish a context for the analysis of contemporary Bible translation theory and practice that is the focus of the book as a whole. I propose to briefly sketch the state of Bible translation for the past fifty years, to suggest what I think is happening currently, and to situate myself in the current debate about what constitutes the best theory of English Bible translation.

THE CONTEXT OF THE DEBATE: BIBLE TRANSLATION FOR THE PAST HALF CENTURY

As I will show in a chapter devoted to the history of English Bible translation, a seismic shift in translation theory and practice occurred in the middle of the twentieth century. Up to that point, most English Bible translations had operated on the premise that the task of English Bible translation was to reproduce the words of the original in the words of the receptor language. Accuracy of translation took precedence over literary style, though compared to modern colloquial translations, it seems from our viewpoint that literary beauty was still accorded a very high position. Certainly dignity and relative formality of language and syntax prevailed.

The person who almost single-handedly changed the course of English Bible translation was Eugene Nida, who championed his theory of "dynamic equivalence." This theory was first introduced by Nida in the mid-twentieth century. Briefly stated, the theory of dynamic equivalence in Bible translation emphasizes *the reaction of the reader* to the translated text, rather than *the translation of the words and phrases themselves.* In simplest terms, dynamic equivalence is often referred to as "thought for thought" translation as compared to "essentially literal" translation (for more on these terms, see the end of this chapter).

The impetus for Nida's theory of dynamic equivalence was his work as a foreign missionary and transcultural Bible translator. Once Nida and his colleagues had formulated their theory of dynamic equivalence, it seemed natural to carry over the same principles as were used for translation into newly discovered languages to the task of translating the Bible into the long-established English language. This is highly significant. In my view, much more thought should have been given to whether translation into the English language—a language in which the Bible had become almost a native book—should follow the same ground rules that prevailed with languages that had just been reduced to an alphabet and written form. It was the apparently automatic carryover of translation practices designed for newly emerging languages to English translation that has had such a deleterious effect on the course of English Bible translation. It is not too much to say that the English Bible had become so familiar to English-speaking Christians (and even cultured non-Christians) that it never seemed foreign until a steady diet of dynamic equivalent translations weaned readers away from the King James tradition.

While I do not believe that Nida's theories would have been sufficient of themselves to turn the tide in English Bible translation, I do wish to acknowledge the extraordinary energy with which Nida pursued his vision as he published numerous books, introductions, and essays. Although I believe that Nida's influence on English Bible translation has been, on balance, negative, depriving current Bible readers of the Bible they need, I nonetheless admire his passion for Bible translation and the scholarly rigor that he brought to the task.

If Nida's influence is not what accounts for the dominance of dynamic equivalent translations today, what does? The current hegemony flowed from two landmark translations based on dynamic equivalence principles. They were The Living Bible, a paraphrase published in 1971, and the New International Version (NIV), published in 1978. While a changing philosophy of translation may have provided the platform for these English Bibles, the way in which they took the evangelical world by storm can be explained at least partly by the cultural trends that coincided with their appearance and that almost guaranteed their success. Before I note the cultural trends that helped both translations, I need to note a crucial difference between them. The Living Bible won its own way as a populist, grassroots success story. The NIV, by contrast, was a triumph of modern public relations and marketing strategy, as representatives from all possible denominations and organizations were deployed in the translation process and as celebrities endorsed the new translation. (I particularly remember an advertisement featuring a seated athlete with a stadium in the background, telling the world that he enjoyed reading the NIV.)

A partial list of cultural forces that paved the way for the triumph of dynamic equivalent Bibles in the 1970s includes these:

• a lack of other alternatives to the King James Bible at a time when the latter was badly showing its age and had become culturally obsolete with its archaic language and deficient scholarship (the RSV might have become the accepted alternative but was shunned as a theologically liberal translation);

• an antiestablishment and antitraditional spirit that welcomed translations that seemed novel and modern (an unconventional Bible was automatically preferred to a traditional one among many evangelicals);

• a loss of appreciation for, or even ability to recognize, literary excellence;

• a new preference for colloquialism over formality in written discourse (perhaps an outgrowth of literary realism); 2

• evangelistic zeal, accompanied by a pragmatic outlook that endorsed whatever religious materials produced the most conversions;

• a consumer-oriented and Gallup poll mentality that led translators and publishers to give readers what they wanted (the "target audience" mentality);

• a general laziness that has increasingly resulted in an obsession with making virtually all pursuits, including Bible reading, easy;

• new marketing techniques that could appeal to target markets (and that could eventually package "niche Bibles" for specific market groups);

• a narcissistic cultural orientation that elevated the reader rather than the author or text to center stage in the reading process (in dynamic equivalence theory, the reader reigns, a view that came into vogue simultaneously with the triumph of reader-response literary theory).

To offer reasons for the sudden popularity of dynamic equivalent translations does not by itself render them illegitimate. It only serves as a caution against an easy assumption that their popularity proves their superiority. I myself believe that English Bible translation took a wrong turn in the second half of the twentieth-century, spurred by certain cultural forces rather than correct translation principles.

For the last three decades, dynamic equivalent translations have had the world of English Bible translation and the English Bible market pretty much to themselves, though I find that laypeople generally do not realize this. Even in the scholarly world, there is some confusion regarding the NIV, which one source incorrectly places in the "verbal equivalence" category.[1] Ray Van Leeuwen rightly says that "if you read a Bible translated in the last half-century, you probably read a Bible influenced by Nida."[2]

During the past half century, there have, indeed, been many Bible readers and scholars who resisted the trend and were unhappy with the dominance of dynamic equivalence theory and practice, but they lacked an organized voice and had no genuine alternative to The Living Bible and the NIV until the publication of the English Standard Version (ESV) in 2001. (I recall reading a review of two books devoted to criticizing the NIV that dismissed the books with the comment that their criticisms, though largely true, were irrelevant because the authors could not point to an adequate alternative to the NIV.) Some of those unhappy with dynamic equivalent translations resisted the times by individually using the New American Standard Bible (NASB) and the Revised Standard Version (RSV), but their resistance had little public visibility. (I myself was surprised and pleased to learn, when I joined the ESV Translation Committee, about evangelical luminaries who had remained closet RSV people for three decades, as had I.)

THE BEGINNINGS OF CURRENT DEBATE

There are currently intimations of a countermovement. The old standby among essentially literal translations, the NASB, was reissued in 1995. The New Revised Standard Version (NRSV, 1990), even though it made the shift to dynamic equivalence, was an attempt to compete with the NIV. The newest English translation, the English Standard Version, is an essentially literal Bible in the King James tradition of fidelity to the original text and commitment to literary excellence. The Holman Christian Standard Bible, still in process, "seeks to provide a translation as close to the words of the Hebrew and Greek texts as possible" (preface).

In the realm of biblical scholarship, too, voices of discontent with dynamic equivalence are beginning to be heard, for example, at the annual meetings of the Evangelical Theological Society (ETS). From the time that I gave the NIV a negative review (in 1978) for its literary deficiencies,[3] I have never wavered in my negative assessment of it; but until I served on a Bible translation committee I lacked the expertise fully to understand *why* my literary intuitions told me that dynamic equivalent translations were inferior. As I was in the process of codifying my objections, I was influenced by a dissertation criticizing Eugene Nida's translation theory.[4]

Although I had formulated the basic position I develop in this book as early as 2000,[5] I subsequently found a kindred spirit in biblical scholar Ray Van Leeuwen, who is much more expert in specialized scholarship than I am and whose outstanding writing on the subject is a good complement to what I attempt in this book.[6] Van Leeuwen believes that dynamic equivalent translations have "made it more difficult for English readers to know what the Bible actually said," and that "we need an up-to-date translation that is more transparent to the original languages."

Other voices of objection are also beginning to appear. The title of one scholarly article sounds the keynote: "Modern English Bible Versions as a Problem for the Church."[7] Y. C. Whang, weighing the question of whether a Bible translator is responsible to the author or the reader, concludes that Nida's "new criteria for translation are . . . untenable."[8] The general drift of a specialized book on translation and relevance is that dynamic equivalent translations have been unable to deliver on their claims to have successfully communicated the meaning of the original.[9] D. A. Carson has written critically about the "limits of dynamic equivalence in Bible translation,"[10] and two books have been critical of the results of dynamic equivalency in the NIV.[11] Among evangelical Bible scholars I find a growing discontent with the dynamic equivalent tradition in general and the NIV, TNIV, and NLT in particular.

I need to be suitably modest in these claims. The NIV remains the dominant evangelical translation, and the NLT has enjoyed a large circulation. The debate is still in its very early stages. This book is my contribution to the debate. I need to underscore that I began my pilgrimage innocent of the context that I have outlined in this chapter. When I was told, upon joining the ESV Translation Committee as its literary stylist, that the new translation was to be an essentially literal translation, I had no conception of what that meant, and I knew nothing about the rival translation theory. My quest had always been simply to delineate the right criteria for excellence in translation and to assess translations by those criteria.

As I pursued my quest to its logical conclusion, I ended up where I had not envisioned—with a wholehearted defense of essentially literal translations in the King James tradition, and as a critic of dynamic equivalence. This book represents the fruits of my labor. I have written in an awareness that many evangelicals will not agree with me, but that has not dampened my enthusiasm for an essentially literal English Bible that preserves both the accuracy and literary excellence of the great tradition of English Bible translation.

DEFINING THE TERMS OF THE DEBATE

Before concluding this chapter, I need to define a number of terms that I will be using throughout this book. The crucial terms, which have been current for only half a century, are these:

• *Receptor language*: the language into which a text written in a foreign language is translated.

• *Native language*: the original language in which a text is written.

• *Dynamic equivalent*: a meaning in the receptor language that corresponds to (is "equivalent" to) a meaning in a native-language text (for example, the "heart" as the modern way of denoting the essence of a person, especially the emotions, which for the ancients was situated in the kidneys).

• *Dynamic equivalence*: a theory of translation based on the premise that whenever something in the native-language text is foreign or unclear to a contemporary reader, the original text should be translated in terms of a dynamic equivalent.

• *Functional equivalent*: something in the receptor language that differs from what the original text says but that serves the same function in the receptor language (for example, "firstfruits" translated as "special offering").

• *Functional equivalence*: a theory of translation that favors replacing a statement in the original text with a functional equivalent whenever the original phraseology or reference is obscure for a modern reader in the receptor language.

• *Equivalent effect*: a translation that aims to produce the same effect on readers of the translation as the original text produced on its native-language readers.

• *Formal equivalence*: a theory of translation that favors reproducing the form or language of the original text, and not just its meaning. In its stricter form, this theory of translation espouses reproducing even the syntax and word order of the original; the formulas *word for word translation* and *verbal equivalence* often imply this stricter definition of the concept.

• *Essentially literal translation*: a translation that strives to translate the exact words of the original-language text in a translation, but not in such a rigid way as to violate the normal rules of language and syntax in the receptor language.

• *Transparent text*: this means two opposite things, and for that very reason I will use this phrase very sparingly, though in the broader world of Bible translation it is common. A text is *transparent to the modern or contemporary reader* when it is immediately understandable in the receptor language; this is the goal of dynamic equivalent translations. A translation is *transparent to the original text* when it reproduces the language, expressions, and customs of the original text; this is the goal of an essentially literal translation.

This whole cluster of terms was apparently unknown until the middle of the twentieth century, which in itself tells us much about Bible translation through the centuries and about developments in the last half century. I will use only two of the concepts defined above regularly. I will refer to Bible translations that follow the theory of dynamic equivalence as *dynamic equivalent Bibles* or (as a variant) *dynamic equivalent translations*. I will refer to translations based on the attempt to translate the very words of the original text as *essentially literal translations*. Although the term *functional equivalent* is in the process of replacing the designation *dynamic equivalent*, it is less accurate to designate the range of topics that I cover in this book.

NOTES

1   Alec Gilmore, *A Dictionary of the English Bible and Its Origins* (Sheffield: Academic Press, 2000), 176. That the NIV has been somewhat slippery is suggested by Gilmore's listing as one of the NIV's "weaknesses" that "it is very literal" and yet claiming that it is "not really a verbal equivalence translation" (118).

2   Raymond C. Van Leeuwen, "We Really Do Need Another Bible Translation," *Christianity Today*, October 22, 2001, 29.

3   Leland Ryken, "The Literary Merit of the New International Version," *Christianity Today*, October 20, 1978, 16-17.

4   Anthony Howard Nichols, "Translating the Bible: A Critical Analysis of E. A. Nida's Theory of Dynamic Equivalence and Its Impact Upon Recent Bible Translations," dissertation, University of Sheffield, 1996.

5   Leland Ryken, "Criteria for Literary Excellence in an English Bible Translation," address at the annual meeting of the Evangelical Theological Society, Nashville, November 14, 2000.

6   Raymond C. Van Leeuwen, "On Bible Translation and Hermeneutics," in *After Pentecost: Language and Biblical Interpretation*, eds. Craig Bartholomew et al (Grand Rapids, MI: Zondervan, 2001), 284-311; "We Really Do Need Another Bible Translation," 28-35.

7   James Barr, "Modern English Bible Versions as a Problem for the Church," *Quarterly Review* 14 (1994): 263-278.

8   Y. C. Whang, "To Whom Is a Translator Responsible—Reader or Author?" in *Translating the Bible: Problems and Prospects*, eds. Stanley E. Porter and Richard S. Hess (Sheffield: Sheffield Academic Press, 1999), 46-62.

9   Ernst-august Gutt, *Translation and Relevance: Cognition and Context* (Oxford: Blackwell, 1991).

10 D. A. Carson, "The Limits of Dynamic Equivalence in Bible Translation," *Evangelical Review of Theology*, July 1985, 200-213. Carson's statement that "dynamic equivalence has won the day—and rightly so" (10) strikes me as a *non sequitur* to the rest of his article.

11 Robert P. Martin, *Accuracy of Translation and the New International Version: The Primary Criterion in Evaluating Bible Versions* (Carlisle, PA: Banner of Truth, 1989); Earl D. Radmacher and Zane C. Hodges, *The NIV Reconsidered: A Fresh Look at a Popular Translation* (Dallas: Redención Viva, 1990).

PART ONE

*Lessons from
Overlooked Sources*

1

LESSONS FROM LITERATURE

I WANT TO BEGIN my analysis far from the act of translating. I intend initially simply to look at what it is like to read and write in the everyday conduct of life. Once we have considered reading and writing in principle, I think it will be obvious that translation in the last half century has taken liberties with the biblical text that would be rejected out of hand in the ordinary world of reading and writing.

The Bible is a written book and as such shares certain qualities with other books. This is not to deny that the Bible is unique, having been inspired by God in a way that other books are not. In format, though, the Bible is an anthology of diverse literary writings, similar to other anthologies. The writers of the Bible themselves signal their awareness of literary genres (types of writing) by referring with technical precision to such forms as chronicle, psalm, song, proverb, parable, apocalypse, and many others. In keeping with the nature of the Bible itself, therefore, there is much that we can learn about how to handle the Bible in translation by paying attention to how we treat literary texts beyond the Bible. If anything, our reverence for the biblical text should be higher than the respect we accord to Shakespeare and Hawthorne.

It will be evident at once that I write as someone who teaches literature and writes literary criticism. While this does not make me an expert on translation theory, it allows me to scrutinize Bible translation from a fresh angle. One of the problems with Bible translation for the last half century is that it has been an "in-group" project in which linguistic specialists have done their work in a self-contained world. They have not been held accountable by scholars in other disciplines. This chapter is my attempt to cast a critical eye at what I regard as license in Bible translation and to call us back to views of translation that once prevailed.

ON HAVING GREAT EXPECTATIONS WHEN YOU READ

Picture yourself settling down to read a novel or short story. It is a weekend refuge. You are settled into a comfortable chair or your bed, and you are in fact "lost in a book." The scenario is so common and seemingly straightforward that we are unaware of the assumptions and implied promises that govern the transaction.

What do we assume when we sit down to read, let us say, *Great Expectations* by Charles Dickens? We assume that the words in the book in our hands are the words that Dickens himself wrote. This is a good-faith promise that the publisher has in effect made when it put Dickens's name on the cover and title page. The words and descriptions and humor that we come to love in this novel forge a bond between us and Dickens. In a very real sense, the two of us are engaged in a conversation, with no one else intruding. In the words of one expert on hermeneutics, "The goal of reading is . . . a meeting of the minds of author and reader."[1]

We not only trust that the author has been fairly represented to us; we also implicitly trust the text—the words on the page. When Dickens describes the hero's return to his hometown after a shallow life of idleness in the city of London, he conducts the description superbly. The protagonist returns to his town of origin hoping to marry someone he had scorned when he was a rich young man bent on being socially respectable. Here is the classic paragraph:

> The June weather was delicious. The sky was blue, the larks were soaring high over the green corn, I thought all that country-side more beautiful and peaceful by far than I had ever known it to be yet. Many pleasant pictures of the life I would lead there, and of the change for the better that would come over my character when I had a guiding spirit at my side whose simple faith and clear home-wisdom I had proved, beguiled my way. They awakened a tender emotion in me; for, my heart was softened by my return, and such a change had come to pass, that I felt like one who was toiling home barefoot from distant travel, and whose wanderings had lasted many years.[2]

Every time I read this passage, my imagination soars, and even a religious sense is awakened in me. This is vintage Dickens, I tell myself.

Now consider a second scenario. An editor has decided that the picture of Pip walking home barefoot is too foreign to most modern readers' experience to resonate with them. Suppose further that the editor has decided that references to "distant travel" and "wanderings" are "not the way we would say it." So the editor has dropped the references that he thinks archaic and has made the passage read simply, "I felt like someone returning home who had been gone for many years." By eliminating the references to "toiling home barefoot from distant travel" and "wanderings [that] had lasted many years" the editor has, of course, wiped out the evocative allusion to Jesus' parable of the prodigal son.

How would we feel if we had been given the modernized edition of the novel? Would it make any difference? If we were familiar with the correct text, would we not feel cheated, and would we not protest at the reductionism represented by the deletion of the allusion to the parable and the loss of evocative language in favor of prosaic language? Of course we would object.

Alternately, suppose the altered text were the edition in which we first read the novel. Suppose additionally that we later read the novel that Dickens wrote. Would we feel a sense of betrayal at what had been offered to us as Dickens's novel but which was in fact quite different from what Dickens had written? I think we would feel that we had been deceived when we had read the altered text. We would also feel in regard to the altered text that an editor had interposed himself or herself between us and Charles Dickens. We had thought that we were meeting the author face to face by the medium of the author's own words, and it turns out that we were not. We were meeting an editor instead, and no matter how much we like editors, they are not the people we expect to meet when someone else is the author.

Slings and Arrows, or Trials and Tribulations?

Words are even more inviolable with poetry than with prose. So I want to take the time to consider another hypothetical reading experience, this time with poetry. Imagine that you have recently seen a performance of Shakespeare's *Hamlet*. You are so caught up in the experience that you decide to read parts of the actual script. Surely any edition of the play is as good as any other one, you think; so you open the one that you found in the local library to the famous "to be or not to be" soliloquy. Here is what you read:

To be, or not to be; that is what really matters.
Is it nobler to accept passively
the trials and tribulations that unjust fate sends,
or to resist an ocean of troubles.[3]

This does not sound quite right. In fact, it is far removed from what you know the speech is supposed to be. Would this bother you? Would you shrug it off, perhaps saying to yourself that you had never thought of the text in this way before? Or would you be sufficiently unsettled that you would ferret out an edition of what Shakespeare actually wrote?

I hope that you would be sufficiently discontent that you would track down the speech in an unaltered edition of Shakespeare. If you did, this is what you would find:

To be, or not to be—that is the question:
Whether 'tis nobler in the mind to suffer
The slings and arrows of outrageous fortune
Or to take arms against a sea of troubles.[4]

Would you say that it makes any difference which of the two versions you read? Of course you would. Would you look upon the first version as being Shakespeare's play? No, you would not. If you were planning to write a piece of commentary on the play—in other words, engage in serious study—would you use the first version? You would not, for the simple reason that you know that it is not what Shakespeare actually wrote. To use the first text as the basis for serious commentary on the play is unthinkable.

Does the paraphrase have any usefulness? Yes, it does. It is useful as a gloss or interpretation on difficult words. In my thinking, this is the usefulness of dynamic equivalent translations of the Bible that claim to convey the meaning but not necessarily the words of the original. But this hints at the chief problem of dynamic equivalent Bibles: They arrogate to translation something that should be left to interpretation and commentary. Whenever a translation abandons translation for interpretation and commentary, it impedes a reader's access to the actual words of a biblical author.

But what about archaic language in a text that comes to us from the past? Or, if not archaic language, then simply difficult words and figurative language? The practice in high school and college literature courses is clear: Teachers explain passages or rely on footnotes in scholarly editions to clue students in. In other words, they initiate students and readers into the meaning of the text, helping them to understand and enjoy the full richness of a text from the past. They do not alter the text itself.

To underscore what I have said about poetry, I offer another example. John Donne wrote a famous sonnet on what it feels like to believe in the immortality of the soul. The two opening lines are these:

> *Death, be not proud, though some have called*
> *Thee mighty and dreadful, for thou art not so.*

The eloquence and forcefulness of these lines depend on their being other-than-ordinary. We can note specifically the use of apostrophe (direct address to an absent being as though it were present), personification, exalted diction, and archaism. If we were to apply the principles of dynamic equivalence and colloquialism to the text as some translators do to the Bible, we end up with this:

> *Don't be proud, death. You're not as great as*
> *some people think you are.*

Do these lines communicate the same thing as the lines Donne wrote? Would Donne's poem continue to be read if it were reduced to prosaic prose? The answer to both questions is no, which explains why the world at large (and not just literary experts) would not tolerate this kind of tampering with the original. Changing Donne's lines as I have done above does not, of course, involve translation from one language into another, but it illustrates *the kind of* distortion that is done consistently in dynamic equivalent translations.

How Do Writers Feel about Their Texts?

Thus far I have viewed the matter of preserving the integrity of a text from the viewpoint of readers. But equally instructive is how writers typically view what they have written. When *you* write something, do you feel a right to protect the integrity of what you have written? More specifically, consider how you would feel if a transcriber decided to do the following things to something that you had painstakingly and consciously composed:

• reduced the level of vocabulary from what you had written to what the translator regarded as a seventh-grade vocabulary level;

 • cut your sentences down into a series of shorter sentences;

 • dropped metaphors because he decided that a target audience did not know how to handle figurative language;

 • changed words that he thought to be old-fashioned;

 • eliminated words that he thought to be technical;

 • changed words to match what he thought you had intended to say.

Do changes like these bother writers? Of course they do. They are also the changes that many modern Bible translations make to the biblical text.

A TECHNICAL CONSIDERATION: CORRUPT TEXTS

Scholars who deal in a serious way with literary texts have a name for texts that do not correspond to the actual words of an author. Such a text is called a corrupt text. It is defined as a text that has been changed from its original and reliable form to something different from that standard. Technically the term is usually reserved for accidental errors made in the process of copying or transcription, but I am extending the concept to cover anything that produces the *effect* of such accidents—namely, a text that has been altered from the original, intentionally or unintentionally. Even deviations in punctuation and spelling are considered forms of corruption, though it is possible for a reliable edition of a text from the past to have its punctuation and spelling modernized.

What is never considered appropriate is to change the words themselves. If Shakespeare wrote, "When in disgrace with fortune and men's eyes," it would be a corruption of the text to make the last phrase read "people's eyes." If T. S. Eliot described a city landscape at twilight as "a patient etherized upon a table," a text that reads "like a patient on an operating table" would be considered unreliable. A version of the Gettysburg Address that begins "eighty-seven years ago" instead of "four score and seven years ago" would be written off as a corrupt text.

A LESSON FROM TEXTUAL EDITING

The positive counterpart to the negative phenomenon of textual corruption is the practice of establishing an accurate text. This is a formal discipline known as textual editing or textual criticism. One of the foremost twentieth-century authorities on textual criticism, Fredson Bowers, defined the aim of textual criticism as "the recovery of the initial purity of an author's text and of its revision . . . and the preservation of this purity despite the usual corrupting process of reprint transmission."[5] What is important in this stated aim is the premise that a writer's own words are the foundation for establishing a reliable written text, and that great care needs to be taken to protect a text from changes.

The standard source on textual criticism in the preceding century, James Thorpe's book *Principles of Textual Criticism*, concurs with the viewpoint of Bowers. How important is the idea of authorial intention to the reliability of a text? Just listen to three statements that Thorpe makes in a chapter entitled "The Ideals of Textual Criticism":

> The ideal of textual criticism is to present the text which the author intended.

> In my way of looking at textual criticism, its value derives only from serving the useful purpose of helping to present the text which the author intended.

> The ideal of textual criticism is to present the text which the author intended [the opening sentence of the chapter is repeated in the conclusion of the essay, suggesting how important it is].[6]

We can hardly miss the point: In establishing the reliability of a text, everything depends on whether the actual words of the author have been accurately preserved.

Biblical scholarship accepts this premise when dealing with the manuscripts of the Old and New Testaments in their original languages. I have not encountered a more impressive body of specialized knowledge than that which surrounds the collating of biblical texts in an effort to establish the most reliable version of the original text. The irony is that in some translation processes this care to preserve the original text is repeatedly and casually disregarded when translators turn the original into English. Words are changed, added, and deleted with apparent ease and frequency. Surely there should be some carryover of principle between the scrupulousness of attention to the actual words of the Bible in the original languages and the way in which that text is transcribed into English.

THE BOTTOM LINE

By now a picture has emerged of how virtually everyone deals with written texts intended for publication or other forms of public circulation. Here are the summary principles:

• The author's own words *matter*.

• Publishers and editors are not ordinarily allowed to change the words of literary texts.

• Readers expect to receive the actual words of an author.

• As changes in language make texts from bygone ages difficult, archaic, and even obsolete, readers are educated into the meanings of the words.

• Figurative language is not changed into direct statement but is preserved, with explanation and interpretation left to notes or commentary beyond the text.

• Authors expect their words to remain unaltered by publishers.

If these are the principles that prevail universally with literary texts, another set of questions naturally arises:

• Should we not treat the words and text of the Bible with the same respect that we show toward Shakespeare and Milton?

• Do not the very words of biblical authors deserve the same protection from alteration that authors ordinarily receive?

• Should we not expect readers to muster the same level of rigor for the Bible that they are expected to summon in high school and college literature courses?

My guess is that if the Bible had originally been written in English, there would be virtual unanimity on the answers to these questions. We would overwhelmingly resist attempts to tamper with the actual words of the Bible. After all, no one has produced editions of the original Hebrew and Greek manuscripts that alter the texts in the ways that many modern translations have done.

So we are brought face to face with the heart of the matter: *The process of translation has been used as the occasion to do all sorts of things with the Bible that we would never tolerate with literary documents as they exist in their original or native language.* The further question thus becomes, can a translation be credible when it does things with the Bible that are considered untenable and unnatural ways of handling untranslated written documents? My answer is that it cannot. Translation should not be the occasion for license. The ordinary rules of textual accuracy, integrity, and reliability still prevail. In fact, I would have thought that the Bible would be the *last* book with which people would take liberties.

Translators are not coauthors and editors. If we were to apply the principles of dynamic equivalence to a text by Dickens or Shakespeare, we would end up with two entirely different texts—one in which the literary features of the original are preserved and one in which the vocabulary has been changed to match the reading level of an audience, the figurative language has been interpreted or removed, interpretation has been intermingled, and archaic language and customs have been updated. This is a totally untenable situation.

The Most Basic Literary Principle of All

There is no more basic literary principle than that meaning is communicated through form. In the words of one literary theorist, "form is meaning."[7] The concept of form should be construed broadly here. It includes anything having to do with *how* content is expressed, including genre. The form of a story consists of such things as plot, setting, and character. The form of a poem consists of imagery and figures of speech. Form precedes and determines meaning. Without interacting with the "how" of an utterance, we cannot ascertain the "what." Before we can know what the parable of the prodigal son communicates, for example, we need to interact with a father and his sons, with a journey and a homecoming.

While most people readily acknowledge this principle of the primacy of form with such genres as stories and poems, it is easy to overlook something even more important: *The most basic of all literary forms through which meaning is conveyed is words.* There is no such thing as disembodied thought. Thought depends on words, and when we change the words, we change the thought. A literary critic has rightly said that "style *is* content; meaning subtly tilts from word to word, and each . . . word, sentence, paragraph depends upon every other part like the cunningly stressed beams leaning together without nails in the tower of the cathedral at Ely. Only by the use of certain words, these and no others, can the writer express his . . . way of seeing."[8]

While logic tells us that this is so, statements of writers confirm it. When a poet lamented his inability to write poetry even though he was "full of ideas," the French poet Mallarmé responded, "One does not make poetry with ideas but with *words*."[9] American poet Robert Frost was of the same opinion when he defined poetry as "a performance in words."[10] Literary effect depends on the very words of a writer. English poet Percy Shelley wrote, "It is impossible to read the compositions of the most celebrated writers of the present day without being startled with the electric life which burns within their words."[11]

When it comes to an understanding of how literature operates and of what is primary in the process of literary communication, writers can be trusted to know best. If they insist on the primacy of words, we can take their word for it. The relevance of this to translating the Bible is obvious: The Bible deserves the same respect for the words of the human authors and the divine Author that ordinary literature does. If we do not feel free to change the words of literary authors, we should not change the words of the biblical writers. Translation of course introduces an element of variability into the situation, so that we can debate whether this or that English word best captures the meaning of the original. But there remains a decisive difference between essentially literal translations that attempt to convey the exact meaning of the original *words* and other translations that do not feel obliged to reproduce the precise wording of the original.

NOTES

1   Kevin Vanhoozer, *Is There a Meaning in This Text?* (Grand Rapids, MI: Zondervan, 1998), 75. The context is Vanhoozer's summarizing of the interpretive theory of Georges Poulet.

2   I have quoted from Charles Dickens, *Great Expectations*, ed. Charlotte Mitchell (New York: Penguin, 1996), 477.

3   I have printed these lines from a parallel text edition, *Hamlet*, ed. John Richetti (New York: Simon and Schuster, 1975), 125.

4   The Pelican edition of *Hamlet*, ed. A. R. Braunmuller (New York: Penguin, 2001), 65.

5   Fredson Bowers, "Textual Criticism," in *The Aims and Methods of Scholarship in Modern Languages and Literatures*, ed. James Thorpe (New York: Modern Language Association, 1963), 24.

6   James Thorpe, *Principles of Textual Criticism* (San Marino, CA: Huntington Library, 1972), 50, 68, 79.

7   Cleanth Brooks, "The Formalist Critic," in *The Modern Critical Spectrum*, eds. Gerald Jay Goldberg and Nancy Marmer Goldberg (Englewood Cliffs, NJ: Prentice-Hall, 1962), 1. Marshall McLuhan's famous formula was, "the medium is the message."

8 Eleanor Cameron, "Into Something Rich and Strange: Of Dreams, Art, and the Unconscious," in *The Openhearted Audience*, ed. Virginia Haviland (Washington: Library of Congress, 1980), 173.

9 I have quoted Mallarmé from Paul Valéry, "Poetry, Language and Thought," in *The Modern Tradition: Backgrounds of Modern Literature*, eds. Richard Ellmann and Charles Feidelson, Jr. (New York: Oxford University Press, 1965), 77.

10 Robert Frost, quoted in Elizabeth Drew, *Poetry: A Modern Guide to Its Understanding and Enjoyment* (New York: Dell, 1959), 19.

11 Percy B. Shelley, *A Defence of Poetry*, in *Criticism: The Major Statements*, ed. Charles Kaplan (New York: St. Martin's, 1964), 380.

2

LESSONS FROM ORDINARY
DISCOURSE

IT IS BY NOW apparent that I am talking about principles of writing in isolation from their application to English Bible translation—or at least to specific English translations of specific Bible passages. There is a very good reason for my proceeding this way. I want to establish the principles of translation as objectively as possible, unclouded by partiality in favor of this or that Bible translation and to some degree unclouded by one's preference for one theory of Bible translation over another. For readers who may have begun to wonder how my discussion is relevant to English Bible translation, my reassurance is simple: Just keep reading, and you will see the relevance when I reach later stages of this book.

The previous chapter argued a point that virtually everyone will accept. It is that literary texts as the author put them into their final form are considered inviolate. All possible efforts are made, supported by a range of scholarly safeguards, to prevent alterations in the very words that an author wrote.

I can imagine someone's thinking that literature is a special case and that in more ordinary kinds of discourse we do not pay such rigid attention to the actual words of an utterance. It is the purpose of the present chapter to dispel this misconception. There are, indeed, everyday situations of reportage where deviation in an author's or speaker's actual words makes virtually no difference. As I hope to show, these situations are actually in the minority. In most everyday written or spoken utterances, it turns out, perhaps to our surprise, that we assign a different type of credibility to someone's actual words than we do to words that are someone else's report of the gist of what was said.

The previous chapter dealt with such formal-sounding matters as authorial intention and textual integrity. The present chapter deals with something much more informal. Here the focus is on the way in which precise wording counts for a lot, even when authorial intention and textual integrity might be non-issues.

The plan for the rest of this chapter is to look at a wide range of everyday written and spoken utterances, with a view toward ascertaining whether they require actual transcription of the exact words of a writer or speaker. Along the way, I will make generalized applications to Bible translation.

Heard a Good Joke or Riddle Lately?

When is a joke not a joke? When does an intended joke fall flat? To answer these questions, all you need to do is remember the last time that you or someone else tried to retell a joke without being able to remember the exact wording of the original. Without the right words, an intended joke becomes a total embarrassment. The gist of the joke's content may have been present, but unfortunately the gist of a joke will not deliver the proverbial goods.

Riddles present a similar case of the importance of exact and careful wording. Consider the riddle of the Sphinx in ancient Greek folklore: "What is it that walks on four feet, two feet, and three feet and has only one voice?" The answer, of course, is "man." Suppose a dynamic equivalent editor decided that this is not how people ordinarily talk and therefore renders the riddle colloquially: "What fits the following description? Sometimes it walks on four feet. At other times it walks on two feet. At still other times, it walks on three feet. In all three instances, it has one voice." What has happened to the original riddle? As it more closely approximates everyday discourse, it loses its punch and actually becomes harder rather than easier to follow.

What lesson lurks in the embarrassment of a joke that failed and the letdown in the riddle that lacks punch because the teller did not closely follow the precise wording of the original? The lesson is that in the everyday "lowbrow" genres of the joke and the riddle, the effect evaporates when the wording is changed.

A further question that we can ask is this: If exact wording matters in supposedly imprecise everyday discourse, would we expect precision to be more important or less important in the Word of Life?

LOVE LETTERS AND MARRIAGE VOWS

Anyone who has carried on a courtship by correspondence knows something of the hallowed genre known as love letters, loosely defined as any letter exchanged by two people in love. Are the very words important? Would a loose summary of sentiments carry the same weight? In a letter from the beloved, especially at critical points in a romance, exact words are crucial. The recipient of the letter pores over the words. He or she wants to read the whole letter. Exact nuances of phrasing can make or break a person's day.

And what about wedding vows? Couples often labor over selecting the exact wording of their vows, regardless of whether they are using an inherited ceremony or writing their own vows. The exact crafting of words needs to reflect a couple's view of marriage and their vision for their life together. How might a couple feel if the officiating pastor decided to change some of the wording to match what he thought was everyday language or in keeping with what he thought the couple's intention was? The couple would probably go into orbit.

Would we not say that the Bible is more like a love letter or marriage vow than an informal account of where a couple went on a date? Correspondingly, we should conclude that preservation of the exact words of biblical authors is very important.

LEGAL DOCUMENTS AND OFFICIAL REPORTS

Have you ever noticed how detailed most legal documents are? It takes a lawyer to figure them out. Why are exact terms so important in legal documents? They are important because they define the issues at stake. Casual terminology and approximate meaning are inadequate to the demands of language in these situations. Contract lawyer Douglas Colber, who has observed in his experience that "big outcomes in court cases regularly hinge on a few words in a contract or a few words in a statute," defines the importance of exact wording in contracts thus:

> Clear, precise language in contracts and laws . . . creates predictability. Contracts are designed to counterbalance the frailty of human memory. They are promises on which we rely to manage resources and relationships.[1]

This equation of a contract with predictability and promise is interesting terminology when we think of the Bible.

I recall an occasion when three out of four homes in my town of residence experienced flooding in their basements. Naturally rumors circulated about whether or not insurance would cover the damage. When I called my insurance company, everything hinged on (a) the exact description I gave of the source of the water in my basement and (b) the terms and definitions in the insurance contract. No matter how vivid the concept of "water in my basement" was to me, it was not sufficiently exact to suffice as the description of my problem. Similarly, whether or not I could receive reimbursement for the damage to my house depended on the exact wording of what was covered and what was excluded by my insurance policy.

Much of daily life is pervaded by specialized language where exactness is expected. To the ordinary person, *income* means "money received." To an accountant, it has a more precise meaning that may not entail the actual receipt of money. In some contexts of life, the loose definition of "income" will suffice, while in others it will not. So the question becomes, how precise do we think the content of the Bible is? Is the case of Galatians 3:16, where the entire argument hinges on the fact that an Old Testament word is singular rather than plural, an exceptional case, or does it project an aura over the entire way in which we view the words of Scripture?

And then there is the category of founding documents for an institution. The most venerable of such documents in the United States are the Constitution and the Bill of Rights. If you take the time to consult these documents, you will find that much of the language is remote from everyday discourse. Some of the words are archaic. The general style is exalted and eloquent, more poetic than prose-like. Do we respond to the difficulty of the language by simplifying the vocabulary and syntax? Do we replace the words of the original with more contemporary words? No. The wording of the documents is considered to be inviolate. The text is interpreted and rendered accessible through commentary, not through changing the original language.

Much the same is true of accident reports. Eventually they need to be in the actual words of the persons involved in the accident, or of eyewitnesses, and they must be in writing. An oral account to an investigating policeman will not suffice. Why not? Because it is not considered sufficiently permanent and reliable. We can return to written words. They are always there. They are the person's own official account of what happened. To change the wording of the person involved in the accident, even if the wording is awkward and the style unpolished, is unthinkable.

Richard Hassert, who is employed as a manager in business communications, has said that in his sphere communicating the general idea is sometimes sufficient, but usually it is not.[2] That is why businesses invest in expensive computer systems that ensure that "static information" is always uniform and accurate. In advertising, moreover, exact wording is considered crucial and liable to legal action if it is wrong. A juice made *with* 100 percent Florida oranges is very different from juice made *from* Florida oranges. The English branch of Hassert's company was forced to change its advertisement of "the most comfortable [computer] mouse that you have ever used" because it could not prove the accuracy of the word *most*. The individual word obviously mattered.

In official documents, then, the exact wording of the original is regarded as crucial. It is worth asking, in this regard, whether the Bible strikes us as being more like a constitution, contract, or legal document, or more like a backyard conversation across the fence between two neighbors. The Bible itself contains treaties, laws, and covenants. Its overall character is that of God's covenant with the human race.

Eyewitness Accounts of Events

Also instructive are the eyewitness accounts of events, especially remarkable events. Does a journalist's version of an eyewitness's account carry the same weight or credibility as the eyewitness's own words? What lies behind the impulse of journalists to provide actual quotations? Surely it is the conviction that nothing is as accurate as a person's own words.

The events surrounding the tragedy of September 11, 2001, provide instructive examples of how important the exact words of a person can be. Consider the hierarchy of credibility that we would give to the following types of reportage:

• A newspaper person's account, in his or her own words, of the conversation between the AT&T telephone operator and Todd Beamer, who called from Flight #93 before it crashed in rural Pennsylvania.

• The AT&T operator's account, in her own words, of the exchange that she had with Todd Beamer.

• A recording of Todd Beamer's words uttered to the operator just before the crash of the airplane.

Which of these is considered most reliable? And would anyone think of changing Beamer's own words to make it more suitable for a target audience? Of course not. What matters is what he really said.

Again, therefore, we need to ask whether the Bible is more like an eyewitness's account, in his or her own words, than it is like a summary of a reporter in his or her own words. In the former case, the words of the original are crucial. In the case of the reporter, one phraseology might be considered as reliable as another, since there is no claim to be retaining anyone's exact observations. It is a commonplace that the Bible, when compared with other religious books, gives unique importance to history. The eyewitness quality of its history requires the exactitude that we require of other historical records.

HAVE YOU HEARD SOMETHING MEMORABLE LATELY?

Consider also the genre of the memorable statement. Proverbs are a good example. Does the exact wording of a proverb matter? Would it pack the same punch if the language were changed to make it more contemporary? Does the statement that "getting to bed on time and getting up on time leads to success" have the same aphoristic flair as "early to bed and early to rise makes a man healthy, wealthy, and wise"? Of course not. The quaint phraseology of the original gives it a meaning and voltage that the prosaic prose statement lacks.

Or how about a memorable statement that we have heard in a sermon or public address? What happens to the power of the original when we try to share the thought with someone later and cannot remember the exact wording? When we put it into our own words, the power of the original usually evaporates into thin air. Why is this? Because the power of a memorable utterance resides in the exact wording of the statement. Trying to express the thoughts without the precise words dissipates the effect.

My wife recalls an era before my mother's death when she codified some of my mother's memories of her immigrant childhood in rural Iowa and her subsequent life there. Why did it prove so important to get my mother to write down her memoirs or to record conversations orally? For several reasons. Recollections in my mother's own words had a greater accuracy and credibility than would be true for someone else putting the recollections into his or her own words. Beyond that, my mother was a walking encyclopedia of proverbs, as well as a master of the vivid and colorful twist of phrase. Changing my mother's way of saying things would not produce the same effect as her own wording produced. A "bare bones" narrative of what happened would have stripped my mother's account of its power.

Is the Bible a book known for its aphoristic flair, its vivid and memorable descriptions, its eloquence and unforgettable twists of thought, or does it possess the eminently forgettable quality of a newspaper article in which one way of stating the information is as good as another? Surely the former.

OF RECIPES AND CRAFT PROJECTS

Recipes provide an interesting insight into the topic we are considering. The simpler and more basic the recipe, the less important it is to have precise wording. My wife assures me that "anyone" can produce an acceptable spaghetti sauce with only approximate directions. A slight deviation in quantities or even ingredients will make little difference in a pizza or a tossed salad.

But what happens when we try to duplicate a treasured family recipe? We need to know *exactly* what Mom said about ingredients and process. Furthermore, a soufflé will not be a soufflé if we do not know the exact instructions. In recent years I have undertaken to type my wife's most treasured recipes on my word processor so whenever food spots and other mishaps render my wife's version illegible I can run off a "clean copy." Why have I learned to have my wife proofread my version and check it against the original? Why are even minor errors in transcription immediately and sternly judged to be deficient? Because the success of the recipe depends on "getting it right."

Much the same prevails with instructions for craft projects. Does it matter whether or not we gather all of the stated ingredients for constructing a plaster of paris model of the Dead Sea terrain? Does it matter if we mix the ingredients in the exact proportions stated in the list of instructions? Or will an approximation be sufficient?

From time to time my wife has written down recipes or instructions for a craft project while watching the home and garden television channel. Sometimes she does not take down exact details, thinking that the gist of the instructions will suffice. Later she finds herself unable to duplicate the results that seemed simple at the time. Exactness of language matters.

I am not saying that the Bible is a recipe book or craft book. I am making the more general point that as societies transact the everyday affairs of life, they repeatedly find it necessary to retain the exact wording of a communication. Having made that disclaimer, I would note in passing that the dietary laws of the Mosaic covenant and the instructions surrounding the building of the tabernacle and temple *do* resemble recipes and building projects.

HAVE YOU BEEN COMPLIMENTED OR CRITICIZED LATELY?

To receive a nice compliment is enough to make one's day. And the day after that as well. Does it matter whether we have the exact wording of the compliment? Yes, it does. First of all, compare the greater impact of having the compliment in written form to having only heard it. Which has the greater impact? The written version has the greater impact because the exact wording is a matter of permanent record, as opposed to having only the gist of the oral compliment. And what do we do with the written compliment? Do we look at it once and toss it into the waste-basket, confident in our assurance that we know the general drift of it? No; we go back and reread the written compliment. Apparently the precise words matter.

What happens when we are criticized illustrates the same principle by negative example. When I give my students written critiques of their papers, I find two common responses:

Students sometimes have a tendency to soften the effect of what I have said. I have been amazed at how often something that should have been interpreted as a serious alarm is reduced in my student's thinking to a slight deficiency. In a student's mind, my critique means a B+ rather than an A, whereas the real message was that the student was at that point failing the course.

At other times students greatly exaggerate my criticism, turning what I intended as a mild statement suggesting that something might profitably have been written differently into a sweeping attack on their character and ability.

I cannot overemphasize how often in these situations the only recourse I have to correct students' misconceptions is to ask them to produce the paper on which my critique appears. My actual words matter a great deal.

The Bible contains many commendations of good behavior and criticisms of bad behavior. The forms in which these appear are often promises, exhortations, and warnings. Is it enough to know simply the gist of God's rules for living, or does a lot hinge on knowing exactly what the original says? Surely the latter.

The Newspaper Interview or Quotation

The journalistic interview or report is yet another example of how we regard it as very important that a person's actual words be quoted verbatim and not tampered with. If you have ever been misquoted in print, you know how it feels. In some measure we feel violated when this happens to us.

From time to time the student newspaper on my own campus revives a column known as "Quotable Quotes." It consists of off-the-cuff humorous or inept statements made by unsuspecting professors and students. Since the element of surprise is partly what renders the quotations humorous, and because the quotations are submitted anonymously, the alleged statements are naturally never run past the people being quoted before they go to print. I have made the column numerous times, and only rarely have the quotations been completely accurate. Does it matter? Not to the public, which enjoys a laugh over a partly inaccurate quip. Does it matter to me? Yes, it does, because I happen to know that the statement is not completely accurate and is therefore to some degree false. But didn't the printed version give the gist of what I said? Yes, it gave the gist, but it was capable of being misinterpreted, and furthermore it did not give the exact nuance of what I had said.

The point is this: In such an everyday genre as a newspaper interview or report, it matters a great deal that we have the exact words of someone. That is why responsible journalists are scrupulous about accuracy and whenever possible run quotations past people they intend to quote before going to print. Here is what columnist Burt Constable of the suburban Chicago *Daily Herald* has to say about the matter:

> Most newspaper reporters consider tinkering with quotes to be a cardinal sin. While we might be the architects of a story, we are simply

the users of quotes. We didn't create them, and they are not ours to craft to meet our needs. . . . One of the reasons I prefer to conduct interviews face-to-face is so the person I'm interviewing can see when I am writing down his quotes.[3]

Constable adds that "technology is changing the way reporters often get quotes. I've had several sources beg out of phone interviews, promising, instead, to answer all my questions by e-mail. That way, they know the quotes we get will be the same as the ones they sent."

There is a counterpart to this in the papers that my students write for me, whether in writing courses or literature courses. I consider it a better form of supporting evidence when my students actually quote from a text or source as opposed to their simply referring to data in a written source in their own words. Why? Doesn't the citation capture the gist of the text's meaning? Presumably it does, but even when it does, it lacks the reliability and (often at least) the verbal force of an actual quotation.

I am not claiming that the Bible is exactly like a newspaper article or essay. The point is that in yet another everyday type of discourse exact wording is preferable to a version in which the language of the original has been changed. The related question is this: Is the Bible a document in which the wording of the original is as important as it is in journalistic or academic writing?

HAVE YOU ASSEMBLED AN APPLIANCE LATELY?

The list of everyday discourses in which exact wording proves crucial could go on indefinitely, but for my purposes I will mention just one more. Instructions for assembling something can, of course, be a great trial. I am no lover of instructions for assembly. Still, they prove my point.

Think of safety instructions first of all. Will a general sense of what to do with a fire extinguisher suffice if it actually needs to be used to put out a fire? I doubt it. One needs to know *exactly* how to activate and aim the extinguisher.

Then there is the genre of the instructions for assembly of a product. Upon unwrapping a product, I usually find the detailed assembly booklet so uninviting that I try to perform the task without reading the document carefully and fully. Does exact wording help or hinder the process? If the instructions are well written, they are an asset. I remember with what despair I unpackaged the kerosene heater I purchased in preparation for the predicted crash of the computers with the transition to the new millennium. I was so intimidated that I enlisted the help of my wife. As she read each instruction, I performed the corresponding function. The result was a revelation to me: The heater started as it was supposed to and functioned as the manufacturer had designed. Did exact wording matter? It did.

Other kinds of instructions belong to the same category. We pore over owner's manuals, operating instructions, and doctors' instructions for postsurgical care. A chemistry or biology teacher standing in front of a class as it is about to perform an experiment is not interested in conveying the gist of the procedure; he or she wants precision in conveying instructions. Parental instructions to children depend for their effect on the exact words: "*If* you finish your vegetables, you may have dessert" is not the same as the loose interpretation, "You said I could have dessert." Teenagers are legalists regarding instructions about when they must return home, so that the instruction "be sure to be home at a decent time" is unlikely to yield the same result as the stipulation "you need to be home by eleven o'clock."

And then there is that ever-important process of passing on messages in a personal or professional context: Getting the person who answers the telephone to get the *precise* message is what matters. This happens to be a charged issue for my wife, who is a counselor. She needs to know *exactly* what a client said, and if possible in what tone of voice. The gist of the message does not suffice.

The Bible is, among other things, a book of instructions—God's instructions to the human race and to those who follow him. It has the same interest in making sure that people do things correctly that a manufacturer of a product does or that a parent giving instructions to a child has. As readers of the Bible, too, we should be as interested in the exact message as we want when receiving an account of a telephone call.

WHAT DOES ALL THIS HAVE TO DO WITH BIBLE TRANSLATION?

I am still moving toward the main subject of this book. For the moment, the important thing is that precise wording is considered highly important in many contexts of life. My guess is that most people think that exact wording is important in just a few kinds of discourse, but that in most situations of life it does not matter. I believe that if we start to survey the discourses that make up everyday life, the reverse is true. It is only in a minority of instances that getting the gist of something is adequate.

This is not to deny that many kinds of everyday communication could have the wording changed without distorting the meaning of an utterance. A summary of last evening's ball game could be successfully conveyed this way or that. A narrative of yesterday's trip to the zoo could be couched in any number of ways that would be equally accurate and effective. On the other hand, if a four-year-old uttered a memorable one-liner about an animal at the zoo, transcribing the exact words into something else would greatly diminish the accuracy and effectiveness of the narrative.

The question for Bible translation runs something like this: Is it likely to be more important or less important to preserve the original wording of the Bible than it is with everyday discourse? Stated another way, if getting the exact wording is important in many kinds of everyday discourse, is it not important to strive for this as far as possible when we translate the Bible from the original into English?

This is not merely an academic question. In later parts of this book it will become apparent that Bible translators were generally scrupulous to remain faithful to the words of the original text of the Bible until dynamic equivalency became the reigning theory in the middle of the twentieth century. We will also have occasion to see how some translations flaunt their deviation from the words of the original in their prefaces.

NOTES

1 Douglas Colber, E-mail to the author, March 1, 2002.
2 Richard Hassert, E-mail to the author, May 27, 2002.
3 Burt Constable, E-mail to the author, February 20, 2002.

3

Lessons from the History of Translation

THE HISTORY OF English Bible translation is an immense subject, and many books have been written on it. I have limited my inquiry to the context suggested by my chapter title: My concern is the lessons that we can learn from the history of translation as we seek to understand Bible translation today.

Because I cover so many specific details, I have not specifically documented every piece of data that I present. Unless I cite a source in my text, I have taken my information from one or more of the sources cited in the footnote that accompanies this sentence.[1]

LANDMARKS IN ENGLISH BIBLE TRANSLATION

Before I extract the relevant "lessons" from the history of English Bible translation, I will briefly trace the leading contours of the history itself. This will provide a useful point of reference, and I invite my readers to compose their own list of conclusions that emerge from the history of English Bible translation before I present my own conclusions. I have limited my survey to translations that have been most important for English-speaking Protestantism.

Wycliffe Bible (1380). I suspect that most people believe that William Tyndale's translation was the first English translation of the Bible, but this is not entirely accurate. Followers of John Wycliffe translated the Bible from the Latin Vulgate into Middle English in the 1380s. Predating the invention of the printing press, the Wycliffe Bible circulated in manuscript form in its own day, and it was so prized that at one point the cost for being allowed to use a copy for one day was the price of a load of hay. It was first printed in the eighteenth century.

Tyndale's New Testament (1525). Modern English Bible translation begins with William Tyndale (1494-1536), a linguistic genius whose expertise in multiple languages dazzled the scholarly world of his day. Because the Bible was condemned by the Roman Catholic Church, Tyndale did most of his work on the New Testament while living on the Continent, finishing the translation of the New Testament in 1525. Copies of the New Testament reached England in 1526, smuggled in bales of cloth or sacks of flour. Catholics burned the copies that came into their possession. Tyndale began translating the Old Testament but was soon lured out of hiding by a Catholic traitor. He met his end by strangling and burning at the stake in 1536.

Tyndale's translation was far more accomplished than one might expect from the somewhat rudimentary state of the English language in the early sixteenth century and the fact that Tyndale was forging new ground. When a Catholic sympathizer said in Tyndale's presence that "we were better without God's law than the Pope's," Tyndale famously retorted, "If God spare my life, ere many years I will cause a boy that driveth the plough shall know more of the Scripture than thou dost." Tyndale's translation has been variously described as "a homely, racy affair," "free, bold and idiomatic," and a translation characterized by "simplicity and directness."[2] Perhaps Tyndale's own use of the plowboy image, coupled with a few famous colloquialisms (see below), has perpetuated a somewhat distorted view of his translation as being essentially colloquial. If 80 percent of Tyndale's translation eventually found its way into the King James Version, it can hardly be as colloquial as the received tradition has portrayed it. Tyndale's translation in any case was the foundation of all subsequent translation of the Reformation era and beyond (except for the Catholic Rheims Douai translation). Tyndale is important, then, for both starting and influencing the tradition of English Bible translation as we know it.

Coverdale's Bible (1535). Miles Coverdale, who had worked as an assistant to Tyndale, produced the first complete Bible in English. Because this Bible had the sanction of the monarch (Henry VIII) and the church hierarchy, it was also the first English Bible to circulate freely in England. Copies of Coverdale's Bible were an early instance of chained Bibles (Bibles chained to a desk in English cathedrals or parish churches, where people could read them). Coverdale's Bible was the first English Bible to include chapter summaries and marginal notes.

Matthew's Bible (1537). "Thomas Matthew" was a pen name or pseudonym for John Rogers, a friend of Tyndale (Rogers, too, died at the stake, in Rogers's case under the reign of the Catholic Queen Mary). This translation was an edited version of the translations of Tyndale and Coverdale. It was the first "authorized version" in England ("Set forth with the kinges most gracyous lycence"). Matthew's Bible divided the material into chapters and paragraphs (but not verses) and included copious notes and cross-references. The first English concordance was based on Matthew's Bible.

The Great Bible (1539). The title of this translation came from its large size. An edict from the king in 1538 charged the clergy to provide "one book of the whole Bible of the largest volume in English, and the same set up in some convenient place within the said church that ye have cure of, whereas your parishioners may most commodiously resort to the same and read it." The Great Bible owed its initiative to Thomas Cromwell, who served Henry VIII as Lord Chancellor of England. Cromwell's desire for a revision of Matthew's Bible was carried out by Miles Coverdale, whom Cromwell put in charge of the revision. The title page to the 1540 edition contained the statement, "This is the Byble appoynted to the use of the churches," meaning that it was the official translation for use in the English church. That its chained presence in the churches made a big hit is suggested by a proclamation from the king (1539) forbidding the reading of the English Bible aloud in church during services. The long-term legacy of the Great Bible, though, is that it became the basis for the Bible passages that appeared in the 1549 Book of Common Prayer (and subsequent versions of the Anglican Prayer Book as well).

Geneva Bible (1560). This is the Bible of the Reformers, produced in Switzerland by Puritan refugees who had fled the persecution of the Catholic Queen Mary. This Bible quickly became the household Bible of English-speaking Protestants, and it was the Bible used by Shakespeare and carried to America on the *Mayflower*. This translation contained copious notes (many of them anti-Catholic) that provided running commentary on the biblical text. It was smaller in size and more affordable than previous English Bibles had been, giving it mass appeal as opposed merely to official church sanction. The Geneva Bible introduced several innovations into English Bible translation: It was printed in a roman typeface instead of the difficult-to-read black gothic letter-

ing, it used italics for words not found in the original text but needed to
make sense in English, and it divided the text into numbered verses.
Because of its rendering of Genesis 3:7 (where Adam and Eve are said
to have sewn "breeches" for themselves), the Geneva Bible has been
known to posterity as the Breeches Bible.

Bishops' Bible (1568). Initiated by Queen Elizabeth and carried out
under the auspices of the Church of England, this volume was intended
to counteract the radical Puritan notes and bias of the Geneva Bible. Its
chief long-term importance is that the committees that produced the
King James Version were mandated to use it as the starting point for
their translation work.

The King James Version (1611). The most famous English Bible of
all time is often called the Authorized Version (AV), a misnomer because
it was never officially sanctioned by either the monarchy or the clerical
hierarchy (though its title page claimed that it was "appointed to be read
in Churches"). The origin of this translation project was the Hampton
Court Conference of 1604, summoned by the new king James I for
"determining things pretended to be amiss in the Church." Puritan
leader John Reynolds proposed a new English translation of the Bible,
and James, hostile as he was to the Puritans, seized upon the suggestion
because, in his words, "I profess I could never yet see a Bible translated
in English; but I think that, of all, that of Geneva is worst."

So six committees of the most knowledgeable biblical and linguistic scholars of England were appointed to work on the project. While
the resulting translation is distinctive for its sheer excellence, it was
nonetheless more a revision of previous translations and the beneficiary
of the earlier evolving history of English Bible translation, as the KJV
translators themselves acknowledged. The KJV is an essentially literal
translation. Alister McGrath claims that a careful study of the way in
which the King James Bible translates the Greek and Hebrew originals
suggests that the translators tried to (1) ensure that every word in the
original had an English equivalent, (2) highlight all words added to the
original for the sake of intelligibility, and (3) follow the word order of
the original where possible.[3] Instead of translating the same Hebrew or
Greek consistently in the English, the King James translators loved the
principles of synonymity (using synonyms instead of verbatim repetition
for the same Hebrew or Greek word) and variety; so they multiplied the
number of English words used for a given Hebrew or Greek word. In

terms of format, the KJV eschewed paragraphing in favor of indenting every new verse.

Stylistically, the KJV is the greatest English Bible translation ever produced. Its style combines simplicity and majesty as the original requires, though it inclines toward the exalted. Its rhythms are matchless. Many of its aphoristic statements passed into common English usage. Beginning with Milton, the KJV has been *the* translation for English-speaking authors and composers. Although never officially licensed by ecclesiastical and governmental agencies, the excellence of the KJV allowed it to supplant the popular Geneva Bible within three or four decades of its appearance, after which it had the field pretty much to itself until the middle of the twentieth century. The best tribute to its uniqueness is that it is often parodied but never successfully paralleled. For all its excellence, the King James translation did not maintain its supremacy after the mid-twentieth century for three main reasons: Its language is now outdated, the translators' knowledge of ancient languages was less reliable than modern knowledge is, and the translation uses a New Testament text (the *Textus Receptus*) that most scholars no longer consider the most reliable.

Revised Version (1881-1885). Although in terms of long-term influence this excessively literal, inartistic translation fell stillborn from the press, the project is actually an important milestone in modern Bible translation, quite apart from the text itself. A symptom of its importance is the eagerness with which the New Testament was greeted: On its first appearance in London, the streets around the publishing house were blocked from dawn to dusk with processions of wagons being loaded with Bibles for transport; leading newspapers in the United States had the text telegraphed for serial printing; and it sold 300,000 copies the first day it hit the streets in New York City.[4]

To explain the significance of the Revised Version, we need to ponder what it represented. The King James translation was the only viable English Bible in Victorian England, and it was two and a half centuries old. Its language was increasingly obsolete. It was not based on reliable manuscript traditions. Viewed thus, the RV is the forerunner of the entire modern translation tradition. Important contributions included arrangement of the content by paragraphs, improved consistency in placing words added to the original in italics, printing Old Testament poetry in indented poetic lines (instead of as prose), and inclusion of marginal notes that alert the reader to variations in wording in ancient manuscripts.

The Revised Version was a British project. Attempts to get American scholars on board failed. American scholars kept working after the British committee disbanded, publishing the American Standard Version (ASV) in 1901. The final text of the ASV was, in the end, almost identical to the RV, and the ASV never caught on with the public either.

J. B. Phillips' New Testament (1947-1957). Although now nearly forgotten, J. B. Phillips's paraphrased New Testament has an importance that makes it belong in this brief history. I remember the excitement that Phillips's New Testament created among English and American readers, partly because of the novelty of the venture, and partly because of the freshness that the translation infused into many people's reading of the New Testament. I believe that dynamic equivalence would never have achieved the prominence that it did if Phillips had not whetted people's appetite for a loose and colloquial English version.

Revised Standard Version (1946 [NT], 1952 [OT], 1957 [complete], 1971 [rev. NT]). As the name of this translation suggests, it was intended as a revision of the American Standard Version, though it would be equally accurate to view it as a revision of the King James translation. As such, it aimed for stylistic excellence within the parameters of modern English usage. Although by later standards the RSV seems old-fashioned, in its original context it was regarded by many readers as too innovative—too destructive of the familiar phraseology and rhythms of the KJV.[5] The RSV is, next to the KJV, the most literary English translation. Some of its literary excellences, though, carry the price tag of being based on emendations that, although they have the support of ancient versions (especially the Septuagint), have lost credibility in more recent exegetical theory. In translation philosophy, the RSV inclined toward verbal equivalence.

The RSV was jettisoned among evangelicals because of alleged theological liberalism, though the number of texts where this can be demonstrated is no more than a handful. On the positive side, the RSV was the first ecumenical Bible translation, enjoying the approval of Protestants, Catholics, and Eastern Orthodox. It also became the most widely used text for biblical scholarship in the scholarly world at large. F. F. Bruce concluded in 1978 that "for the English-speaking world as a whole there is no modern version of the Bible which comes so near as the R.S.V. does to making the all-purpose provision which the A.V. [the KJV] made for so many years."[6]

Although a New Revised Standard Version appeared in 1989, this translation is not the genuine heir to the RSV, being instead a dynamic equivalent translation that regularly turns the concretion of the original into abstraction and takes liberties with gender references to accommodate feminist concerns. In terms of translation philosophy and literary excellence, the true heir to the RSV is the English Standard Version (see below).

New American Standard Bible (1971). For evangelicals who wanted a modern Bible and were distrustful of the RSV, the NASB was the translation of choice until the NIV appeared, after which it became largely neglected except among scholars who knew the difference between an essentially literal translation and a dynamic equivalent translation. The NASB was a revision of the American Standard Version of 1901. Its great virtue is its reliability and fidelity to the language of the original. Its corresponding weakness is that it ranks low among modern translations regarding readability and literary style. Additionally, its printing of verses as individual units results in a fragmented text (though more recent editions are available in paragraph format).

Good News Bible (1976). Also known as Today's English Version, this translation is important because it was the first thoroughgoing outgrowth of Eugene Nida's dynamic theory of translation. In fact, it pushed the new translation philosophy to its limits. Within the family of dynamic equivalent translations, it is a colloquial translation that strives to sound like contemporary American speech. The GNB was sponsored by the American Bible Society, which in 1995 also produced the Contemporary English Version, which is even freer than the GNB, including adoption of gender inclusive language and avoidance of theological terms like *atonement, redemption,* and *righteousness.*

New International Version (1978). Within a few years after its appearance, the NIV became the most widely used English translation among American evangelicals. The project began with dissatisfaction with the RSV among American evangelicals. Claiming to be eclectic, the NIV is in fact on the dynamic equivalence side of the continuum (as the rest of this book will repeatedly show). It regularly moves beyond what the original text says to the interpretation preferred by the translators. Readability was a high priority, and one tabulation considers its reading level as being at the seventh-grade level.[7] Since the NIV will repeat-edly be used in my illustrations of deficiencies in modern translations, I want the record to show that among dynamic equivalent translations, it is consistently on the "conservative" or literal side of the dynamic equivalent half of the translation spectrum. That statement ceases to be true with the subsequent gender-inclusive *Today's New International Version*, with its multitudinous changes to gender references.

Having acknowledged that the NIV falls on the conservative end of the dynamic equivalent spectrum, I want to highlight something that will happen in the second half of this book. I will repeatedly contrast how representative literal translations have rendered a passage with how dynamic equivalent translations have rendered it. The NIV will almost invariably appear in the dynamic equivalent cluster. To anyone who might complain about this placement of the NIV with other dynamic equivalent translations, let me say forthrightly that I am not the one who places it there; the NIV places itself with the dynamic equivalent trans-lations, as my illustrations will plainly show.

New English Bible (1970), Revised English Bible (1989). These dis-tinctively British translations have had little influence in the United States, but they are important to English Bible translation because both translations have had the sanction of leading religious bodies in England and have accordingly enjoyed a kind of official status there. When the NEB appeared, it was the first dynamic equivalent translation produced by a committee whose members were regarded as the best British lin-guists in the scholarly world at large. Even in scholarly circles, though, both translations have been regarded as adventuresome and somewhat experimental. Gilmore's verdict on the NEB is instructive: "Though it tended to finish up largely as a text for scholars, it was originally directed at three groups of people: churchgoers who had become too familiar with the text to 'hear it fresh', young people who wanted a more con-temporary translation, and people who rarely attended church and were put off by the language of the AV."[8]

New Living Translation (1996). Published by Tyndale House, the NLT was based on a desire to refute charges that its predecessor, *The Living Bible*, was unscholarly. The NLT was therefore a new translation based on the ancient texts, but firmly committed to the principle of dynamic equivalence. It is a colloquial translation.

English Standard Version (2001). The English Standard Version began with discontent over both the content and style of modern English Bible translations in the dynamic equivalent tradition. In particular, the Translation Committee wanted a more literal translation than most of the versions produced during the twentieth century, combined with greater stylistic flair than the essentially literal NASB provided, as well as more accuracy than the New King James Version possessed. The committee took the RSV (as slightly revised in 1971) as its starting point. The entire Bible was subjected to comparison with the original texts, and the committee ended up changing about 6 percent from the RSV text, more than originally envisioned, chiefly because of the propensity of the RSV to emend (a feature that includes its reliance on the Septuagint). A notable feature of the translation process was that the entire oversight committee of twelve members met in full for all deliberation on spadework done by specialists, with literary interests fully represented at the table in all deliberations. The result is the highest possible degree of consistency and unity throughout the Bible.

SUMMARY

The foregoing overview has been highly selective, suggesting at once how multiple the attempt has been to give English readers a Bible in their own language. This multiplicity reflects an ongoing discontent with any single Bible that English-speaking readers have available to them. With the lack of consensus goes a degree of uncertainty and potential confusion. The acceleration of translations during the past four decades doubtless signals a restlessness and quest for novelty.

As A. C. Partridge has noted, "There were two dynamic periods of English biblical translation."[9] I myself would fix the two eras as 1520-1611 and 1950 to the present (though one can argue for 1880-1901 as a mini-era of translation ferment). Approximately two and a half centuries lie between the two eras of greatest translation activity. The first era represented an evolutionary process in which each translation built upon the previous ones until the story reached its climax in the King James translation. The story of translation in the past half century is not such a story of cooperative collaboration but is instead a story of individual attempts to be innovative and different.

For the rest of this chapter, I propose to explore the most obvious lessons that the history of English Bible translation offers for contemporary Bible readers and translators. I found that the material fell naturally into a series of dichotomies, as signaled in the headings I have assigned to the material.

Literal vs. "Dynamic"

If we take the entire history of Bible translation into account, it is obvious that the two poles present from the beginning have been literal vs. free translation. Although the "essentially literal" principle dominated English Bible translation until the mid-twentieth century, the alternate principle (without its modern terminology of equivalency) was present from the beginning. One of the very earliest English translators, King Alfred the Great (whose language was Old English), claimed that he translated "sometimes word for word, and sometimes meaning for meaning."[10] In this statement we have the two tendencies laid out to view.

Martin Luther, whose vernacular German translation influenced the English pioneer Tyndale, reflects the same tension between literal and dynamic. In his preface to the German Psalter, Luther speaks of his practice "sometimes to hold rigidly to the words, and sometimes only to give the meaning."[11] Luther adds, "We have sometimes translated word for word, though we could have done it otherwise and more clearly, and for this reason: the words have something important in them. . . . To honor such teaching, and for the comfort of our souls, we must retain such words, must put up with them, and so give the Hebrew some room where it does better than German can."[12] But we get a different impression when Luther writes,

> Whoever would speak German must not use Hebrew idioms; but if he understands the Hebrew writer, he must see to it that he grasps his meaning and must think: Now let me see. How does a German speak in this case? When he has the German words that serve the purpose, then let him dismiss the Hebrew words and freely express the sense in the best German he is capable of using.[13]

William Tyndale shows the same dichotomy at work. On the one hand, as C. S. Lewis puts it, "he naturalizes his originals in a way that will seem quaint to modern readers."[14] Thus in Tyndale's New Testament we find to our surprise that there are shire towns in Palestine and that Paul sailed from Philippi after the Easter holidays. On the other hand, in arguing that the original Hebrew and Greek syntax have more affinity with native English than with Latin, Tyndale makes the statement that "the manner is both one; so that in a thousand places thou needest not but to translate it into the English, word for word."[15]

This dichotomy between literal and free translation quickly became resolved in the direction of fidelity to the very language of the Bible. Some translators (including those who produced the Geneva and King James translations) were so scrupulous not to mislead their readers as to what the original really said that they italicized words that were not in the original but that were needed to make the English version more intelligible. Of course the penchant for literalness reached its climax in the Revised Version.

Although there had been hints of dynamic equivalence in the very early translations, its explosion in the middle of the twentieth century represents a distinctly new development. Until that time the main tradition had favored literal translation. Suddenly literal translation fell out of favor. The prefaces to the new translations show exactly *what* was new. One thing that was new was the claim of the translation to be faithful to *the meaning* of the original. This was code language for "dynamic equivalent rather than literal." The second thing that suddenly appeared in the prefaces and surrounding documents was an emphasis on the target audience for which the translation was intended. Previous translations had not elevated the audience to the role of who should determine how words would be translated. Up to that point the assumed arbiter was (a) what the original really said and (b) a desire that the language of the translation be current and understandable (but not immediately understandable to people with low linguistic abilities and comprehension).

I will note in passing another historical curiosity regarding who is primarily addressed in the prefaces to translations. In the Reformation era, translation committees bent over backward to ingratiate themselves to the ruling monarch, who singlehandedly (though usually in consultation with selected church leaders) controlled permission to print English Bibles. The Puritan Geneva Bible includes a dedicatory epistle to Queen Elizabeth, which reads in part,

> The eyes of all that fear God in all places behold your countries as an example to all that believe, and the prayers of all the godly at all times are directed to God for the preservation of Your Majesty.... The Lord of lords and King of kings ... strengthen, comfort and preserve Your

Majesty, that you may be able to build up the ruins of God's house to his glory.

The King James translators dedicated their work "to the most high and mighty prince James," expressing their gratitude for the king's active interest in the translation of the Bible and for his protection of their work. Modern translators do not need to please a monarch but instead the paying public, and they accordingly elevate the interests of the reader to center stage. This is one way among several in which translation of the Bible has become democratized in the modern era.

Formal Language vs. Colloquialism

A second dichotomy that runs as a unifying theme through the history of English Bible translation is the continuum of formality that exists. At one end of the continuum we find a prevailing formality of expression and literary polish, where smoothness of style is preferred to roughness. At the other end of the spectrum we find an urge to render as much of the Bible as possible into colloquial language and simple syntax. While it is doubtless true that both impulses combine in most English translations, it is also demonstrable that translation committees commit themselves to one of the two options as their guiding principle.

Both impulses were present from the beginning. Tyndale is capable of stately dignity when the original calls for it:

> Blessed are the poor in spirit: for theirs is the kingdom of heaven. Blessed are they that mourn: for they shall be comforted. Blessed are the meek: for they shall inherit the earth. Blessed are they which hunger and thirst for righteousness: for they shall be filled.

This is the Beatitudes as we know them, coming to us via the King James translation, which took them over verbatim from Tyndale. If one reads Tyndale in an edition with modernized spelling, the prevailing impression is one of dignity and relative formality close to what we find in the KJV, while reading Tyndale's translation in an edition with the original spelling makes Tyndale's style seem rather difficult and scrappy. Certainly Tyndale's prevailing syntax is in a formal rather than conversational style. Yet there is a side of Tyndale that likes to indulge in the colloquial and daring. Thus in Tyndale's handling, the serpent says to Eve, "Tush, ye shall not die," Joseph "was a luckie felowe," Pharaoh's "jolly captains" drowned in the Red Sea, and Jesus told his disciples to "babble not much" when they prayed.

With the relative formality of Tyndale as the foundation, sixteenth-century translation, partly under the influence of the oral reciting of biblical passages from the Prayer Book in Anglican worship services, moved in the direction of polished diction, masterful rhythm, and accomplished rather than choppy syntax. I need to urge a caution regarding the KJV: It *combines* the simple and the majestic. As a literary scholar has rightly noted, "A stylistic virtue of K.J.V. is the tact with which it uses stately, sonorous Latin-root abstract words *and* humble, concrete Anglo-Saxon words, each in its appropriate place."[16]

The preference for a dignified Bible prevailed until the middle of the twentieth century. Again, therefore, we can see what a watershed happened at that moment in English Bible translation. The NIV held the line for a relatively dignified level of language, but most other translations in the dynamic equivalent tradition have preferred informality. It is easy to see why: On the logic of wanting to be immediately understandable by readers with low linguistic abilities, translators will naturally translate in the idiom that is most familiar to such a readership. Readability is here synonymous with colloquial informality:

> One day, Adonijah went to see Bathsheba, Solomon's mother, and she asked, "Is this a friendly visit?"
>
> "Yes. I just want to talk with you."
>
> "All right," she told him, "go ahead." (1 Kings 2:13-14, CEV)

Continuity and Tradition vs. Innovation and Originality

A final dichotomy that emerges from the survey of Bible translation is the contrast between maintaining continuity with the earlier tradition of English Bible translation and the urge to break with tradition and be original. Here, too, even though the two impulses are always present, a seismic shift occurred in the middle of the twentieth century.

The story of English Bible translation from Tyndale through the King James Version is a story that has all the shapeliness that Aristotle attributed to literary narrative: It has a beginning, a middle, and an end.

The foundation on which everything rests is Tyndale's New Testament and the early books of the Old Testament. Of course that leaves much of the Old Testament unaccounted for, which needed to be completed by Coverdale after Tyndale's martyrdom. Partly because associates of Tyndale produced some of the subsequent translations, but partly also because a community spirit imbued translators in that era, there was a conscious assimilation of previous translations in the versions that followed them.

The result was an evolution toward the King James Version. Here is how various scholars have helpfully described the process:

• The KJV "was no sudden miracle but rather the harvesting or refining of the previous century's experience in translating the Bible into English. Tyndale, Coverdale, and their successors stand behind it."[17]

• "Tyndale and Coverdale remain the base: but after Tyndale nearly all that is of real value was done by Geneva, Rheims, and Authorized. Our Bible is substantially Tyndale corrected and improved by that triad—almost in collaboration."[18]

• "The 'Authorized' Version represents a slow, almost impersonal evolution. For it is, in reality, itself a revision, resting upon earlier versions, and these, in turn, depend in varying degrees upon each other, so that through the gradual exercise of something which approaches natural selection, there has come about, in both diction and phraseology, a true survival of the fittest. . . . The style of the King James version then is . . . an evolution . . . and the long process of version upon version served (to use Dante's phrase) as 'a sieve for noble words.'"[19]

The King James preface to the reader confirms these descriptions: "Truly (good Christian Reader) we never thought from the beginning, that we should need to make a new Translation, nor yet to make of a bad one a good one . . . ; but to make a good one better, or out of many good ones, one principal good one."

The story of this evolution is like an adventure story. It is particularly interesting to see the felicities that successive translations contributed to the eventual climax. To Tyndale we owe the words *peacemaker, passover, intercession, scapegoat,* and *atonement,* and the phrases *die the death, the Lord's Anointed, flowing with milk and honey, the powers that be, my brother's keeper,* and *a law unto themselves.* Miles Coverdale contributed *the valley of the shadow of death, thou anointest my head with oil, baptized into his death, tender mercies, lovingkindness, respect of persons,* and the beautiful *even, neither,* and *yea* to introduce a Hebrew parallelism. From the Geneva Bible came *smite them hip and thigh, vanity of vanities, except a man be born again,* and *Comfort ye, comfort ye my people.*

Something to note in passing is the influence of Bible translation on the development of the English language. The influence, of course, worked the other way as well, with the development of the English language providing the materials for ever better English translations. But Alister McGrath, in noting that Tyndale invented the term *atonement* to convey the idea of reconciliation, observes additionally that "it can be seen immediately that biblical translation thus provided a major stimulus to the development of the English language, not least by creating new English words to accommodate biblical ideas."[20]

The continuity of the King James tradition persisted until the mid-twentieth century. If one reads the prefaces to such translations as the Revised Version, the American Standard Version, and the Revised Standard Version, and even more if one reads the books and documents that those committees produced about their translation, it is obvious that the translators had a continuous eye on continuity with the King James tradition and tried to retain as much historic and literary similarity to the received tradition as accuracy of translation allowed. The statement of the preface to the Revised Standard Version can serve as a summary for this tradition of translation:

> The Revised Standard Version seeks to preserve all that is best in the English Bible as it has been known and used through the years. It is intended for use in public and private worship, not merely for reading and instruction. We . . . have sought to put the message of the Bible in simple, enduring words that are worthy to stand in the great Tyndale-King James Tradition.

I note in passing that the preferred name for new translations until the mid-twentieth century was *revised.* The whole climate changed around 1970. To understand which way the wind was now blowing, all we need to do is look at the names of versions as they appeared: New American Standard Bible, New Century Version, New English Bible, New International Version, New King James Version, New Living Translation, New Revised Standard Version. The fashionable term is now *new.*

Most of the resulting translations have striven to be original and innovative, consciously breaking with the King James tradition. The opening sentence of the NIV preface sounds the keynote: "The New International Version is a completely new translation of the Holy Bible." When we pick up new translations as they appear, it is as though the impulse has been to be as original as possible. One thing that is new is the new theory of translation—dynamic equivalence rather than essentially literal.

But this by itself does not explain the degree of originality that we find in most modern translations. There is a prevailing quest for novelty—novelty in language, in style, in interpretation of what the original "really means." Modern translations have participated in the spirit of the times—a spirit restless for change, iconoclastic in its disrespectful attitude toward what was venerated in the past, granting automatic preference to what is new and original. A common commendation of a new translation is a reader's comment that "I have never thought of the Bible in this way before." Indeed.

Several things have been lost in the change from continuity to innovation. One is the diminishing of literary effect, both because literary values are no longer highly regarded and because to depart from the King James tradition is to depart from the touchstone of literary excellence. We have also lost continuity with the liturgical and literary past as modern translations have drifted from the once-standard King James tradition. We have lost a common Bible for English-speaking Christians. The Christian community no longer speaks a universal biblical "language." And with the loss of a common Bible we have lost ease in memorization of the Bible. After all, when a common Bible exists, people hear it over and over and "memorize" it virtually without consciously doing so, but this ease is lost when translations multiply. Furthermore, with the proliferation of translations, churches and organizations find it difficult to know which translation to choose for purposes of memorization; and even after they choose, there is such variety that a person faces the prospect of having to memorize from different translations in different settings.

SUMMARY

The history of English Bible translation is a story of both triumph and loss. It is a stirring history of courage, energy, sacrifice, and reverence before the sacred Word of God. In regard to the last of these, to read the concluding paragraphs of virtually all prefaces as the translators offer their final labor to the believing community is invariably moving, even when one has reason to lament the principles on which the translation has been based or the suspected liberalism of a few of the translation committees. Through the long history, despite all the lapses that human products invariably carry, God's Word has been available to English-speaking readers. The main outlines of the message have been clear. Readers can honestly say regarding the Word of God:

> *"It is not in heaven, that you should say, 'Who will ascend to heaven for us and bring it to us, that we may hear it and do it?' Neither is it beyond the sea, that you should say, 'Who will go over the sea for us and bring it to us, that we may hear it and do it?' But the word is very near you. It is in your mouth and in your heart, so that you can do it." (Deuteronomy 30:12-14, ESV)*

On the other hand, I believe that there is much to lament in recent developments. The English-speaking world has not been brought closer to the ideal translation with the proliferation of modern translations. Readers are less sure than ever of what the original text actually says. Many of these readers carry Bibles that lack dignity and that have reduced the Bible to the level of colloquial discourse. The general tendency has been to demote literary beauty and eloquence. We are not in a golden era of English Bible translation.

NOTES

1   These are the books on which I have drawn for information about Bible translations: *The Cambridge Bible Handbook* (no author listed) (Cambridge: Cambridge University Press, 1996); Benson Bobrick, *Wide as the Waters: The Story of the English Bible and the Revolution It Inspired* (New York: Simon and Schuster, 2001); F. F. Bruce, *History of the Bible in English* (New York: Oxford University Press, 1978); Alec Gilmore, *A Dictionary of the English Bible and Its Origins* (Sheffield: Sheffield Academic Press, 2000); C. S. Lewis, *English Literature in the Sixteenth Century Excluding Drama* (Oxford: Oxford University Press, 1954); Jack P. Lewis, *The English Bible from KJV to NIV: A History and Evaluation* (Grand Rapids, MI: Baker, 1981); Bruce M. Metzger, *The Bible in Translation: Ancient and English Versions* (Grand Rapids, MI: Baker, 2001); A. C. Partridge, *English Bible Translation* (London: Andreé Deutsch, 1973); Robert L. Thomas, *How to Choose a Bible Version: An Introductory Guide to English Translations* (Ross-shire, UK: Christian Focus, 2000).

2   The three quotations are, seriatim, from C. S. Lewis, *English Literature in the Sixteenth Century Excluding Drama*, 207; Bruce, *History of the Bible in English*, 42; and Metzger, *The Bible in Translation: Ancient and English Versions*, 60.

3   Alister McGrath, *In the Beginning: The Story of the King James Bible and How It Changed a Nation, a Language, and a Culture* (New York: Doubleday, 2001), 250.

4   Samuel Hemphill, *A History of the Revised Version of the New Testament* (London: Elliot Stock, 1906), 86-88.

5   A collection of reviews on the RSV (as well as the NEB) shows how overwhelmingly the RSV was regarded as too modernizing. See *Literary Style of the Old Bible and the New*, ed. D. G. Kehl (Indianapolis: Bobbs-Merrill, 1970). The irony of the viewpoints expressed in this volume is that half a century later, after the advent of dynamic equivalent and contemporary translations, the very appeals to the KJV as the standard of literary excellence in criticism of the RSV could now be advanced *in favor of* the RSV when compared to more recent translations.

6   Bruce, *History of the Bible in English*, 203.

7   Thomas, *How to Choose a Bible Version: An Introductory Guide to English Translations*, 127.

8   Gilmore, *A Dictionary of the English Bible and Its Origins*, 117.

9   Partridge, *English Bible Translation*, 230.

10 Quoted by Bruce, *History of the Bible in English*, x.

11 Franz Rosenzweig, "Scripture and Luther," in Martin Buber and Franz Rosenzweig, *Scripture and Translation* (Bloomington, IN: Indiana University Press, 1994), 49.

12 Ibid.

13 Ewald M. Plass, ed., *What Luther Says: An Anthology*, Vol. 1 (St. Louis: Concordia, 1959), 106.

14 C. S. Lewis, *English Literature in the Sixteenth Century Excluding Drama*, 207.

15 Quoted in Bobrick, *Wide as the Waters: The Story of the English Bible and the Revolution It Inspired*, 117.

16 Dwight Macdonald, "The Bible in Modern Undress," in *Literary Style of the Old Bible and the New*, ed. D. G. Kehl (Indianapolis: Bobbs-Merrill, 1970), 40.

17 Craig R. Thompson, *The Bible in English, 1525-1611* (Ithaca, NY: Cornell University Press, 1958), 27.

18 C. S. Lewis, *English Literature in the Sixteenth Century Excluding Drama*, 214.

19 John Livingston Lowes, "The Noblest Monument of English Prose," in *Literary Style of the Old Bible and the New*, ed. D. G. Kehl, 14.

20 McGrath, *In the Beginning: The Story of the King James Bible and How It Changed a Nation, a Language, and a Culture*, 79.

PART TWO

Common Fallacies of Translation

4

FIVE FALLACIES ABOUT THE BIBLE

ALL TRANSLATION THEORIES presuppose certain things about the Bible. While these presuppositions do not necessarily govern specific choices that translators make along the way, there is good reason to believe that the starting premises do exercise a formative influence on the actual translation process.

It is the purpose of this chapter to examine what I believe to be fallacies about the Bible that underlie some modern translations of the Bible. In casting a critical eye at these fallacies, I will also sketch out what I think is true of the Bible in the areas that I introduce.

FALLACY #1: THE BIBLE IS A UNIFORMLY SIMPLE BOOK

The drift in modern translations is to produce a colloquial Bible with a simple vocabulary and syntax. What lies behind this drift? Some of the prefaces answer the question. The assumption is that the Bible itself is a simple book intended for people of limited education and intelligence. Here, for example, are statements from prefaces and other documents:

• Since God "stooped to the level of human language to communicate with his people," the translators' task is to set forth the "truth of the biblical revelation in language that is as clear and simple as possible."[1]

• "Jesus talked plainly to people. . . . Jesus, the master Teacher, was very careful not to give people more than they could grasp. . . . We are trying to re-capture that level of communication. . . . Jesus was able to communicate clearly, even with children" (SEB).

• "After ascertaining as accurately as possible the meaning of the original, the translators' next task was to express that meaning in a manner and form easily understood by the readers" (GNB).

If we take the time to unpack the claims here, the lapses of logic begin to emerge. First, the fact that God stooped to human under-

standing when he revealed his truth in human words does not itself settle the question of how simple or sophisticated, how transparent or complex, the Bible is. Human language encompasses an immense range of
simplicity and difficulty. Nor does the fact that God accommodated himself to human understanding in itself say anything about the level of
intelligence and artistic sophistication possessed by the writers and
assumed audience of the Bible.

The preface quoted above that cites the example of Jesus to support
the claim that the Bible is simple shows how winsome the claims can be
on the surface and yet how wrong they actually are when we stop to analyze them. Contrary to the implication of the statement that "Jesus was
able to communicate clearly, even to children," we have no recorded
statements of Jesus to children. And what about the claim that Jesus
"was very careful not to give people more than they could grasp"? This
is directly contradicted by Jesus' explanation of why he spoke in parables: "To you [the disciples] it has been given to know . . . but to them
[the unbelieving masses] it has not been given. . . . This is why I speak
to them in parables, because seeing they do not see, and hearing they do
not hear, nor do they understand" (Matthew 13:11, 13, ESV). This is
indeed a mysterious statement, already giving the lie to the claim that
Jesus' statements are simple and easy to understand. My interpretation
of Jesus' statement is that he did *not* intend his statements to carry all
of their meaning on the surface. I would also speak of "delayed action
insight" as summing up Jesus' strategy, by which I mean that those who
ponder Jesus' sayings will come to an understanding of them, whereas
people who are unwilling to penetrate beneath the surface will not.

If we stop to consider what the implied opposites of "simple" are, it
becomes obvious that multiple qualities can be set over against simplicity. Something can be simple as opposed to complex and intricate. It can
be simple as distinct from sophisticated. Or it can be simple and easy to
understand instead of difficult. As we turn now to look at specimens of
biblical passages, all of these qualities—simple, complex, difficult, sophisticated—will be present, for the Bible is all of these in different passages.

To test how simple or complex and difficult the Bible is, we need
only to look at the text itself. To begin, a cursory glance at any scholarly Bible commentary will reveal at once how difficult a book the Bible
often is. Scholars pore over it, write whole books on it, write articles on
the minutest details, and disagree with each other (or admit perplexity

themselves) over what the text says and means. Even when the vocabulary is translated into simple terms, the very arrangement and content of the material show that the Bible is not a simple book. Consider the following (randomly selected) passage (Isaiah 38:12-13, ESV):

> *My dwelling is plucked up and removed from me*
>   *like a shepherd's tent;*
> *like a weaver I have rolled up my life;*
>   *he cuts me off from the loom;*
> *from day to night you bring me to an end;*
>   *I calmed myself until morning;*
> *like a lion he breaks all my bones;*
>   *from day to night you bring me to an end.*

This is not a simple passage. It requires one's best powers of concentration to follow the flow of thought and images. In what sense is the speaker's dwelling plucked up? How can a person roll up his or her own life like a weaver? How can God cut a person off from a loom? Exactly how does God bring the speaker to an end? Why does the speaker claim to have calmed himself "until morning," specifically? What does it mean that God brings the speaker to an end "from day to night"? What are we to make of the way in which the speaker shuttles back and forth between referring to God as "he" and "you"? I repeat—this passage is not simple. On the contrary, it is a difficult passage. Let me note in passing that the relative difficulty of the passage is not a matter of vocabulary, and thus merely scaling down the language in translation will not make the passage easy to assimilate.

Related to the claim that the Bible is a simple book is the assumption that the Bible carries all of its meaning on the surface. The passage from Isaiah that I have quoted belies this claim too. One cannot read quickly through the passage. It requires stopping and pondering. This is the normal situation with the Bible, which is a meditative book, often elusive on a first reading.

The relative difficulty of the passage from Isaiah is a literary difficulty in the sense that it consists of the flow of thought and the presence of figures of speech. Another type of difficulty that we encounter in many passages of the Bible is the presence of weighty and intricate theological content. Here is a random specimen: "For the wrath of God is revealed from heaven against all ungodliness and unrighteousness of men, who by their unrighteousness suppress the truth" (Romans 1:18, ESV). There are some big words and big ideas here: *wrath, revealed, ungodliness, unrighteousness, suppress the truth*. A lot of the theological teaching of the Bible is like this. It inclines toward technical theological terminology. It is impossible to retain the full theological meaning if one removes all vestiges of technical vocabulary.

Much of the Bible is intricately and artistically organized. There is a lot of chiasm in the Bible, for example. Chiasm, from the Greek word for "crossing," consists of a passage that repeats the main elements of the first half in reverse order in the second half. Here is an example (with key terms highlighted to show the balance and symmetry):

> *Seek me and live;*
> *but do not seek Bethel,*
> *and do not enter into Gilgal*
> *or cross over to Beersheba;*
> *for Gilgal shall surely go into exile,*
> *and Bethel shall come to nothing.*
> *Seek the LORD and live. (Amos 5:4-6, ESV)*

Modern biblical scholarship has repeatedly shown how rhetorically sophisticated a book the Bible is.

This is not to say that the Bible is not sometimes simple. It is. Here is a type of passage that we find throughout the Bible:

> *We give thanks to God always for all of you, constantly mentioning you in our prayers, remembering before our God and Father your work of faith and labor of love and steadfastness of hope in our Lord Jesus Christ. (1 Thessalonians 1:2-3, ESV)*

But writing that is this simple and direct comprises relatively little of the Bible. In fact, I had to look a relatively long time to find a passage that was totally devoid of figurative language or statements that require interpretation. Totally transparent passages are the exception rather than the rule in the Bible.

The Bible encompasses an immense range of style and content. Someone has said that in the waters of Scripture a lamb can walk and an elephant can swim. Victorian poet Francis Thompson called the Bible "the most elastic of all books," adding that "whoever opens it, learnéd or simple, equally finds something . . . appropriate to his understanding."[2]

What is the result when translation committees begin with the assumption of a simple Bible that carries its meaning on the surface and is devoid of sophisticated technique? When translators begin with the premise that the Bible is uniformly simple, they use the process of translation to produce the Bible that they envision. They simplify the vocabulary and syntax. They modify or eliminate figurative language. They add explanatory commentary in their translation. They eliminate theological language. Rhetorical patterning often evaporates. The end product is a Bible that deviates significantly from the original.

Contrariwise, if translators begin with no presuppositions about the level of difficulty represented by the Bible, they are free to follow the actual contours of the writing and to be faithful to whatever they find in the biblical text. Sometimes the text before them will, indeed, be simple. At other times it will be difficult, complex, or elusive. The task of translators is simply to reproduce in English whatever they find in the original. When they do, they will have created a translation that is transparent to the original text—not necessarily transparent to a modern reader, but to the original text.

FALLACY #2: THE BIBLE IS A BOOK OF IDEAS RATHER THAN CONCRETE PARTICULARS

Because the Bible is a religious book, designed to impart religious and moral content, a prevalent misconception is that the Bible is predominantly a book of ideas. The best index to this is the commentary that has grown up around the Bible. This commentary leans heavily toward the ideational. Its preference is for the theological proposition. I see this bias among my students, whose first impulse when writing about a Bible passage is to translate the Bible into a series of theological ideas.

Let me forestall a possible misunderstanding by saying that I do not question that the Bible does, in fact, embody ideas, and that it is both possible and necessary to extract theological and moral ideas from biblical texts. That is not the issue in question. My concern is what the actual text is like *before* we extract religious meaning from it and transform the details of the text into a set of ideas.

What kind of texture do we encounter when we read the Bible? Let me quote brief specimens from some leading biblical genres. Narrative typically yields this type of material:

Then Jacob went on his journey and came to the land of the people
of the east. As he looked, he saw a well in the field, and behold, three
flocks of sheep lying beside it, for out of that well the flocks were
watered. (Genesis 29:1-2, ESV)

Here is the type of material that we virtually always encounter in
poetry:

Save me, O God!
    For the waters have come up to my neck.
I sink in deep mire,
    where there is no foothold. (Psalm 69:1-2a, ESV)

Proverbs similarly incline toward the concrete and imagistic:

For they [the wicked] eat the bread of wickedness
    and drink the wine of violence.
But the path of the righteous is
    like the light of dawn,
which shines brighter and brighter until full day.
    (Proverbs 4:17-18, ESV)

Prophecy shares the same bias:

Then the LORD will appear over them,
    and his arrow will go forth like lightning;
the Lord GOD will sound the trumpet
    and will march forth in the whirlwinds of the south.
    (Zechariah 9:14, ESV)

Only expository (informational) writing prefers abstraction, and it
is not as wholly free from concretion as we might think:

Now before faith came, we were held captive under the law, impris-
oned until the coming faith would be revealed. So then, the law was
our guardian until Christ came, in order that we might be justified by
faith. (Galatians 3:23-24, ESV)

What difference does it make when translators begin with the
premise that the Bible is a predominantly ideational book? As always,
the tendency will be to use translation from one language into another

as the occasion to produce the kind of biblical text that corresponds to the translators' conception of what kind of book the Bible is. The evidence of this happening is plentiful in some modern translations, as I will show later in this book. One of the most consistent results of dynamic equivalent translations is to rob the Bible of its literary qualities, since literature always resists reduction to abstract ideas.

FALLACY #3: THE BIBLE IS A MODERN BOOK

While no one would state baldly that the Bible is a modern book, the belief that it is such is clearly implied by the prefaces and practices of some modern translations. According to these, the important thing is how *we* would phrase things, not how the authors said them. In many modern translations, references to ancient customs and idioms that are foreign to modern readers are replaced by formulations that are immediately accessible. Details in the biblical text that belong to antiquity are updated and phrased in terms of modern counterparts. Here are specimen statements from prefaces to English translations:

• "Ancient customs are often unfamiliar to modern readers. . . . So these are clarified either in the text or in a footnote" (New Century Bible).

• "This version of the New Testament in a contemporary idiom keeps the language of the Message current and fresh and understandable in the same language in which we do our shopping, talk with our friends, worry about world affairs, and teach our children their table manners" (*The Message*).

• "We have sought to translate terms shrouded in history or culture in ways that can be immediately understood by the contemporary reader" (NLT).

How does such contemporizing look in actual translation? In the following rendition, the arrival of the two spies in Jericho reads like an event happening in modern-day Israel: "Then Joshua sent two spies from the Israeli camp at Acacia to cross the river and check out the situation on the other side, especially at Jericho. . . . Someone informed the king of Jericho. . . . He dispatched a police squadron to Rahab's home" (Joshua 2:1-3, *The Living Bible*). There is no doubt that this ranks high on readability. There is also no doubt that it obscures the precise details of what actually happened.

I need again to forestall a possible misunderstanding of my conviction in this matter. I do, indeed, believe in "bridge building" or "bridging the gap" between the world of the text and our own world. If Mordecai was a courtier, it is helpful for us to know that the counterpart is a member of the President's cabinet. The story of Joseph's ill treatment by Potiphar's wife suddenly assumes shape when we think of it in terms of a hostile work environment, sexual harassment on the job, and imprisonment on trumped-up charges. Helpful as such bridging of the gap is, however, the crucial point is that it is the proper domain of interpretation and exposition, not of translation.

I feel almost foolish in making the case for something as self-evident as that the Bible is an ancient document that belongs to a world remote from our own world; yet the prefaces of some modern translations and the translations themselves require me to make the case. The facts of the matter are that the Bible is two and three millennia old. For all its universality, the Bible is a book whose particulars consistently transport us to another time and another place. Abraham did not ride in airplanes but on camels. When Jesus attended dinner parties, he did not sit at a dining room table but reclined at a table. Ancient warriors fought with swords, not machine guns.

The ramifications of the Bible's status as an ancient book—and a book of the Middle East rather than the West—will occupy me in later chapters. My purpose in this chapter is simply to clear the air of misconceptions about what kind of book the Bible is. The sheer fact of the matter is that the Bible is an ancient book, not a modern book. To translate it into English in such a way as to make it appear a modern book is to distort it.

FALLACY #4: THE BIBLE NEEDS CORRECTION

In an ever-increasing arc, biblical scholars and translators during the past half century and ordinary readers more recently have viewed the Bible as a book that stands in need of correction. Consider the following statements from prefaces and surrounding documents of modern English translations:

• "It was recognised that it was often appropriate to mute the patriarchalism of the culture of the biblical writers" (NIVI [Inclusive Language NIV]).

• "Metaphorical language is often difficult for contemporary readers to understand, so at times we have chosen to translate or illuminate the metaphor" (NLT).

• "In everyday speech, 'gender generic' or 'inclusive' language is used, because it sounds most natural to people today. This means that where the biblical languages require masculine nouns or pronouns when both men and women are intended, this intention must be reflected in translation, though the English *form* may be very different from that of the original" (CEV).

• "Sentences are purposely kept short, transparent, and uncomplicated to promote greater understanding. Complex sentence structures are often unnecessary anyway" (SEB).

• "The unsophisticated" reader "is likely to be grateful . . . at being delivered from theological subtleties" in this translation.[3]

• This translation "*breathes new life* into the enduring wisdom of the ancient biblical texts" (dust jacket of *The Message*; italics added to highlight the implication that the Bible needs resuscitation).

Despite a range of motivations in these statements, all of the quotations have something in common: They begin with the premise that there are things about the Bible that need to be changed for the contemporary reader. Further, the translations based on these principles do, in fact, change the Bible to bring it into alignment with the specific criticisms or dislikes that are voiced. In short, they "correct" the Bible.

Against the view of the Bible as a book that needs to be corrected, I believe that the Bible is the book that God intended the human race to have. If it contains a large amount of poetry, I conclude that God wanted us to be able to read, interpret, and enjoy poetry. Where pronouns and nouns are masculine, I believe that God wanted us to come to grips with the implications of that formulation. And where, incidentally, terms that have been traditionally rendered masculine but that according to the context imply that there is no gender distinction, I believe that the older formulations can be changed to accurately reflect in English the "dual reference" language of the original. If God ordained that the Bible be written two and three thousand years ago, it seems plausible to believe that he designed as his sacred book a book that is for us an ancient book, not a contemporary book.

FALLACY #5: THE BIBLE IS A BOOK DEVOID OF MYSTERY AND AMBIGUITY

My concern in this chapter is not miscellaneous misconceptions about the Bible but rather misconceptions that specifically impinge on Bible translation. The final one of these is that the Bible is a book devoid of mystery and ambiguity, a book in which everything is immediately clear and in which statements mean one thing only.

This view of the Bible has been the cardinal principle of modern dynamic equivalent Bibles. Here are specimen statements:

• "Every effort has been made to use language that is natural, clear, simple, and unambiguous" (GNB preface).

• "Jesus talked plainly to the people" (SEB preface).

• "The translators have made a conscious effort to provide a text that can be easily understood by the average reader" (NLT preface).

• "The writers of the Bible ... intended one meaning and not several."[4]

What all of these theories rule out is the possibility that the Bible in its original text might *not* have been unambiguous, simple, direct, and easily understood.

Yet if we look at the actual text of the original Bible, we find that most of it consists of statements that require interpretation, pondering, and analysis. Some of this mystery comes in the form of figurative language. Consider this proverb, which is one of my favorites (Proverbs 4:18, ESV):

> *But the path of the righteous is like the light of dawn,*
>   *which shines brighter and brighter until full day.*

What is this metaphoric path of the righteous? How can a path be like the light of dawn? What is the light that brightens the path of the righteous (obviously it is not the physical light of the sun, which shines on the good and evil alike)? And what happens to a righteous person when the brightness of his or her path has reached full day? Much of this utterance remains mysterious and requires a reader to think through what the statement means. And after the statement has thus teased a reader into pondering the meanings, much remains elusive.

A random opening of the pages of John's Gospel yields this familiar passage:

> *Truly, truly, I say to you, unless a grain of wheat falls into the earth and dies, it remains alone; but if it dies, it bears much fruit. Whoever loves his life loses it, and whoever hates his life in this world will keep it for eternal life. (John 12:24-25, ESV)*

This is mysterious even at a literal level. In what sense does a grain of wheat die and remain alone unless it falls into the earth? But of course this is a metaphor that says something about people. In what sense does a believer die in order to follow Christ? Surely this requires our best thinking, and just as surely the meanings are multiple. Bearing fruit is likewise multiple rather than single in meaning. What does it mean to hate one's life? How can we square that with other teachings in the Bible? Paradox is one of the most mysterious of all rhetorical forms, and surely no paradox is as stark as the idea of losing one's life to gain it.

But isn't the perspicuity or clarity of Scripture a cornerstone of Protestant biblical interpretation? Yes, it is, but there is reason to believe that the doctrine is easily misunderstood. The statement should not be taken out of its historical context. The Protestant Reformers insisted on the clarity of Scripture and the right of the layperson to have access to the Bible as a way of countering the Roman Catholic practice of making the Bible the exclusive property of the clergy. So extreme was this removal of public access to the Bible that the official Bible was the Latin Vulgate, with the result that laypersons could not read the Bible even if they could get their hands on one. In asserting the right of laypeople to read the Bible in their own language, Protestants naturally formulated a theory that Scripture was sufficiently clear that ordinary people could be trusted to understand the message of the Bible.

This does not mean, however, that ordinary people can completely understand all the details in the Bible. If they could, why would a library of scholarly commentary have grown up around the Bible? Here is what the perspicuity of Scripture really means:

> In the estimation of the Church of Rome the Bible is obscure and is badly in need of interpretation even in matters of faith and practice. For that reason an infallible interpretation is needed, and this is supplied by the Church. Over against this position of Rome the Reformers emphasized the perspicuity or clearness of Scripture. By doing this they did not deny that there are mysteries in the Bible which the human mind cannot fathom, did not claim that man can very well dispense with the labours of commentators, and did not even mean to assert that the way of salvation is so clearly revealed in Scripture that every one can easily understand it, irrespective of his spiritual condition. Their contention was simply that the knowledge necessary unto salvation, though not equally clear on every page of Scripture, is yet communicated to man throughout the Bible in such a simple and comprehensive form that anyone who is earnestly seeking salvation can easily gather this knowledge for himself, and need not depend for it on the Church or the priesthood.[5]

As we ponder the matter, an odd paradox emerges. The very translators who make so much of the need to translate the Bible into immediately understandable terms, with all interpretive problems removed from readers, have themselves become the counterparts to medieval Roman Catholic priests. By means of preemptive interpretive strikes, these translators take to themselves the power of making readers' minds up for them, deciding for "ignorant readers" what they think the text means and then doling out only those interpretations that they think correct. The reader is just as surely removed from the words of the text as the medieval Christian was.

SUMMARY

My purpose at this stage of this book is theoretic. I am not yet looking at actual translations of Bible passages. I am attempting to gain a hearing for principles that can be understood more clearly and dispassionately before we look at actual translations.

In this chapter I have looked chiefly at prefaces and surrounding documents of modern translations to show that these translations reveal attitudes about the Bible that I believe to be fallacious. The fallacies are that the Bible is a uniformly simple book, that it is predominantly a book of ideas, that it is essentially a modern book, that it needs correcting in some areas, and that it was intended to be without mystery and ambiguity. I believe all of this to be the reverse of what is actually true. The truth is that the Bible is sometimes simple and sometimes difficult and complex. It is a book of stories and poetic images more than a book of abstract propositions. Furthermore, the Bible is an indisputably ancient book. As such, it is the book that in its original form is the book that God wants us to have, including much that is mysterious and requires careful pondering and unpacking.

NOTES

1   This statement was made by a member of the Bible Society that produced the Good News Bible, in a letter to the editor of *Theology*, May 1978, quoted in Stephen Prickett, *Words and the Word* (Cambridge: Cambridge University Press, 1986), 6.
2   Francis Thompson, *Literary Criticisms* (New York: E. P. Dutton, 1948), 544.
3   See footnote 1, above.
4   Eugene A. Nida and Charles R. Taber, *The Theory and Practice of Translation* (Leiden: E. J. Brill, 1969), 7.
5   L. Berkhof, *Manual of Christian Doctrine* (Grand Rapids, MI: William B. Eerdmans, 1953), 47-48.

SEVEN FALLACIES ABOUT TRANSLATION

IN THIS CHAPTER I will look at translation theory more directly than at any other point in this book. I propose to look critically at the claims that have dominated translation theory for half a century. It is time to question some principles that have been accepted as axioms for too long.

FALLACY #1: WE SHOULD TRANSLATE MEANING RATHER THAN WORDS

No principle has been more central to the dynamic equivalent project than the claim that translators should translate the meaning or ideas rather than the words of the original. Eugene Nida has been the definitive exponent of this view, nowhere more clearly than when he writes about the priorities that should govern translation. Among Nida's priorities is "the priority of meaning. . . . This means that certain rather radical departures from the formal structure are not only legitimate but may even be highly desirable."[1] A corollary to this principle is a relative disparagement of words themselves, as in Nida's statement that "words are merely vehicles for ideas,"[2] a view of language that A. H. Nichols stigmatizes as "docetic."[3]

Once we are clued into this context, the prefaces to dynamic equivalent translations say more than most readers think, partly by virtue of what they *omit*. When these translations claim to give "the meaning of the original" (GNB) or "the thought of the biblical writers" (NIV), they signal that the translators were committed to translating what they *interpret* the meaning of the original to be *instead of* first of all preserving the language of the original. The premise is that "a thought-for-thought translation . . . has the potential to represent the intended meaning of the original text even more accurately than a word-for-word translation" (NLT).

The fallacy of thinking that a translation should translate the meaning rather than the words of the original is simple: There is no such a thing as disembodied thought, emancipated from words. Ideas and thoughts depend on words and are expressed by them. When we change the words, we change the meaning. An expert on Bible translation has expressed the matter thus:

> Language is not a mere receptacle. Nor does the Bible translator work with some disembodied 'message' or 'meaning.' He is struggling to establish correspondences between expressions of the different languages involved. He can only operate with these expressions and not with wordless ideas that he might imagine lie behind them. Translators must not undervalue the complex relationship between form and meaning.[4]

The whole dynamic equivalent project is based on an impossibility and a misconception about the relationship between words and meaning. Someone has accurately said that "the word may be regarded as the body of the thought," adding that "if the words are taken from us, the exact meaning is of itself lost."[5]

It is easy to illustrate the dependence of meaning on words by comparing English translations of identical Bible passages. Psalm 1:3 ends with a statement of the complete prosperity of the godly person. Presumably all translators begin in agreement on the gist or general meaning of the statement. But once they commit themselves to the words of a translation, it turns out that the meaning is not independent of the words that express it but instead is determined by those words. Here is how a range of translations express the agreed-upon meaning:

- "Whatsoever he doeth shall prosper" (KJV).
- "In all that he does, he prospers" (RSV, ESV; NASB similar).
- "In all that they do, they prosper" (NRSV; NLT nearly identical).
- "Whatever he does prospers" (NIV).
- "They succeed in everything they do" (GNB).

Do these translations communicate the same meaning? No. To project prosperity into the future with the formula "shall prosper" is not the same as to assert the present reality that the godly person "prospers." To locate the prosperity in the person by saying that in all that the godly person does "*he* prospers" (italics added for emphasis) is different from saying that "whatever he *does*" or "they *do*" prospers (italics added for emphasis). To paint a portrait of the godly *person* (singular) communicates a different meaning from the communal or group implication of the plural "they." It is not my purpose to arbitrate among these translations but simply to make the point that meaning depends on words. When the words differ, the meaning differs. To claim that we can translate ideas *instead of words* is an impossibility.

Second Timothy 3:16 furnishes another example of how statements on which translators probably agree in principle turn out looking quite different when translators commit the statement to actual words. The core of common agreement is that this verse ascribes the origin of Scripture to God and that it uses the key verb *breathe* to state this idea. Yet the range of actual renditions is extensive:

- "All scripture is given by inspiration of God" (KJV)
- "All scripture is inspired by God" (NASB; GNB; NLT).
- "Everything in the Scriptures is God's Word" (CEV).
- "All Scripture is God-breathed" (NIV, TNIV).
- "All Scripture is breathed out by God" (ESV).

For a verse that probably began in agreement as to its basic idea, this is a very large range of translation. The formulas do not all say the same thing. Only the last rendition clearly states that the words of Scripture are breathed *out by God* as opposed to being breathed *into the human authors*. To repeat my main point: One cannot translate ideas rather than words. When the words differ from other formulations, so does the meaning.

Something else that needs to be said is that dynamic equivalent translations ordinarily show a much greater range of variability than essentially literal translations display. This is a way of saying that dynamic equivalence lacks an internal set of controls on the translation process. Here is the range of meanings that essentially literal translations find in the central part of 1 Thessalonians 1:3:

- ". . . your work of faith, and labour of love, and patience of hope in our Lord Jesus Christ . . ." (KJV).
- ". . . your work of faith and labor of love and steadfastness of hope in our Lord Jesus Christ" (RSV).
- ". . . your work of faith and labor of love and steadfastness of hope in our Lord Jesus Christ" (NASB).

• "... your work of faith and labor of love and steadfastness of hope in our Lord Jesus Christ" (ESV).

The reason for the nearly identical renderings is that these translations are based on the primacy of words. Fidelity to the words of the original has here served as a curb on translation, sparing the translators from straying from the path that the original text itself sets out.

Here is the range of dynamic equivalent translations of 1 Thessalonians 1:3:

"... your work produced by faith, your labor prompted by love, and your endurance inspired by hope in our Lord Jesus Christ" (NIV, TNIV).

"... how you put your faith into practice, how your love made you work so hard, and how your hope in our Lord Jesus Christ is firm" (GNB).

"... your faithful work, your loving deeds, and your continual anticipation of the return of our Lord Jesus Christ" (NLT).

"... your faith and loving work and ... your firm hope in our Lord Jesus Christ" (CEV).

Two things are obvious. First, it is difficult to correlate these renditions individually with the essentially literal versions quoted earlier. We are looking at major deviations from the literal rendering of the original. In fact, if we did not know that these were all translations of the same passage, that fact might easily escape our notice.

Secondly, the sheer range of variability in the dynamic equivalent translations of this verse shows that once fidelity to the language of the original is abandoned, there are no firm controls on interpretation. The result is a destabilized text. Faced with the range of dynamic equivalent translations, how can a reader have confidence in an English translation of this verse? And if it is possible to translate more accurately by abandoning the words of the original for its ideas, why do the dynamic equivalent translations end up in such disagreement with each other? Instead of enhancing accuracy, dynamic equivalence subverts our confidence in the accuracy of the translations.

Essentially literal translation is based on linguistic conservatism. It seeks to conserve the actual words of the original text as much as translation into English allows, and it resists wandering from those words. The result of this conservative impulse, let me say again, is to produce a stable text because there are reliable controls on the translation process—controls exerted by the very words of the original. A literal translation yields this rendition of Psalm 139:5a (NRSV, ESV; NIV nearly identical; KJV, NASB, NKJV very similar):

> *You hem me in, behind and before,*
> *and lay your hand upon me.*

In contrast to linguistic conservatism is linguistic license and antinomianism. Once translators adopt the principle that only the thought of the original needs to be communicated, with the words of the original being dispensable, linguistic license sets in because there is nothing to control the actual words that are chosen to communicate what a translation committee regards as the meaning of the text. As an illustration of linguistic antinomianism, here is what dynamic equivalent translations do with Psalm 139:5a:

> *You are all around me on every side;*
> *you protect me with your power. (GNB)*

> *You keep close guard behind and before me*
> *and place your hand upon me. (REB)*

> *You both precede and follow me.*
> *You place your hand of blessing on my head. (NLT)*

> *. . . with your powerful arm you protect me*
> *from every side. (CEV)*

These translations introduce an unsettling range of meanings, but within the logic of dynamic equivalence they are all commendable for doing exactly what the "thought-for-thought" philosophy prescribes: The translators decided what they thought the imagery of God's hemming in and placing his hand over the speaker *means*, and they then dispensed with the actual words of what the original *says*, choosing their own words to express the thought. In my experience, defenders of a given dynamic equivalent translation stigmatize the other dynamic equivalent translations as being "an abuse" of the theory, but this simply points up the problem of dynamic equivalent translations—namely, that there are no linguistic controls on the translation. In the case of Psalm 139:5, a translation that retains the imagery of hemming in and placing the hand over the speaker *allows for* the interpretations proposed by the quoted translations without *imposing* those interpretations on the reader. As I will argue elsewhere, dynamic equivalence is based on an elementary confusion of translation with interpretation.

Let me say in passing that I am increasingly impatient with translators who claim to embrace the "thought for thought" theory and then choose all of their examples from the NIV, the most conservative of the dynamic equivalent translations. Those who endorse dynamic equivalency as a theory need to "own" the tradition that has flowed from the theory, just as advocates of essentially literal translation must do. The NIV stood near the beginning of the dynamic equivalence experiment and was a mild version of dynamic equivalence theory. The trajectory from that early point has been toward greater and greater removal from the original text. One need only compare the NIV with its successor the TNIV, which has deviated far from the original with its gender changes, its changing of singular/individual references to plural references (a seismic shift), and its grammatical aberration of mingling singular nouns with plural modifiers (e.g., "rebuke the offender; and if they repent, forgive them").

Dynamic equivalence shows its weakness partly in the variability that stems from the theory. Proponents of dynamic equivalency need to do more than defend their preferred dynamic equivalent translation. If it is the theory itself that proponents wish to endorse, they need to offer a defense of the variability that stems from their theory, or formulate controls on the wide-ranging renditions that typically characterize the dynamic equivalence tradition. Until they can produce such controls, the far-flung variability that we find in dynamic equivalent translations constitutes a linguistic antinomianism, with every translation committee a law to itself in the sense that once it decides what the meaning of a passage is, the translators are free to express that meaning without attention to the words of the original.

The result is that readers are at the mercy of the particular dynamic equivalent translation they happen to have chosen. Without recourse to what the original said, they have access to only one interpretation. As Ray Van Leeuwen says with his usual good sense, "It is hard to know what the Bible *means* when we are uncertain about what it *says*. . . . The problem with [functional equivalence] translations (i.e., most modern translations) is that they prevent the reader from inferring biblical *mean-*

ing because they change what the Bible *said*."[6] In the example cited above, it is impossible for a reader to assess whether the proposed interpretations that God "protects" and "blesses" the speaker are right or wrong because what the passage *says* (the imagery of hemming in and placing a hand over) has been removed from sight. The only reliable curb on the tendency of dynamic equivalence to multiple contradictory interpretations is to render the *words* of the original and not abandon them for interpretive license in the translation process.

Before I leave this discussion of the fallacy that we can translate ideas rather than words, I want to guard against the possible misconception that I reject the now-common linguistic axiom that thought resides in complete thought units (phrases and sentences) rather than in individual words. We all know that discourse depends on complete thought units. But units of thought *begin* with words, and in the process of translation, words need to be translated *before* we can move to the interpretive level of determining thought. Let me also say that I do not deny that the translation of words must occur *within the context of* a translator's understanding of the meaning of a passage. I am only disputing that understanding of meaning can *replace or render unnecessary* fidelity to the actual words of the original—the mistaken notion of "thought-for-thought" *rather than* "word-for-word."

FALLACY #2: ALL TRANSLATION IS INTERPRETATION

There is, of course, a sense in which the statement that all translation is interpretation is true. Whenever a translator decides that a given English word best captures the meaning of a word in the original text, the decision implies an interpretation. But there is a crucial difference between *linguistic* interpretation (decisions regarding what English words best express Hebrew or Greek words) and *thematic* interpretation *of the meaning* of a text. Failure to distinguish between these two types of interpretation has led to both confusion and license in translation.

Linguistic interpretation is a judgment that translators make regarding which English words best render the meaning of the words in the original biblical text. Is the Hebrew word *zera* best rendered as "seed" or "offspring"? This is an issue of linguistic interpretation. So is a decision that a translator reaches on how to render the verb in the genealogies of Genesis. Did Seth "beget" Enosh, "father" him, or "become the father of" him? Were the Israelites led through the "desert" or the "wilderness"?

At this linguistic level, translation is indeed a continuous process of interpretation. But this is not the type of interpretation that is usually in view when translators invoke the principle that "all translation is interpretation." In my experience, this motto is invoked almost uniformly by devotees of dynamic equivalence theory and practice, or when a translator in a given instance wants to "go dynamic" (that is, change the words of the original in ways that explain the meaning of the text or influence a reader's choice of one possible meaning over another option). In other words, the motto that "all translation is interpretation" is almost invariably part of a translation philosophy that wants to take liberties with the original text. This does not make it automatically wrong, but it does signal that the motto is invoked in the service of a specific translation theory.

We can see the difference between linguistic interpretation and thematic interpretation of meaning by looking at varied translations of Psalm 1:1. Linguistic interpretation determines whether a translation speaks of the wicked as "scoffers" or as "mockers." An entirely different level of interpretation occurs when a translation drops the metaphor of the godly person's not "stand[ing] in the way of sinners" and replaces it with the statement that godly people "won't follow sinners" (CEV), or drops the metaphor about not "walk[ing] in the counsel of the wicked" and instead uses the formulation "never follows the advice of the wicked" (Jerusalem). This is one common type of interpretation that dynamic equivalent translations perform—interpreting the meaning of figurative language, sometimes removing the figurative language in the process, and often changing the meaning of the original.

The other main type of interpretation in which dynamic equivalent translators engage is thematic interpretation of the theological meaning of a passage, achieved by going beyond the literal statement of the original. Romans 1:17 says that in the Gospel "the righteousness of God is revealed" (RSV, NASB, ESV). This literal translation of what the original says does not proceed to interpret whether this righteousness of God is an attribute of God's character or whether it is God's gift of righteousness conferred on those who believe leading to salvation. Obviously not *all* translation is theological interpretation. But for *dynamic equivalent translators* the translation of this verse is, indeed, theological interpretation. These translators go beyond the literal rendering and make a theological decision for the reader:

• "For in the gospel a righteousness *from* God is revealed" (NIV, italics added to highlight the element of theological interpretation).

• "This Good News tells us how God makes us right in his sight" (NLT).

• "For the gospel reveals how God puts people right with himself" (GNB).

• "The good news tells how God accepts everyone who has faith" (CEV).

We have wandered so far from the literal meaning of the original that I need to restate it: "the righteousness of God is revealed." *That* is translation; the other renditions are interpretation.

It is demonstrably untrue that *all* translation is interpretation. Essentially literal translations do not continuously abandon verbal translation to offer the reader what the translators think the meaning of a statement is. The goal of an essentially literal translation is to keep the line of demarcation clear between translation and interpretation of meaning. For dynamic equivalent translations, on the other hand, all translation *is* potentially interpretation—interpretation defined as we define it hermeneutically to mean interpreting the thought of a statement or passage.

A lot of mischief has been done by the indiscriminate airing of the motto that "all translation is interpretation." Because this statement is demonstrably true at the linguistic level (determining what English words best render the original words), it seems perverse to deny the axiom at other levels. The self-evident level of what the axiom means has been the channel for silencing anyone who does not endorse what the motto means for dynamic equivalence.

To prove that not *all* translation is interpretation, we can also look at how the rival translation theories handle the story of Mary and Martha in Luke 10:38-42. The key statement in the story is Jesus' reply to Martha after she had complained about Mary's not helping in the kitchen. Here is how essentially literal translations render the key statement (Luke 10:42):

• "Mary hath chosen that good part" (KJV).

• "Mary has chosen the good part" (NASB).

• "Mary has chosen the good portion" (RSV).

- "Mary has chosen the good portion" (ESV).

I have printed these nearly identical translations because I want the point to sink in that they all follow the principle that translation is translation, not interpretation. They give us the original text in an uninterpreted form. Classical scholar J. I. Packer claims that the original is unambiguous in saying "good thing."[7] On this interpretation, Martha's error is not in having been active in preparing a meal but in implying that Mary has been negligent in not helping. Jesus defends Mary as having chosen a good thing. The passage need not be construed as saying anything beyond that.

If dynamic equivalent translators try to tell us that *all* translation is interpretation, their statement is verifiably untrue. What they really mean is that *their* translation has gone beyond translation and forced a specific interpretation on the story. Their rendering of the key verse makes the story a contrast between Martha's activism and Mary's contemplative spirit, an interpretation that the original does not make explicit and that J. I. Packer regards as incorrect. Here is how dynamic equivalent translations interpret (notice that I did not say "translate") Jesus' statement:

- "Mary has chosen what is better" (NIV, TNIV)
- "Mary has chosen what is best" (CEV).
- "There is really only one thing worth being concerned about" (NLT).
- "The part that Mary has chosen is best" (NEB).

It is not relevant to my purpose of the moment to defend one translation over another. I wish only to call attention to the fact that the first family of translations, which everyone will immediately recognize as essentially literal translations, agrees upon what might be called a minimalist rendering in the sense of straightforward linguistic translation, unburdened by anxiety about making sure that the overall interpretation of the passage will accord with the translators' preferences. It is equally obvious that the second cluster of translations goes beyond linguistic interpretation in such a way as to control the interpretation of the passage as a whole (and we might note additionally that these translations do not agree among themselves).

Rival translations of Psalm 23:5b illustrate the same division between versions that translate what the Bible *says* and those that bypass that and express what the translators think it *means*. A literal translation reproduces what the original says: "you anoint my head with oil." Expositors disagree on whether this is a picture of a human host's hospitality toward a guest or a shepherd's anointing the scratches of a sheep with olive oil in the sheepfold at the end of the day. A literal rendition does not prejudge the interpretation of the verse but preserves its full interpretive potential. By contrast, some (but not all) dynamic equivalent versions move beyond translation to interpretation: "you welcome me as an honored guest" (GNB); "you welcome me as a guest, anointing my head with oil" (NLT); "you honor me as your guest" (CEV).

It is time to call a moratorium on the misleading and ultimately false claim that all translation is interpretation. For essentially literal translations, translation is translation, and its task is to express what the original *says*. Only for dynamic equivalent translations is all translation potentially interpretation—something added to the original or changed from the original to produce what *the translators think the passage means*.

One more thing needs to be said about dynamic equivalence: It tends toward paraphrase, despite the way in which even the freest translations try to avoid that label. "This is *not* a paraphrase," declares the preface of the Simple English Bible. Are claims like this really true? We can answer that question by comparing what free translations do with the Bible to what hymn-writers do when they paraphrase passages from the Bible. Here is part of George Herbert's paraphrase of Psalm 23, with added elements italicized to clarify what is going on:

> The God *of love* my Shepherd is,
> And he that doth me feed;
> *While He is mine and I am His,*
> What can I want or need?
>
> He leads me to the tender grass,
> Where I *both feed and* rest;
> Then to the streams that gently pass,
> In both I have the best. . . .
>
> Yea, in death's shady, black *abode*
> Well may I walk, not fear,
> For Thou art with me, and Thy rod
> *To guide,* Thy staff *to bear.*

It is easy to surmise *why* songwriters expand the scriptural text: They need to do so for line length, rhythm, and rhyme. But I want to look past the reason for paraphrase and simply observe what it is that poets do. They expand and clarify beyond what the original text says.

Here is a sampling of specimens from dynamic equivalent translations that show the kind of interpretive moves that they continuously employ and that, in fact, their theory commits them to do (and again I have italicized the added or changed elements):

• "*The oppressed* look to him and are *glad*" (Psalm 34:5, GNB).

• "Those who look to him *for help* will be radiant *with joy*; *no shadow* of shame will *darken* their faces" (Psalm 34:5, NLT).

• "You will shine *like the sun and never blush* with shame" (Psalm 34:5, CEV).

• "My cup overflows *with blessings*" (Psalm 23:5b, NLT).

• "*You . . . fill* my cup *until it* overflows" (Psalm 23:5b, CEV).

• "On him God the Father has placed his seal *of approval*" (John 6:27, NIV).

• "Have the salt *of friendship* among yourselves" (Mark 9:50, GNB).

Dynamic equivalent translators do exactly what hymn-writers do: They paraphrase by adding explanatory material beyond what the original does, and they substitute terms for what the original contains. The cumulative effect of such expansion is that it is "almost a homily" on the original text.[8] Someone has correctly compared the effect of dynamic equivalent translations to that of "hearing a poet read his verses while someone stands by and paraphrases."[9]

We might profitably pause to consider all of this adding to and subtracting from the biblical text in light of the following comments from the Bible itself:

• "You shall not add to the word that I command you, nor take from it . . ." (Deuteronomy 4:2, ESV).

• "Everything that I command you, you shall be careful to do. You shall not add to it or take from it" (Deuteronomy 12:32, ESV).

• "Every word of God proves true. . . . Do not add to his words" (Proverbs 30:5-6, ESV).

Surely these cautions from Scripture have *some* implication for Bible translation.

The root of the matter is that the rival theories of translation have differing metaphors by which they understand the translator's task. For essentially literal translators, the translator is *a messenger* who bears someone else's message and "*a steward* of the work of another" whose function is "to be faithful to what is before him" and "not . . . to change the text."[10] Dynamic equivalent translators assume the roles of both *exegete* and *editor*. In those roles, they perform exactly the same functions that exegetes and editors perform—they offer interpretations of the biblical text right in the translation, and they make the stylistic changes that they think will improve the biblical text for a target audience.

FALLACY #3: READABILITY IS THE ULTIMATE GOAL OF TRANSLATION

I recall an early encounter after the NIV made its appearance with someone who attempted a put-down of my preference for the RSV by asking, "What do you do with the fact that surveys show a higher rate of comprehension for the NIV than the RSV?" (To this person's credit, she also regularly acknowledged in Bible studies that the NIV was unfaithful to the original.) In a day when polls and surveys carry automatic persuasive effect, the claim that *surveys show* that the NIV is easier to understand than are translations in the King James tradition of dignified language seemed on the occasion of my "cross-examination" to carry the day.

Because dynamic equivalence has dominated the field for half a century, the criterion of readability (code language for "easy to read") has become the chief selling point for modern translations. This comes out not only in the prefaces to the translations but in the commendations that are urged by partisans of easy-reading translations.

Having had a quarter of a century to ponder the matter, I have concluded that the criterion of readability, when offered as a criterion by itself, should be met with the utmost resistance. To put it bluntly, *what good is readability if a translation does not accurately render what the Bible actually says?* If a translation gains readability by departing from the original, readability is harmful. It is, after all, the truth *of the Bible* that we want. The farther a translation feels free to depart from the original text, the more readable contemporary readers find it, just as a seventh-grade reading book is easier to read than a novel by Dickens or C. S. Lewis's space trilogy.

Here is an eminently readable selection from *The Message*: "You're blessed when you're at the end of your rope. With less of you there is more of God and his rule. You're blessed when you feel you've lost what is most dear to you. Only then can you be embraced by the One most dear to you" (Matthew 5:3-4). The problem is that this readable passage is so far removed from what the original says as to render the original nearly invisible. A literal translation reads, "Blessed are the poor in spirit, for theirs is the kingdom of heaven. Blessed are those who mourn, for they shall be comforted." We might note in passing that the rendition from *The Message* does what dynamic equivalency often does: It forecloses interpretive options, such as the possibility that the blessings stated in the Beatitudes are eschatological promises for the coming age.

The only legitimate appeal to readability comes *within* the confines of a translation's having been truthful to the language of the original. Faithfulness to what the Bible actually says is like a qualifying exam. If a translation does not give us that, it has failed the test, and we can be excused from inquiring into its readability. Within the confines of accuracy to the original text, a translation should strive to achieve maximum readability by avoiding obsolete words and demonstrably archaic language, and by using with discretion and where necessary words that are slightly archaic and words in a reader's passive as distinct from active vocabulary (words that are understood by readers though not regularly used by them).

We need to remember that readability exists relative to the linguistic level of a given reader or group of readers. One cannot help noticing the discrepancy between dynamic equivalent translations and their prefaces. The prefaces are written in what is commonly known as "standard formal English"—the language used by college-educated users of English. It is more demanding than most dynamic equivalent translations. In fact, if subjected to the standards of readability by which translations are tested, these prefaces would rank low on readability.

Why, then, do translation committees produce such prefaces? Because the issues being discussed require a more sophisticated vocabulary, syntax, and logic than are represented by a lowest-common-denominator style. We should learn a lesson from this: An effective piece of writing needs to be answerable to the demands of what it is designed to do. *Within those demands*, it must be as readable as possible. Readability in an English Bible translation should not be defined in terms of being the simplest English prose that we can produce. It should always be defined in terms of maximum readability *within the parameters of the true nature of the biblical text as it stands in the original.* As I said in an earlier chapter, the Bible is not, on balance, a simple and easy book. It is frequently difficult, complex, and sophisticated. If it were not, it would not have occasioned so many learned commentaries and books. Simplifying this complexity for the sake of readability does not increase understanding; instead of *clarifying* the original text, it *obscures* it.

FALLACY #4: THE IMPORTANT QUESTION IS HOW *We* WOULD SAY SOMETHING

Another common fallacy that reigns among dynamic equivalence translators is the notion that the task of translators is to express the content of the Bible as we today would express that content. How would *we* say the things that the biblical writers said? is regarded as the important question.

I was first introduced to the "how *we* would say it" fallacy one day at church as I overheard two people who are expert in the Bible's original languages talk in the hall after a Sunday school class devoted to the study of biblical Greek. Since this was the first time I had heard the principle articulated so baldly, the objection that I intruded into the conversation yielded little. Having had time to digest the argument, I can say that whereas some dynamic equivalent principles have a surface appeal to me, this one does not. To say that we should translate the Bible in terms of how *we* would express the Bible's content is contrary to all of the facts of the matter.

First, there is an elementary confusion here regarding authorship of the Bible. To ask how *we* would express things is to elevate ourselves to the status of writing the Bible, in effect putting ourselves in the place of the biblical writers. Authors are the ones who decide how they want their content expressed. I feel almost foolish to make the elementary point that it is the biblical authors who wrote the Bible, not we. The relevant question is not how we would say something but how the writers of the Bible, guided by the Holy Spirit, *did* say it.

Secondly, to make the Bible approximate our own contemporary idiom is to remove the world of the biblical text from view. As I discuss in other parts of this book, the Bible achieves its effect by first confronting the modern reader with the "otherness" of the text. Without that removal from our own vantage point, we run the risk of not being challenged as we should. In the words of Ray Van Leeuwen, "The danger of [functional equivalent] translations is that they shape the Bible too much to fit our world and our expectations."[11]

Thirdly, to make the Bible sound as modern as possible is to obscure an obvious fact about the Bible, namely, that it is an ancient document. People back then did *not* express things as we express them today. To conceal the antiquity of a text that comes to us from two and three millennia ago with a veneer of modernity provided by a contemporary idiom is to cut against the grain. The final product is a confusing hybrid, part ancient, part modern.

Fourthly, when the formula "how *we* would say it" is invoked, the question needs to be asked, What is meant by "we"? The ordinary educated English-speaking person? In my experience, people who appeal to the formula have in mind the colloquial idiom of informal American discourse. People who speak a different kind of discourse from this would obviously express themselves differently from how lowest-common-denominator translations express their content. In fact, often people who speak in ungrammatical and unsophisticated form in life's most informal settings usually speak much better than that on more formal occasions. The point is that it is not our prerogative as *readers* of the Bible (rather than its authors) to express the content of the Bible according to *our* customary way of speaking. Furthermore, there is no single and definitive norm for how "we" speak and write.

Fallacy #5: Koiné Greek Was Uniformly Colloquial

It has become a commonplace that the New Testament was written largely in an idiom known as koiné ("common") Greek rather than classical, academic Greek. This is sometimes used to defend the practice of translating the Bible into informal, colloquial English. For example, in laying down the translation rule "pay careful attention to the Koiné," one translator asserts that the right procedure in translating the New Testament consists of simply "sticking with the 'newspaper' marketplace Greek of the first century A.D., in which the New Testament is written. God wrote the New Testament in such a way that the *average* person of that day could easily understand."[12]

It is beyond the scope of this book to explore the ramifications of the koiné of the New Testament for Bible translation in detail. All that I wish to do is question the blanket attempt to defend a colloquial English translation on the basis of the fact that the New Testament was written in koiné. In brief, here are considerations that resist such a facile equation of koiné with modern colloquialism.

First, the fact that the New Testament was written in koiné by itself says little about the level of formality or informality of what was spoken and written *in* that language. All that it means is that the New Testament was written in a vernacular language rather than in classical Greek, comparable to Dante's writing *The Divine Comedy* in the vernacular Italian and Chaucer's writing *The Canterbury Tales* in Middle English rather than in Latin, the language of international ecclesiastical and scholarly discourse at the time Dante and Chaucer were writing. *Every* language has its own continuum of formality and informality. If koiné was the language of the street and marketplace and shopping list, it was also the language of the synagogue and public prayer and theological treatise. When my father, who had not finished grade school, prayed at the table, he prayed in the high style, not in the language he used when the "haying" crew sat down to coffee.

Secondly, the Old Testament is *not* written in a dialect but in the mainstream language of Jewish culture. The importance of this for the New Testament is that much of the New Testament incorporates the Old Testament (including its formal poetic passages) into its very vocabulary and network of allusions. The result is that New Testament koiné Greek is not just like everyday colloquial discourse of the New Testament era. As a Greek scholar notes, "The Greek of the New Testament is . . . set apart from the Greek of the marketplace throughout the Mediterranean world by the large Semitic element which it contains."[13] The result is a passage such as this (Hebrew 1:3-5, ESV):

> *He is the radiance of the glory of God and the exact imprint of his nature, and he upholds the universe by the word of his power. After making purification for sins, he sat down at the right hand of the Majesty on high, having become as much superior to angels as the name he has inherited is more excellent than theirs. For to which of the angels did God ever say,*

> *"You are my Son,*
> *today I have begotten you"?*

This is not the vocabulary and syntax of the street. It is exalted prose with a poetic allusion tossed in as well.

Thirdly, that New Testament koiné is capable of exaltation is confirmed by the view of some specialists of the language of the New Testament, who conclude that the language of the New Testament is frequently different from that of koiné used in everyday conversation and commercial transaction. Classicist Nigel Turner wrote an article that surveys the wide range of ways in which the Greek language of the New Testament rises to literary status, including parallels to contemporary writers considered accomplished literary and philosophical figures.[14] A. H. Nichols surveys the work of Rydbeck, Silva, Horsley, and Porter in arguing that "few scholars, now, would give unqualified assent" to the earlier view of Kenneth Pike that the language of the New Testament is the language of the street.[15]

Similarly, a translator of the New Testament concluded that "diction alone is not all that counts; and when I talk of the Gospels as 'supreme works of literary art,' I am thinking rather of the skill with which their very miscellaneous contents were put together. . . . The Greek gospels . . . are majestic, and I think we must strive to convey this effect in the best contemporary English at our command, and never to write down."[16] E. K. Simpson believed that in the wake of Adolf Deissmann's emphasis on the linguistically low level of New Testament language, "the balance needs to be somewhat redressed," noting in his discussion the need "to recognize that *literary element* which transcends the plebeian level."[17]

Bruce Metzger's extensive survey of the language of the New Testament consistently produces such statements as these:[18]

- ". . . a careful and skillful author, whose work is easily recognized as coming closer to the definite literary style of a master of the Greek language than anything else in the New Testament."
- ". . . written in excellent Greek and in a strikingly elevated and picturesque style resembling that of the Hebrew prophets."
- "Another author whose literary abilities were of a superior order was Luke . . . a capable littérateur."
- "The language of 1 Peter is nearer to the standards of classical Greek than the vernacular koine."
- "Borne along by his earnest and spirited emotions, Paul's colloquial Greek sometimes becomes elevated and dynamic."

• Nonliterary koine varies from a "crude and frequently ungrammatical form of Greek to the standard literary form."

One thing that Metzger and others have emphasized is the degree to which the Greek of the New Testament has been suffused with Hebraic terminology from the Old Testament. Regarding this liturgical flavor in the New Testament, Albrecht Ritschl claimed that "the Old Testament is the lexicon of the New Testament."[19] This casts a new light on the King James Version, which is so scorned by dynamic equivalent translators for its strangeness. Someone has written that "the New Testament was written in Hebraized Greek. The KJV with its literalism is Hebraized English."[20] The import of this is that a contemporary colloquial translation of the New Testament that makes everything sound "natural" might be the very translation that is farthest from the original text.

The most systematic analysis of New Testament language is Detlev Dormeyer's book *The New Testament Among the Writings of Antiquity*.[21] Dormeyer concludes that "the stylistic level of the language of the New Testament corresponds only partially to the high style of artistic prose, but it is nevertheless of a middle-level literary Koine throughout."[22] According to the same source, "Paul strove to attain a sophisticated rhetorical and literary level of Koine."[23] Again, "Like the Septuagint, the New Testament contains a mixture of lower and higher literature. But it clearly came closer to mastering the subtle style than did the Septuagint."[24]

I have made no attempt to cover all that can be said on a complicated issue. My purpose has been only to counter a naive oversimplification of the presence of koiné Greek in the New Testament that regards the presence of koiné as a blanket rationale for producing a colloquial English translation of the Bible. The koiné Greek of the New Testament actually displays a broad range of literary style and sophistication.

FALLACY #6: IF BIBLICAL WRITERS WERE LIVING TODAY . . .

Another fallacy that underlies much modern Bible translation is the belief that translation should be governed by the question, "How would the biblical writers express their content if they were living today?" A specimen statement of the theory is the statement in a preface that "the purposes of this adaptation is to present Paul's message in words that he himself would use if he were writing for you and me today."[25] I would call that statement a well-intentioned but presumptuous statement.

Once again we need to state the obvious: The biblical writers are *not* writing today. They wrote millennia ago. To picture them as writing in an era when they did not write is to engage in fiction, and it distorts the facts of the situation.

The real objection to claiming to know how a biblical writer would have expressed himself if he were writing today is that it is totally speculative. There is no verifiable way by which we can know how biblical writers would express themselves if they were writing today. In my experience it is invariably translators who want to produce a colloquial Bible expressed in a contemporary English idiom who propose to know how biblical writers would have expressed themselves if they were living today. To engage in such speculation is to remake the Bible in our own image.

Paul serves as an example. What is characteristic of Paul's writing? A good starting point is to ask what we know about Paul's educational and cultural background. He was an intellectual. He was learned in both Jewish and Greek thought. He was a theologian among theologians. He was a master of rhetoric, even though he eschewed the ostentation of classical orators. All of these features converge in Paul's speech to the Areopagus (Acts 17). The Areopagus was the intellectual elite of Athenian society. Paul's speech begins with all of the rhetorical formulas of classical rhetoric.[26] The syntax is elaborate and formal. The language is dignified. There are allusions to Greek poets, showing Paul's acquaintance with them.

If we were to transport a speaker and writer like Paul into our own day, whose style would Paul's style most clearly resemble? A seminary-educated preacher's? A seminary professor's? A national leader's when making a formal address? Or the style of the local garage mechanic and check-out clerk? My answer is the former rather than the latter. People who evoke the formula "how Paul would have expressed himself if he were writing today" regularly and in my view incorrectly assume that Paul would have spoken in contemporary colloquial speech.

Those who imagine Paul as approximating the idiom of the sports talk in the office might well object that my picture of the formal and learned Paul does not match their conception. That very objection proves my point: It is pure speculation how Paul would have expressed himself if he were speaking and writing today. We do not *know* how he would have expressed himself in modern terms. We do not want a speculative Bible. We need a Bible based on certainty. What is certain is what the biblical writers *did actually say and write*.

FALLACY #7: ANY DIFFICULTY IN READING THE BIBLE IS THE FAULT OF THE TRANSLATION

It is well known that the primary goal of dynamic equivalent translations is to make the Bible immediately understandable. Correspondingly, translators in that tradition attempt to remove anything that might impede immediate understanding. The goal is that the Bible will be "*easily* understood by the readers" (GNB preface; italics mine) and "*immediately* understood by the contemporary reader" (NLT preface; italics mine).

The natural corollary of this translation philosophy is that any difficulty readers might have in understanding a Bible passage is the fault of the translation they are using. Conversely, according to this theory, any easily understandable translation is regarded as being a good translation. Eugene Nida relishes the anecdote of the reader of Today's English Version who exclaimed, "This must not be the Bible; I can understand it."[27]

To assert that easy and immediate comprehension is the sign of a good translation involves a double fallacy. As I showed in the previous chapter, the Bible is on balance a difficult rather than an easy book to read. Secondly, one of the points I will develop in the next chapter is that it is wrong to assume that the original audience of the Bible was somehow exempt from the difficulties that modern readers face. My concern here is with the implications of this for the translator.

The reasons for believing that the Bible was not immediately and easily understandable for its first readers and hearers have been admirably summarized by Wayne Grudem:

> Lest we think that understanding the Bible was somehow easier for first-century Christians than for us, it is important to realize that in many instances the New Testament epistles were written to churches that had large proportions of Gentile Christians. They were relatively new Christians who had no previous background in any kind of Christian society, and who had little or no prior understanding of the history and culture of Israel. The events of Abraham's life (around

2000 B.C.) were as far in the past for them as the events of the New Testament are for us! Nevertheless, the New Testament authors show no hesitancy in expecting even these Gentile Christians to be able to read a translation of the Old Testament in their own language and to understand it rightly.[28]

If this is an accurate assessment of the relative difficulty of the biblical text and the difficulty that its original audience experienced when reading or hearing it, then we can see how fallacious it is to blame the difficulty that a modern reader might find in the Bible on a given English translation.

But the fallacy does not stop there. As Tony Naden has correctly observed, to use the translation process as the occasion to render the biblical text easily understandable actually violates the translation principle of faithfulness to the original: "To iron out everything in the Bible to a uniform easy cognitive intelligibility is surely to be guilty of a failure of translation principle. It may even be necessary to render 'heaviness' or 'difficulty' in the original by a different sort of heaviness or difficulty more appropriate to the TL [target language] stylistic resources."[29] In other words, there are parts of the Bible for which we can unequivocally say that the easier a translation is to read, the more inaccurately it has translated the original text.

SUMMARY

The positive counterpart to the fallacies I have delineated are as follows: The only way to keep a translation from wandering into subjective variability and to remain subject to verifiable criteria of reliability is to render the words of the original into English. There is a decisive difference between linguistic interpretation and thematic interpretation of meaning, and a reliable translation sticks to the main task of translation— namely, determination of linguistic meaning. An English Bible translation should strive for maximum readability only within the parameters of accurately expressing what the original actually says, including the difficulty inherent in the original text. The crucial question that should govern translation is what the original authors actually wrote, not our speculations over how they would express themselves today or how *we* would express the content of the Bible. The fact that the New Testament was written in koiné Greek should not lead translators to translate the Bible in a uniformly colloquial style. Finally, a good translation does not attempt to make the Bible simpler than it was for the original audience.

NOTES

1 Eugene A. Nida and Charles R. Taber, *The Theory and Practice of Translation* (Leiden: E. J. Brill, 1969), 13.

2 Eugene A. Nida, *Bible Translation* (New York: American Bible Society, 1947), 12.

3 Anthony Howard Nichols, "Translating the Bible: A Critical Analysis of E. A. Nida's Theory of Dynamic Equivalence and Its Impact Upon Recent Bible Translations," dissertation, University of Sheffield, 1996, 295.

4 Ibid., 283.

5 Erich Sauer, *From Eternity to Eternity*, trans. G. H. Lang (London: Paternoster, 1954), 103.

6 Raymond C. Van Leeuwen, "We Really Do Need Another Translation," *Christianity Today*, October 22, 2001, 30.

7 James I. Packer, sermon preached at Bethel Presbyterian Church, Wheaton, Illinois, February 26, 1984.

8 Frances R. Steele, "Translation or Paraphrase," in *The New Testament Student and Bible Translation*, ed. John H. Skilton (Phillipsburg, NJ: Presbyterian and Reformed, 1978), 72.

9 Dwight Macdonald, "The Bible in Modern Undress," in *Literary Style of the Old Bible and the New*, ed. D. G. Kehl (Indianapolis: Bobbs-Merrill, 1970), 40.

10 John H. Skilton, "Future English Versions of the Bible and the Past," in *The New Testament Student and Bible Translation*, ed. John H. Skilton, 190.

11 Van Leeuwen, "We Really Do Need Another Translation," 30.

12 Clarence E. Mason, Jr., "Normative Principles of New Testament Translating (As I See It)," in *The New Testament Student and Bible Translation*, ed. John H. Skilton, 50.

13 Nigel Turner, *Grammatical Insights into the New Testament* (Edinburgh: T. & T. Clark, 1965), 183. Bruce M. Metzger is of the same opinion: "To a greater or less extent the idiom of the New Testament manifests traces of Semitic coloring in vocabulary, syntax, and style," "The Language of the New Testament," in *The Interpreter's Bible*, Vol. 7, ed. G. A. Buttrick et al (Nashville: Abingdon, 1951), 46.

14 Nigel Turner, "The Literary Character of New Testament Greek," *New Testament Studies*, 20 (1974): 107-114.

15 Nichols, "Translating the Bible: A Critical Analysis of E. A. Nida's Theory of Dynamic Equivalence and Its Impact Upon Recent Bible Translations," 215-220.

16 E. V. Rieu, "Translating the Gospels" (interview of E. V. Rieu and J. B. Phillips), *The Bible Translator*, 6 (1955). 154-155.

17 E. K. Simpson, *Words Worth Weighing in the Greek New Testament* (London: Tyndale, 1946), 6, 13.

18 For my quotations, I have ranged throughout Metzger's essay, "The Language of the New Testament," which appears on pages 43-59 of the source cited in note 13 (above).

19 Quoted by Metzger, ibid., 55.

20 Noel K. Weeks, "Questions for Translators," in *The New Testament Student and Bible Translation*, ed. John H. Skilton, 108.

21 Detlev Dormeyer, *The New Testament Among the Writings of Antiquity*, trans. Rosemarie Kossov (Sheffield: Sheffield Academic Press, 1993).

22 Ibid., 12.

23 Ibid., 78.

24   Ibid., 81.

25   Kenneth N. Taylor, *A Living Letter for the Children's Hour* (Chicago: Moody Press, 1959), 8.

26   For more on this, see Leland Ryken, *Words of Delight: A Literary Introduction to the Bible*, 2nd ed. (Grand Rapids, MI: Baker, 1992), 468-473.

27   Eugene A. Nida and Charles R. Taber, *The Theory and Practice of Translation*, 7. Nida repeats the anecdote in *Good News for Everyone* (Waco, TX: Word, 1977), 10.

28   Wayne Grudem, *Bible Doctrine: Essential Teachings of the Christian Faith* (Grand Rapids, MI: Zondervan, 1999), 51.

29   Tony Naden, "Understandest Thou What Thou Readest?" *The Bible Translator*, 33 (1982): 33.

6

EIGHT FALLACIES ABOUT BIBLE READERS

IN THIS CHAPTER I will discuss what I consider to be fallacies that some modern translations make about contemporary readers of the English Bible. The assumptions that I question are made by most dynamic equivalent translations and are, in fact, inherent in dynamic equivalence theory. I need to clarify that I have not set out to discredit these translations themselves, as though they are on my hit list. My concern throughout this book is correct principles of Bible translation, a topic that inevitably raises questions about the relative merits of various translations. As I have pursued the quest for correct principles, I have indeed ended with a profound distrust of dynamic equivalent translations.

The most salient impression that I receive from reading the prefaces of modern translations is how patronizing they are toward their readers. The premise is that modern readers are inept—people with low abilities in reading and comprehension. A number of specific premises about English Bible readers make up this condescending attitude, and these constitute the headings of the current chapter.

FALLACY #1: CONTEMPORARY BIBLE READERS HAVE LOW INTELLECTUAL AND LINGUISTIC ABILITIES

At the heart of the dynamic equivalence project has been an assumption that English Bible readers are relatively uneducated, with low reading and comprehension abilities. One preface claims that its reading level is that of a seventh grader, and another speaks of a vocabulary of three thousand words. The specific ramifications of this assumption will yield a host of further premises that make up the rest of this chapter. Underlying all of these premises, though, is the assumption of a grade-school reading level or slightly higher. One source lists the reading level of various translations this way: fifth grade level, CEV and *The Message*; sixth grade level, NLT; seventh grade level, NIV, NKJV, NRSV; tenth grade, NASB; twelfth grade, KJV.[1]

A grade-school Bible is great—for grade-schoolers. But it is emphatically not great for readers of normal adult reading and thinking ability. The fallacy is not that we need a Bible for readers of low ability. In a day of declining reading ability, we do, indeed, need simplified translations for *some* early readers *en route to more accurate and more dignified translations* as an ultimate goal. The fallacy addressed here is that of assuming impaired readers to be the norm for readers of the English Bible. It is the principle of the thing that needs to be questioned.

It is time to ask bluntly, who are these alleged readers who cannot rise above a grade-school reading level? What do they read? They obviously do not read *Sports Illustrated*, as represented by the following excerpt from an article on mountain climbing:

> Not that these were four heedless thrill-seekers plucked from a Mountain Dew commercial. Each had a wealth of experience and was prominent in the skiing-mountaineering subculture. The team comprised two sets of longtime friends. Martin and Sanders, both 30, had met in the sandbox in Los Gatos, Calif., when they were two and had been as close as siblings ever since. Martin, a world-renowned adventure skier who claimed several first descents—including some in Alaska's Chugach Mountains in the late '90s—cut a larger-than-life figure, standing 6'5" and sporting a mane of blond hair. Sanders was a stoic whose poise and levelheadedness complemented Martin's exuberance.

Easy-read translation committees would set immediately to work on paring down the vocabulary and syntax of this passage.

Nor does the target audience of most modern translations read *The Wall Street Journal*:

> Yesterday, the New York City board of education unveiled survey results indicating that the emotional toll of 9/11 on area children may be broader than first thought. The sampling of 8,000 kids in roughly 100 city schools indicates that 60,000 to 80,000 or more schoolchildren may be in distress. . . . Among the maladies: post-traumatic stress disorder, major depression and anxiety, along with strikingly high

rates of agoraphobia, or the fear of venturing outdoors. A greater risk factor than geographical proximity, like attending a school near the World Trade Center, the survey found, is psychological proximity, in the sense of suffering personal loss or knowing someone who did.

Here, too, the level of vocabulary and syntactical sophistication falls outside the pale of modern easy-read Bibles, as it does for the following specimen from the populist *USA Today*:

> Defense Secretary Donald Rumsfeld has told the White House that the United State is vulnerable to an attack by cruise missiles, *The Washington Post* reported Sunday. It cited a confidential memo in which Rumsfeld says that adversarial countries have stepped up efforts to obtain cruise missiles. Those missiles can be launched from air, sea or land and fly low to the ground to evade radar detection. The newspaper said Rumsfeld also urged that the United States mount an intensified effort to defend the country against possible attacks by such missiles.

Nor do the assumed readers of these Bibles read mainstream Christian magazines like *World*:

> He died in 1900, but philosopher Friedrich Nietzsche, along with fellow German atheists Sigmund Freud and Karl Marx, cast a long shadow over the 20th century. The latter two assumed religion was a mere fantasy, but for Nietzsche, who denied there was any reality outside our minds, religion was a more powerful fantasy than most. Perhaps that is why he hated it so much. "I call Christianity the one great curse, the one enormous and innermost perversion, the one great instinct of revenge, for which no means are too venomous, too underhand, too underground and too petty," he wrote in his 1888 diatribe, *The Antichrist*.

Readers of mainstream Christian magazines obviously have a higher reading ability than what is presupposed by reader-friendly modern Bible translations. They should not be patronized when they come to read the "Book of books."

The assumed readers of modern Bible translations apparently do not read a classic like Stephen Crane's novel *The Red Badge of Courage*:

> The cold passed reluctantly from the earth and the retiring fogs revealed an army stretched out on the hills, resting. As the landscape

changed from brown to green, the army awakened, and began to trem-
ble with eagerness at the noise of rumors. . . . A river, amber-tinted in
the shadow of its banks, purled at the army's feet; and at night, when
the stream had become of a sorrowful blackness, one could see across
it the red, eyelike gleam of hostile camp-fires set in the low browns of
distant hills.

And the assumed audience of simplified translations will not read a
typical movie review (the following one coming from *Christianity Today*):

The Nash equilibrium posits that there are circumstances in which we
are better off if we settle for something other than that which we most
desire. This may be counterintuitive, but the mathematical proof . . .
is quite elegant. Indeed, the implication of the Nash equilibrium is that
sometimes the entire community is better off when we choose not to
pursue that which we want most desperately.

The point here is not that it is illegitimate that there be a Bible translation for people who cannot read a mainstream magazine or newspaper. The fallacy is instead that we need to make most Bible readers settle
for a simplified Bible. Most of the English-speaking adult world operates at a level of vocabulary and style beyond the grade-school or even
high-school level. It is a dishonor to the Bible to expect less of people
when they read the Bible than when they read their favorite magazine
or newspaper.

My own conclusion is that we have fabricated a hypothetical audience for English Bibles that represents only a relatively small minority
of Bible readers. Most Americans—and therefore most American Bible
readers—operate at a higher level of literacy and thinking ability than
the readership presupposed by contemporary easy-read Bible translations. Some specific questions that need to be asked include these:

• Why should we expect less of people when they read the Bible
than when they read magazines and books?

• Why should we not expect readers of the Bible to rise to the levels of difficulty that they summon for academic courses and literary
works required in high school and college courses?

• Why should we require a majority of English-speaking readers to
descend to the level of comprehension and linguistic ability represented
by a minority of Bible readers?

• Instead of lowering the Bible to a lowest common denominator, why should we not educate people to rise to the level required to experience the Bible in its full richness and exaltation?

Instead of expecting the least from Bible readers, we should expect the most from them. The greatness of the Bible requires the best, not the least. I do not object to making sure that every reader has access to an English Bible commensurate with his or her level of ability. But the operative phrase here is *commensurate with*. Easy-read Bibles are below the reading and comprehension ability of most English-speaking readers. If we coddle Bible readers, they will remain at the low level at which we position them. One preface links "the average reader of modern English" with "the reading level of a junior high student" (NLT). The average American, English-speaking reader is *not* a junior high reader. He or she has graduated from grade school, high school, and in many cases college. But formal education is not the only consideration. All education is ultimately self-education. The most difficult of modern English translations—the King James—is used most by segments of our society that are relatively uneducated as defined by formal education.

There was a time when the English Bible itself raised the linguistic and cultural level of English-speaking societies. In the sixteenth century, Bible translation actually helped increase English vocabulary. There is no reason why English Bibles should not serve the same purpose in our own day. John Skilton writes in this regard:

> Far from pampering or patronizing the reader by reducing all things . . . the translator will not stand in the Bible's way as it enlarges the reader's horizon, acquaints him with a culture not his own, and challenges him to break the bonds of parochialism and insularity. He will not impede the Scriptures in their educative work; he will not try to bring the Bible down to where its readers may be; but will rather let the Bible bring them up to where it is.[2]

A final thing that needs to be said is that research has shown repeatedly that people are capable of rising to surprising and even amazing abilities to read and master a subject that is important to them. They can perform feats of mastery when it comes to specialized vocabulary and detailed information—*if* they are genuinely interested in the subject. In fact, learning a new vocabulary is part of the excitement of mastering a subject. I have begun to wonder if some Bible translations have fabricated an imaginary dilettante audience for the Bible—a hypothetical audience that does not actually read the Bible. It may be time to become realistic not only about the assumed abilities of Bible readers but also about who actually reads the Bible. This leads naturally to the next fallacy.

FALLACY #2: THE BIBLE IS READ MAINLY BY PEOPLE UNFAMILIAR WITH IT

The assumption that the Bible should be translated primarily for non-Christians who need to be evangelized has cast a long shadow over contemporary Bible translation. We need to recall at this point where the impulse for dynamic equivalence began. It began with a missionary concern to make the Bible available to people groups with newly discovered languages. The tragedy is that without serious questioning the same translation theory was applied to English translation theory and practice. Only one translation comes right out and claims that it is especially for "those who have never read the Bible" (SEB), but a similar assumption lies behind other translations. One of Eugene Nida's translation principles is that "non-Christians must have priority over Christians."[3]

We can contrast this assumption with the statements of scholars who say things like this:

• "The Bible . . . is primarily, though not exclusively, oriented to the people of God. The Bible primarily is the church's book, regulating her faith and practice. . . . No other claim on the Bible supersedes the church's claim. The church's need of an accurate and reliable standard of faith and practice supersedes every other claim."[4]

• "God's written revelation was not directed to or primarily intended for the general mass of unregenerate humanity. . . . The Bible is . . . a *covenant document.* . . . Many things therein always have and always will mystify the outsider. Our Lord declared this with regard to His own teaching in parables."[5]

• "The truth of the matter is that many New Testament messages were not directed primarily to the man in the street, but to the man in the congregation."[6]

I need to clarify that these writers are not trying to be prescriptive; they are being *descriptive*, simply stating the obvious fact that the Bible is primarily read and understood by Christian believers, not by unbelievers. In a famous monograph entitled *The Literary Impact of the Authorized Version*, C. S. Lewis correctly wrote, "I predict that [the Bible] will in the future be read, as it always has been read, almost exclusively by Christians."[7] Let me again say that the issue is not whether we need and want translations that might win the uninitiated to consider the claims of the Bible. The fallacy is to assume that most readers of the Bible *are* non-Christians who are encountering the Bible for the first time.

FALLACY #3: BIBLE READERS CANNOT HANDLE THEOLOGICAL OR TECHNICAL TERMINOLOGY

There is, of course, a range in the degree to which dynamic equivalent translations excise theological vocabulary from their translations, but all of them do *some* excising, and all of them accordingly share the premise that modern readers have a limited ability to understand theological concepts and terms. One preface claims that "a special effort was made" to translate "some traditional 'religious' words" into "expressions which can be understood by everyone" (SEB). A member of the American Bible Society claimed that the *Good News Bible* was designed for the "unsophisticated" or "average" reader, who would be grateful for "being delivered from theological subtleties."[8]

Of course it is the translations themselves that are the crucial pieces of evidence here. The CEV is committed to "the avoidance of traditionally theological language and biblical words like 'atonement', 'redemption', 'righteousness' and 'sanctification.'"[9] Other parts of this book will show some of the ways in which dynamic equivalent translations delete theological and technical vocabulary from the Bible to preserve the modern reader from encountering it. My purpose here is to question the assumption that modern readers cannot negotiate theological concepts and vocabulary.

Previous generations did not find the King James Bible, with its theological heaviness, beyond their comprehension. Nor do readers and congregations who continue to use the King James translation find it incomprehensible. Neither of my parents finished grade school, and they learned to understand the King James Bible from their reading of it and the preaching they heard based on it. We do not need to assume a theologically inept readership for the Bible. Furthermore, if modern readers are less adept at theology than they can and should be, it is the task of the church to educate them, not to give them Bible translations that will permanently deprive them of the theological content that is really present in the Bible.

Ours is a day of ironies, but few are more striking than some of those surrounding modern Bible translations. These translations sometimes defend their scaled-down level of translation with an appeal to the assumed educational level of the biblical writers and their first audience. Yet these same translations find it necessary to *pare down* the difficulty of the original text, sparing high school and college-educated readers from the difficulties of the text that the original authors expected the common people of their day to understand. Nor should we ignore the irony of assuming less and less theological ability from a culture that is more universally educated than previous centuries in which the King James Bible was the standard English Bible. Finally, after a quarter century of easy-read Bible translations designed to make the Bible accessible to the masses, biblical illiteracy continues to spiral.[10] Instead of solving the problem, modern translations, with their assumption of a theologically inept readership, may have become a self-fulfilling prophecy.

Fallacy #4: Figurative Language Is beyond the Grasp of Bible Readers

The assumptions that modern translations make about readers are actually an interlocking set of premises. It is an easy step from what I have said thus far to the assumption that figurative language is something modern readers cannot understand or relish. One preface states that "metaphorical language is often difficult for contemporary readers to understand" (NLT). Even translations that are not that transparent about the bias against poetry in their prefaces show by their practice that they agree with it (examples appear elsewhere in this book).

Several things are inaccurate about the premise that modern readers cannot understand poetry. First, why do we single out "contemporary readers" (NLT)? What is different about modern readers in regard to poetry? After all, modern readers have had more high school and college literature courses than did most readers of previous centuries. Furthermore, if people cannot understand poetry, why did God give us a Bible that is one-third poetry? Did God miscalculate the Bible's readership? Surely not.

Furthermore, we should not conclude too quickly that people cannot understand metaphor. Someone who wrote a dissertation on the use of metaphor in preaching found in a survey that a majority of sermon listeners rated metaphor as not only more beautiful and affective but also clearer than abstract propositions.[11] Finally, the way to master an idiom is to familiarize oneself with it. People learn to understand and enjoy poetry when they read it, just as they learn to love good music when they listen to it and good art when they look at it. Translations that shield readers from the poetry of the Bible deprive them of the opportunity to master it.

FALLACY #5: MODERN READERS REQUIRE SHORT SENTENCES

I know that I am inviting exasperation by elevating syntax to a point of individual consideration. After all, how much difference can the length or shortness, the complexity or simplicity, of sentence structure make in a Bible translation? The answer is that apparently it can make quite a lot of difference. This is not my idea alone. Modern easy-read translations have been obsessed with syntax. One preface states that "sentences are purposely kept short, transparent, and uncomplicated. . . . Complex sentence structures are often unnecessary anyway" (SEB). Translations in this tradition have uniformly simplified the syntax in English Bible translations by chopping up long sentences into a series of short sentences.

Why have they done so? Because of their assumption that modern readers require a simple syntax consisting of short sentences and as few subordinate clauses and phrases as possible. Before I ask what the results of this simplification are on the Bible, I want to challenge the premise that educated readers require short sentences and simple syntactical patterns. It is true that we live in a day of short attention spans, and that English style has increasingly adapted itself to that mind-set. But this is not uniformly true even of contemporary prose in everyday genres. Here is a specimen paragraph from an article entitled "The Jesus Scandal":

> Along with the shift from Christology to creation is a shift away from the doctrines of sin and repentance, which according to the preaching of the Cross are indispensable for receiving new life in Christ. The new theology often assumes that what *is* is essentially good. The paradigm shift changes the theological proclamation of the church from a call to *transformation* according to the image of Jesus Christ to one of *affirmation* of who I am as I am. The proclamation of the saving grace of the gospel has usually been expressed in transitive verbs of change—

believe, turn, repent, follow. The new theology is couched in intransitive verbs of affirmation—being and becoming. [12]

This is written in a moderately complex syntactical pattern, appropriate to the subject being addressed. I will also note in passing that the modern easy-read Bibles not only shorten the sentences but also the paragraphs, until paragraphing has virtually lost its original function of separating units of thought into their logical units. The rationale of paragraphing in many modern Bible translations is not to keep the logic of argument intact but simply to divide the material into short units for supposed ease of processing by the reader.

I have suggested that much modern prose does not adhere to the short and disjointed sentence structure of modern Bible translations, but of course a whole further sphere is the writing that comes to us from the past. Perhaps we can take John Donne's prose as an example that is like the Bible in being a religious prose text that comes to us from the past:

> No man is an island entire of itself; every man is a piece of the continent, a part of the main. If a clod be washed away by the sea, Europe is the less, as well as if a promontory were. . . . Any man's death diminishes me, because I am involved in mankind, and therefore never send to know for whom the bell tolls; it tolls for thee.

The point is that if modern readers cannot read the Bible in anything other than short sentences, they will necessarily be deprived of centuries of Christian and literary writing from the past, a situation that few would accept.

What are the effects of assuming that Bible readers can handle only short sentences? The most obvious quality that is at once diminished is the unity and coherence of a writer's line of thought. Also lost is the ability to show the subordination of parts of a writer's thought to the whole. With subordination removed from sight, all thoughts become coordinate, placed on the same plane even when the writer clearly placed them into a hierarchy of primary and secondary. This necessarily results in a distortion of the nuances of an author's intended meaning. Furthermore, if sentence structure in an English translation is dictated by the supposed syntactic abilities of the modern reader, the stylistic variety of the biblical authors is flattened out to a single, "cookie cutter" monotone. Lack of variety leads to a loss of beauty. Finally, the disjointedness produced by an endless and monotonous succession of short sentences and clauses is not only stylistically inferior, it also reflects a distinctly modern mindset in which continuity and interconnectedness have been replaced by fragmentation.

FALLACY #6: BIBLE READERS CANNOT BE EDUCATED BEYOND THEIR PRESENT LEVEL OF ABILITY

Of course no Bible translation committee would declare in a preface that they believe their readers cannot be educated, but this is a necessary inference from what the prefaces *do* say. Here is a gleaning of assumptions from several dynamic equivalent prefaces (and translation committees who do not advertise these premises nonetheless operate on the basis of them):

• readers find figurative language difficult to understand;

• the vocabulary of Bible readers is distinctly limited (even to a vocabulary of 3,000 words, according to one preface);

• the style of an English translation must be at a grade-school or high-school level;

• readers are inept at theological terminology and concepts;

• readers are unfamiliar with the Bible.

Even if these premises were true, which I disbelieve, a further, unstated assumption renders the entire train of thought fallacious. When translators fix the level of translation within the parameters noted above, they apparently believe that Bible readers will forever be stuck at their current low level of ability. Alternately, even if readers advance beyond a low level of ability, their new mastery will do them no good when they come to read the Bible because the translation has been fixed at a lowest-common-denominator level. Paul's admonition, "do not be children in your thinking" (1 Corinthians 4:20, ESV) surely has *some* application to Bible translation.

The whole orientation here is wrong. In what other areas of life do we make the assumption that people will remain at a grade-school level of understanding? What are high schools and colleges for if not to educate people beyond the grade-school level? If we were to apply to the rest of life what lowest-common-denominator translations espouse for the Bible, we might as well close our schools and give up on the hope of educating citizens and workers in various specialized spheres of knowledge.

According to educational research expert James Wilhoit, research shows that people can master difficult concepts and specialized vocabulary in areas that interest them strongly.[13] Our own experiences confirm this. It is entirely appropriate to expect Christians to summon for the Bible at least as much as they do for purposes of baking and computer usage and car ownership and hobbies. Let us also notice the irony of translators assuming a lower level of mastery for Bible readers than they themselves use in their everyday conduct of life (and their writing of prefaces and other documents about their translations), and also the irony that the most difficult Bible, the King James Version, continues to be used primarily by people who are less educated rather than more educated.

FALLACY #7: THE BIBLE IS MORE DIFFICULT FOR MODERN READERS THAN FOR THE ORIGINAL READERS

Underlying some prefaces and other defenses of dynamic equivalent translations is the premise that modern readers are somehow special when compared to the readers of earlier centuries. Because they are special, they require special concessions in the translation of the Bible. So far as I can tell, many modern readers are so agog at being told that they deserve special treatment that they do not bother to ask what their specialness consists of. If they made that inquiry, they would find that the claims of specialness are variations on the theme that modern readers are especially deficient: They can't read well, they are inept at theological understanding, they can't handle poetry, and they are the first generation of readers to find the Bible difficult.

It is the last of these that is my concern in this section. There is only one way in which modern readers find the Bible more difficult than the original readers. The farther history moves from Bible times, the more remote the customs, idiomatic expressions, and thought patterns of the original biblical world become for subsequent generations of readers. In every other way—the incidence of poetry, of formal style, of unusual or specialized vocabulary, of theological terms—the original audience faced exactly what the modern reader encounters when reading the Bible. Here are three scholars who state the matter with admirable clarity:

> One cannot escape the fact that the Bible contains many concepts and expressions which are difficult for the modern reader. There is no evidence that they were much less so for the original readers. They, too,

had to cope with technical terminology, with thousands of OT allusions and with Hebrew loan words, idioms and translation that must have been very strange to many of them.[14]

Did the average speaker of *koine* Greek find no difficulty in 2 Peter 2:4-9 or Romans 2:14-21? And if he did, is a non-difficult version of those passages a good translation? Did all the congregation of the Galatian church grasp the whole of Paul's letter to them when it was first read (let alone the street-corner literate. . .)? If "front-heavy sentences" and "distance between subject and predicate" are constructions which "strain the memory capacity of the reader" . . . then they must have been an equal strain to the Greek audience.[15]

Was the Bible written without technical terms? Are rare and difficult words lacking in the original? . . . Like any other discipline or field of study which has a unique or specialized message, the Christian faith has a technical vocabulary.[16]

As noted in the previous chapter, the corollary of thinking that modern readers are the first to find the Bible difficult is the claim, totally unwarranted, that any difficulty that modern readers experience with the Bible is the fault of the English translation they happen to be using. The fault may or may not be with the translation. Some of the difficulty is inherent in the original text, and to the extent that a modern translation removes the difficulty from sight, it has mistranslated.

It is time to call a moratorium on instilling a stance of helplessness in modern readers of the Bible. As Robert Martin has aptly said, "It is better to teach each new generation the meaning of the Bible's technical terms than to eliminate them and produce a generation [of people who] are biblically and theologically illiterate from having suffered long-term exposure to inaccurate and imprecise versions of the Bible."[17]

FALLACY #8: READERS, NOT AUTHORS, DETERMINE MEANING

The theorist who has exerted the strongest influence on evangelical hermeneutics has been E. D. Hirsch. In championing the role of authorial intention in interpretation, Hirsch claimed that if authors do not determine meaning, readers will. His specific formulation was, "When critics deliberately banished the original author, they themselves usurped his place."[18] When I first read this claim, it struck me as an exaggeration, and I still believe that by making the author and reader the only two determinants Hirsch overlooks the even more decisive role that the text itself plays as determiner of meaning.

Hirsch's statement came alive for me, though, when I ventured into the realm of Bible translation theory and practice. Suddenly the formula "if not the author, then the reader/translator" was all too true. The emphasis on matching a translation to a target audience repeatedly determines what is put into dynamic equivalent Bible translations.

We can begin with Eugene Nida's forthright elevation of the reader over the author. One of Nida's translation principles is "the priority of the needs of the audience over the forms of language."[19] Nida then caters to readers even more specifically: "The use of language by persons twenty-five to thirty years of age has priority over the language of the older people or of children"; "in certain situations the speech of women should have priority over the speech of men."[20]

With this explicit elevation of the reader over what the text literally says, certain statements in prefaces to English translations fall at once into place. Consider the following specimens:

• ". . . to express that meaning in a manner and form easily understood by *the readers*" (GNB; italics added).

• "Metaphorical language is often difficult *for contemporary readers* to understand, so at times we have chosen to translate or illuminate the metaphor" (NLT; italics added).

• "Because *for most readers* today the phrases 'the Lord of hosts' and 'God of hosts' have little meaning, this version renders them 'the Lord Almighty' and 'God Almighty'" (NIV; italics added).

• "Ancient customs are often unfamiliar *to modern readers*" (New Century Version; italics added).

Who is calling the shots here? The authors and their original text? No; the modern reader is dictating the translation. A survey of the prefaces of Bible translations will reveal that the contemporary preoccupation with the reader did not surface until the rise of dynamic equivalent translations in the middle of the twentieth century. Until then, the original text of the Bible was what was emphasized, as it still is in the prefaces to essentially literal translations.

It is the actual translation *practice*, however, that verifies the degree to which dynamic equivalent translations allow readers to determine what the translators put forward as the meaning of the biblical text.

Whenever a translation committee makes a decision on the basis of an assumed audience, it has elevated the reader to the role of determiner of meaning. If the biblical text says "who walks not in the counsel of the wicked" (Psalm 1:1, ESV) and a translation adapts to its readership by making it read "who reject the advice of evil men" on the ground that the literal translation "is not understood" by modern readers,[21] the translators have made the reader rather than the original author and his text the arbiter of meaning.

Once again I feel foolish to state the obvious: It is the writers of the Bible who wrote the biblical text, not the modern reader. We need to remind ourselves that we are here talking about linguistic meaning, not thematic meaning. If Zechariah in his song of praise said that God "has raised up a horn of salvation for us" (Luke 1:69, ESV), that is what he meant to say. To change the statement to read "has given us a mighty Savior" (CEV) because translators think that is what a reader needs or wants is to distort the text and reverse the order of authority that should prevail. The proper line of authority is that the writer presents meaning to the reader, not vice versa. This direction of the flow of meaning, I might add, is the one that we insist on in other areas of life, including statements that we ourselves have authored.

What are the results of elevating the Bible reader to the status of the one who determines the shape of an English translation? Well, what are customary commendations of this or that English translation? "I like this translation. It speaks to me." "I find this translation refreshing." "This translation makes the Bible come alive for me." All of these commendations assume that the ultimate court of appeal is the reader. None of them is rooted in fidelity to the biblical text and its authors. This is, indeed, the apotheosis of the reader.

The very proliferation of English translations feeds the syndrome of readers as the ones who determine the shape of translation. The result of the multitude of translations has been a smorgasbord approach to choosing a Bible translation. The assumption is that there are no longer objective or reliable standards for assessing a Bible translation; so readers can simply take their pick. Carried to its extreme, this mentality produces *The Amplified Bible*, which multiplies English synonyms for words in the biblical text, leaving readers to simply pick the word that pleases them, with no attempt to pin a preference to what the original text actually says.

Summary

The fallacies that some modern translations foster have resulted in a chaotic and inconsistent picture. On the one hand, these translations are embarrassingly patronizing toward their readers. They make it clear that the translators have accommodated their translation to readers characterized by low linguistic abilities, impaired comprehension and thinking skills, deficient theological capabilities, inability to read poetry, and impatience with any piece of writing that is not immediately understandable. Yet it is these very readers that modern translations have regularly elevated over the biblical author and text to the role of determining what is put forward as the meaning of the original text.

There is only one way out of this morass, and that is to expect the same standards from Bible readers that we expect of readers in other contexts of life, to lend at least the same authority to the biblical authors and their texts that we expect of our own utterances, and to let the writers of the Bible (and ultimately God) say what they said. This is tantamount to saying that the antidote to the fallacies I have outlined in this chapter is to produce an essentially literal translation of the Bible and to educate (or simply expect) English readers to understand what they read and hear preached.

Notes

1   Robert L. Thomas, *How to Choose a Bible Version* (Ross-shire, UK: Christian Focus, 2000), 127.

2   John H. Skilton, "Future English Versions of the Bible and the Past," in *The New Testament Student and Bible Translation*, ed. John H. Skilton (Phillipsburg, NJ: Presbyterian and Reformed, 1978), 191.

3   Eugene A. Nida and Charles R. Taber, *The Theory and Practice of Translation* (Leiden: E. J. Brill, 1969), 31.

4   Robert Martin, *Accuracy of Translation* (Edinburgh: Banner of Truth, 1989), 3.

5   Milton C. Fisher, "Normative Principles for Bible Translating," in *The New Testament Student and Bible Translation*, ed. John H. Skilton, 20-21.

6   Eugene A. Nida, *Toward a Science of Translating* (Leiden: E. J. Brill, 1964), 170.

7   C. S. Lewis, *The Literary Impact of the Authorized Version* (Philadelphia: Fortress, 1963), 33.

8   Quoted by Stephen Prickett, *Words and the Word: Language, Poetics and Biblical Interpretation* (Cambridge, NJ: Cambridge University Press, 1986), 6.

9   Alec Gilmore, *A Dictionary of the English Bible and Its Origins* (Sheffield: Sheffield Academic Press, 2000), 54.

10 Gary Burge, "The Greatest Story Never Read," *Christianity Today*, August 9, 1999, 45-49.

11 Michael Holcomb, "The Use of Metaphor in Preaching," dissertation, Bethel Theological Seminary, 1982. Ray Van Leeuwen similarly offers the opinion that "it is not clear to me that replacing metaphors with abstractions makes it easier for

readers" (Raymond C. Van Leeuwen, "We Really Do Need Another Translation," *Christianity Today*, October 22, 2001, 32).

12   James R. Edwards, "The Jesus Scandal," *Christianity Today*, February 4, 2002, 77.

13   James Wilhoit, E-mail to the author, August 20, 2002. Wilhoit writes that "especially in areas of verbal learning . . . students can master difficult concepts and specialized vocabulary in areas that interest them strongly." Sources include these: D. Ausubel, *The Psychology of Meaningful Verbal Learning* (New York: Grune and Stratton, 1963); T. E. Good and J. E. Brophy, *Educational Psychology: A Realistic Approach*, 3rd edition (New York: Longman, 1986); E. R. Hilgard and G. H. Bower, *Theories of Learning* (Englewood Cliffs, NJ: Prentice-Hall, 1975).

14   Anthony Howard Nichols, "Translating the Bible: A Critical Analysis of E. A. Nida's Theory of Dynamic Equivalence and Its Impact Upon Recent Bible Translations," dissertation, University of Sheffield, 1996, 298.

15   Tony Naden, "Understandest Thou What Thou Readest? *The Bible Translator*, 33 (1982): 33.

16   Martin, *Accuracy of Translation*, 29.

17   Ibid., 37-38. Fisher writes similarly, "Lowering the terminology of the Bible for each succeeding generation with the well-intentioned aim of communicating in the words of everyday conversation would end in a paucity of expression that would amount to depletion of the vital content it is desired to communicate" ("Normative Principles for Bible Translating," in *The New Testament Student and Bible Translation*, ed. John H. Skilton, 21).

18   E. D. Hirsch, Jr., *Validity in Interpretation* (New Haven, CT: Yale University Press, 1967), 5. Elsewhere Hirsch writes that the meaning in a text has "to represent *somebody's* meaning—if not the author's, then the critic's," 3.

19   Nida and Taber, *The Theory and Practice of Translation*, 31.

20   Ibid., 32.

21   Eugene A. Nida, *Good News for Everyone* (Waco, TX: Word, 1977), 10.

PART THREE

Theological, Ethical, and Hermeneutical Issues

7

THE THEOLOGY AND ETHICS OF BIBLE TRANSLATION

HOW DO THEOLOGY and ethics enter into the translation process? It is easy to give lip service to the importance of theology in the translation process while actually treating the process of translation as only a linguistic science or a marketing venture directed to a target audience. Translation *is* a linguistic science, to be sure, but the translation of the Bible inevitably occurs within a theological and moral framework.

This chapter represents my best attempt at a difficult and sensitive subject. Because of the sensitivity of the issues involved and the seriousness of the claims I am about to make, I want to record at the outset my respect and friendship toward translators and publishers whose translation theory and practice I believe to be theologically and ethically deficient. I can summarize my conclusions in this way: The theology of translation concerns the obligations of translators *to the text of the Bible*, while the morality of translation relates to the obligations of translators *to their readers*. The theology of translation relates a translator to God; the morality of translation, to fellow humans.

THEOLOGY *IN* THE BIBLICAL TEXT

The simplest way in which Bible translation intersects with theology concerns the theology that resides within the Bible itself. The Bible is the source of Christian theology. What English Bible translators put forward as an accurate version of what the Bible says becomes the basis of the theological beliefs of multitudes of people.

The obligation that this imposes on translators is both simple and profound. It is the obligation to express the actual words of the original text as accurately as the process of translation allows. The more theologically-laden a biblical passage is, the more far-reaching the theological ramifications are likely to be. There is no room for casualness or imprecision, no place for a margin of error. What this means practically is that translators need to be alert at every point to how a given rendition of a word, phrase, or passage might be construed theologically.

It is a truism that writers of whatever type need to include material and choose phraseology that helps to safeguard their writing against misreading. While there is no way in which to ensure absolutely that readers will not do something with a text contrary to a writer's intention, the chances of misreading are reduced when writers think ahead and anticipate readers' responses. The same thing is true of Bible translators: They need to be aware of how a given translation of a passage might affect the theological thinking of readers.

Two strictures need to be placed on dynamic equivalent translations at this point. First, these translations typically defend their simplified approach—their desire to remove difficulties from the text and make it immediately accessible—on the ground that this is what first-time or uninitiated readers need. The problem is that no provision is made to move such readers to a more accurate and theologically sophisticated translation when readers have become familiar with the Bible. The typical Bible reader becomes fixed at the level of the simplified translation. The theological problem here, as D. A. Carson notes, is that "the receptor group will likely use this new translation of the Bible for decades to come, maybe a century or two."[1]

Equally troublesome is the way in which some dynamic equivalent translations avoid or modify theological language. The obvious question is this: How can an adequate theology be construed from, or built upon, a translation that deprives the reader of theological vocabulary? As an example, consider how different the theology will be that is based on each of the following translations of Romans 3:24:

• "[We] are justified by his grace as a gift, through the redemption that is in Christ Jesus" (ESV).

• "But by the free gift of God's grace all are put right with him through Christ Jesus, who sets them free" (GNB).

• "Yet now God in his gracious kindness declares us not guilty. He has done this through Christ Jesus, who has freed us by taking away our sins" (NLT).

• "But God treats us much better than we deserve, and because of Christ Jesus, he freely accepts us and sets us free from our sins" (CEV).

• "Out of sheer generosity he put us in right standing with himself. A pure gift. . . . And he did it by means of Jesus Christ" (*The Message*).

Once we remove the theological vocabulary of justification and redemption from the agenda, we are hamstrung in our attempt to formulate a theology as we ordinarily conceive of it. The principle is simple: One cannot formulate a theology without theological vocabulary. Consider what happens when the statement that God "counted it to him as righteousness" (Genesis 15:6, ESV) is rendered as "the LORD was pleased with him" (CEV) or "the LORD was pleased with him and accepted him" (GNB). A doctrine of imputed righteousness can be built on the first translation; the vocabulary of pleasing God does not yield a doctrinal vocabulary. Scholars and preachers who teach their charges theological doctrines like justification and redemption should never have allowed a discrepancy to develop between their own theological vocabulary and the Bibles they themselves use and encourage their students and congregations to read.

How Theology Influences Bible Translators

Translators come to the biblical text with their own theological beliefs, which inevitably influence how they choose to translate some words. There is no such thing as total objectivity here, and James Barr is a bit quick to pin the label "sectarian" on translations produced by evangelical scholars, apparently thinking that liberal translations are somehow more objective than others.[2] There is a legitimate sense in which translators are theological guardians of the truth as they see it, though one's theology, in turn, should be derived *from* the Bible. The number of passages where one's theology directly influences translation is relatively small.

Whenever new translations appear, reviewers pore over them for evidences of theological bias. The most that this scrutiny has usually yielded is *groups* or *families* of translations. For the English-speaking Christian world, they are three in number—evangelical, liberal Protestant, and Catholic. Sometimes the basis for this classification is theological, but in other instances it is simply a matter of choosing terminology that is familiar to a given tradition, such as the Anglican preference for translating the word *episkopos* (1 Timothy 3:2) as "bishop" (NEB) and the evangelical preference for translating it as "overseer" in order to avoid the appearance of Catholic and Anglican church hierarchy.

This is not to deny that theological biases also occur. The RSV doomed itself with many evangelicals by its translation of a handful of theologically-laden verses. The most famous is the use of "young woman" instead of "virgin" in Isaiah 7:14. Another example is the RSV's abandonment of the word *propitiation* (Romans 3:25; Hebrews 2:17; 1 John 2:2; 1 John 4:10) in favor of *expiation*. While the preference of "young woman" may have been a linguistic rather than theological choice, abandoning the word *propitiation* probably reflects the translators' disbelief that God could be angry with sinful humanity to the point of needing to be appeased. We should not overlook the irony, though, that modern dynamic equivalent Bibles (including the NIV) have done exactly what the RSV did on this score with impunity, an obvious case of double standards.

The average reader is doubtless innocent of the theological biases of translations. It is important to know, therefore, that certain passages constitute a virtual code language that signals where a given translation falls. Reviewers quickly pounce on Genesis 1:1 as a signpost. If a translation prefers, "In the beginning God created the heavens and the earth," the translation is broadly evangelical. Liberal translations prefer the formulation, "In the beginning when God created the heavens and the earth . . ." If God's covenant to Abraham reads, "In you all the families of the earth shall be blessed" (Genesis 12:3), the translation accords with evangelical preferences. If it reads, "By you all the families of the earth shall bless themselves" (RSV), or "All the families on earth will pray to be blessed as you are blessed" (NEB), the translation reflects a more liberal bias, even though both translations are linguistically possible. The most obvious lesson to be learned from this is that Bible readers should read translations in an awareness of families of translation.

TOWARD A THEOLOGY OF THE WORD

I have thus far discussed the way in which theology is embedded *in* the Bible and the implications of this for translation. Equally important is the theology *of* the Word—that is, the bearing on translation of what we believe to be true about the Bible and its inspiration.

Three interrelated doctrines are particularly relevant to Bible translation. They are the authority of the Bible, the inspiration of biblical authors by the Holy Spirit, and the verbal or plenary ("full, complete") inspiration of the Bible. I will make my own position clear right at the outset: I believe that these three doctrines lead logically to a translation that is essentially literal. Correspondingly, I believe that dynamic equivalent translations have led many evangelicals to compromise (perhaps unwittingly) the very doctrines of the Word that they theoretically espouse.

The Authority of the Bible

The doctrine of the authority of the Bible affects translation at such a generalized level that my discussion of it will be correspondingly brief. The Bible itself claims to be the supreme authority for faith and practice. The direct and indirect biblical data that attest the Bible's authority is so extensive that for my purposes I will make the case by quoting from secondary sources.

My personal favorite among discussions by theologians has always been J. I. Packer's book *Fundamentalism and the Word of God*, which surveys the biblical data and surrounds it with incisive commentary of the most winsome type. At one point Packer writes, "What Scripture says, God says; and what God says in Scripture is to be the rule of faith and life in His Church. . . . Scripture, 'God's Word written,' is the final authority for all matters of Christian faith and practice."[3]

The same codification of what the Bible says about its own authority was made at the time of the Protestant Reformation. While the resulting theological formulations are embedded in the historic creeds of the Reformation, I am going to share my partiality toward the English and American Puritans by quoting from them:[4]

• "The word of God must be our rule and square whereby we are to frame and fashion all our actions; and according to direction received thence, we must do the things we do, or leave them undone" (William Perkins).

• "This is the glory and sure friend of a church, to be built upon the Holy Scriptures. . . . The foundation of the true church of God is Scripture" (John Lightfoot).

• "The rule according to which conscience is to proceed is what God has revealed in the Sacred Scriptures" (Cotton Mather).

• ". . . a perfect rule of faith and morals" (William Ames).

While it would be wrong to say that dynamic equivalent translators have questioned the doctrine of the authority of Scripture, I would nonetheless say that I myself would not feel comfortable doing the things with the Bible that they customarily do. In fact, I would not feel comfortable making the kinds of changes that dynamic equivalent translations make to the original text with *any* book that I hold in high esteem. For example, if I were to distribute excerpts from a work of literature, the Gettysburg Address, or even an article from *Newsweek* to a class of students, I would never think of changing the wording. I have too high a regard for the authority of even secular texts to do so. The same principle is even more important in Bible translation, where the words of the Bible are the very words of God. Every possible nuance of meaning that resides in the words of the original must be carried over into the words of a translation.

Quite apart from my view of the inviolability of written texts, it seems self-evident to me that if the Bible is authoritative in the way that it claims to be and as the evangelical Christian tradition has regarded it as being, it should be unthinkable that we would exert such aggressive tampering with the biblical text as dynamic equivalent translations do. I can imagine dynamic equivalent translators saying that they do not think of themselves as tampering with the text. My reply is that they need to start viewing it in those terms. If this seems a stretch, they need to ponder the implications of the fact that they themselves would object if an editor or translator or a speaker quoting them did with their statements what they do with the Bible during the process of translating. I refer to such customs as dropping metaphors, changing words, adding explanatory commentary, and changing gender references to match what the editor or translator or speaker prefers. Surely we would think that this constitutes a disrespect for our authority as author. I would just note in passing that the words *authority* and *author* come from the same root word.

My mention of gendered language leads me to observe in passing that Christians who have a high view of the authority of the Bible consistently hold it up as a normative authority by which the fashions of contemporary culture must be assessed. The desire to change the gender references in the Bible did not arise until the arrival of modern feminism on the cultural scene. This does not make gender sensitivities an illegitimate issue. It only means that the impetus for changing gender references in the Bible did not flow from the Bible but from contemporary culture.

The Inspiration of Biblical Authors by the Holy Spirit

Behind the authority of the Bible stands the process by which the Bible came into existence. According to certain key passages in the Bible, the authors of the Bible were guided and inspired by the Holy Spirit to write what they wrote. The most important statements to this effect are the following:

> *And we impart this in words not taught by human wisdom but taught by the Spirit. (1 Corinthians 2:13, ESV)*

> *All Scripture is breathed out by God. (2 Timothy 3:16, ESV)*

> *... no prophecy was ever produced by the will of man, but men spoke from God as they were carried along by the Holy Spirit. (2 Peter 1:21, ESV)*

The result of such a process of inspiration is that the Bible as it stands is what God wanted us to have:

> *And we also thank God constantly for this, that when you received the word of God, which you heard from us, you accepted it not as the word of men but as what it really is, the word of God. (1 Thessalonians 2:13, ESV)*

It is not part of my purpose here to explore the intricacies of the far-reaching doctrine of the inspiration of the biblical writers by the Holy Spirit. So far as Bible translation is concerned, the crucial principle is this: *We can rest assured that the Bible as it was written is in the form that God wants us to have.* This may seem like a platitude, but when we put that principle into the climate produced by dynamic equivalence, it is not platitudinous but revolutionary. To believe that the Bible as we have it is what God wants us to have directly contradicts a number of common practices of dynamic equivalent translation, including the following:

- changing concrete images into abstractions;
- dropping figurative language and changing it into direct statement;

- adding explanatory material beyond what is in the original text;
- deleting theological vocabulary and replacing it with non-theological wording;
- changing singular references to make them plural in the interests of getting rid of masculine gender references.

As I ponder this degree of casualness toward the actual words that the biblical authors wrote, my mind goes back to a question that Clyde Kilby posed in a Wheaton College faculty address and subsequently in a magazine article: "Did God inspire the form or only the content of the Bible? Is its form only a man-made incidental?"[5] This is something that Bible readers and translators rarely ask, but they need to ask it. If the writers of the Bible were at some level guided and even "carried along" by the Holy Spirit (2 Peter 1:21), it is a logical conclusion that the Holy Spirit moved some biblical authors to write poetry, others to imagine prophetic visions, and so forth. The very *forms* of biblical writing are inspired, and to the fullest extent possible the forms of the original need to be carried into the syntax and structure of the receptor language.

If this is true, certain implications for Bible translation follow. If the Holy Spirit moved a given writer to produce poetry replete with concrete imagery, it is inappropriate to turn the images into abstractions and offer the altered text to the public as an accurate translation. If under the Holy Spirit's guidance a biblical poet or epistle writer expressed his thought in a metaphor or theological term, a translation that removes the metaphor or theological term from sight has tampered with something that the Holy Spirit thought good to give to the human race.

I can imagine derisive labels like *purist* and *elitist* and *nitpicker* starting to whiz past me, but the issue deserves to be taken a great deal more seriously than many translators have taken it. In essence, the question is this: *Did the writers of the Bible express God's truth in the exact forms that God wants us to have them*? And if the biblical doctrine of the inspiration of the Scripture by the Holy Spirit prompts the answer "yes," the logical conclusion is that the very images and metaphors and technical terms that we find in the Bible are inspired. We are not free to correct or adapt the text to the perceived abilities or tastes of a contemporary readership. Did God give us the Word as he wants us to have it? That is the question. I was pleased to see Ray Van Leeuwen pick up on this usually overlooked point:

The translator who removes biblical metaphors to make the text "easier" for readers may defeat *the purpose of the Holy Spirit, who chose a metaphor in the first place* [italics added for emphasis].[6]

We need to take seriously what we believe about the inspiration of the Bible by the Holy Spirit. I do not feel free to change the words of Wordsworth or Dickens or C. S. Lewis, and the stakes are considerably higher with a book that I believe to be inspired by God.

Verbal Inspiration of the Bible

In the preceding section I discussed inspiration at a general level as the process by which the Holy Spirit moved and guided the writers of the Bible to say what God wanted said. In this section I intend to narrow the focus to a more specific doctrine of inspiration.

The evangelical Protestant theology of inspiration has traditionally espoused verbal or plenary ("complete, full") inspiration of the Bible. This view holds that God inspired not only the thoughts of biblical writers but their words. I should note that in the past century the impetus for revisiting and vigorously defending the doctrine of plenary inspiration came from a need on the part of evangelicals to resist the claims of theological liberals that only the general thought or ideas of the Bible are inspired, not the actual words and minute details.

What, then, constitutes the doctrine of verbal or plenary inspiration of the Bible? Here are four specimen definitions and explanations of the doctrine:

• "It would . . . be impossible to divorce the thoughts of the Bible from its words. The thoughts are indeed 'God-breathed' thoughts. . . . In what manner, however, has God seen fit to reveal those thoughts to us? To ask the question is to answer it. He has revealed them through the media of words. . . . Only one doctrine of inspiration is taught in the Bible, namely, that of a plenary and verbal inspiration to which the modern mind is so hostile" (Edward J. Young).[7]

• "The point that *plenary* and *verbal* make is that the biblical words themselves (in Hebrew, Aramaic, or Greek) are to be seen as God-given. . . . The Lord who gave the Word also gave the words. It was not just the writers' thinking but 'all Scripture,' the written product, that is inspired by God (2 Timothy 3:16; cf. 2 Peter 1:21). It is critically important, therefore, that . . . we make certain that we know what the God-given words are. Words, after all, are the vehicles and guardians of meaning; if we lose the words, we shall have lost the sense too" (J. I. Packer).[8]

• "It is a well-known fact that many who profess to believe that the Bible is inspired are emphatic in their denial of verbal inspiration. They find satisfaction in the acceptance of partial inspiration, as, for instance, that only the thoughts and not the words . . . were inspired. . . . [The] supernatural guidance of the Holy Spirit extended to the very words, for this is certainly taught in the Bible, both by express statement and by implication" (Louis Berkhof).[9]

• *"The Inspiration of the Scriptures extends to the words. . . . The thoughts are in the words. The two are inseparable. . . . Christ and his Apostles argue from the very words of Scripture. . . . [This view] is known as the doctrine of plenary inspiration"* (Charles Hodge).[10]

I have taken the space to quote at length because I want the weight of what is being said to sink in. Within the context of dynamic equivalent thinking, the descriptions of verbal inspiration are an implied rebuttal to the prevailing ideology of dynamic equivalence, because translators in that camp do not regard it as essential to retain the actual words of the original.

As the last of my quotations hints, the testimony of the Bible itself gives priority to the very *words* of the Bible, not to the thoughts. At a global level, the sheer tabulation of statistics speaks volumes. The formulas "the word of the Lord" and "thus says the Lord," along with their variants, occur well over a thousand times in the Bible. By comparison, the references to the thoughts of God are statistically insignificant. This is not to say that God does not have thoughts. It is to say that the human race cannot know God's thoughts apart from his words. Furthermore, the common formula by which Jesus and biblical writers appeal to an earlier part of Scripture is "it is written" (or a variant), which calls attention to the very language in which Scripture is expressed and not simply the ideas or thoughts contained in it. Luther noted that "Christ did not say of His thoughts, but of His words, that they are spirit and life."[11]

Equally instructive are some specific instances in which the very words of the Bible are highlighted. Here are a few specimens selected with a view toward showing the range of such references (emphasis added to draw attention to the importance of words):

Aaron spoke all the words *that the* LORD *had spoken to Moses.* (Exodus 4:30, ESV)

Then the LORD *put out his hand and touched my mouth. And the* LORD *said to me, "Behold, I have put* my words *in your mouth."* (Jeremiah 1:9, ESV)

And you shall speak my words *to them. (Ezekiel 2:7, ESV)*

*"The words *that I have spoken to you* are spirit and life. (John 6:63, ESV)*

And we impart this in words *not taught by human wisdom but taught by the Spirit. (1 Corinthians 2:13, ESV)*

Now the promises were made to Abraham and to his offspring. It *does not say, "And to offsprings," referring to many, but referring to one, "And to your offspring," who is Christ. (Galatians 3:16, ESV)*

At that time his voice shook the earth, but now he has promised, "Yet once more I will shake not only the earth but also the heavens." This phrase, *"Yet once more," indicates the removal of things that are shaken. (Hebrews 12:26-27, ESV)* (The exact phrase from the Old Testament is highlighted as carrying the author's argument.)

What is the general picture that emerges from these passages? Surely that the very words of God and the words of the Bible matter a great deal. As we read the Bible, we move in a world in which *the word* has a special sanctity—a world in which even the difference between singular and plural can be the basis for an entire theological argument and in which God is said to impart the words, not the thoughts. Someone who wrote a book on plenary inspiration rightly asks, "Without God's word, how can you be sure of possessing his thoughts?"[12]

The application of the doctrine of verbal inspiration to Bible translation should be obvious: If the words rather than just the thoughts of the Bible are inspired by God, it is the words that a translation should reproduce. If we set the biblical data and the theological discussions of verbal inspiration alongside the prefaces and practices of English Bible translations, a dichotomy at once emerges between translations that give priority to the words of the original text and those that claim only to reproduce the thoughts of the original text. Here are quotations from a cluster of prefaces to English Bible translations (italicizing has been added to highlight the point under consideration):

• This translation "seeks to provide a translation as close to the *words* of the Hebrew and Greek texts as possible" (Holman Christian Standard Bible).

• "The attempt has been made to render the grammar and *terminology* [of the original text] in contemporary English" (NASB).

• "Dynamic equivalence . . . commonly results in paraphrasing where a more literal rendering is needed to reflect a specific and vital sense. . . . Complete equivalence *translates fully*, in order to provide an English text that is both accurate and readable" (NKJV).

• This translation "is an 'essentially literal' translation that seeks as far as possible to capture the precise *wording* of the original text and the personal style of each Bible writer" (ESV).

Here are quotations from another cluster of prefaces (italicizing has been added to highlight the point being emphasized):

• The translators' "first task was to understand correctly *the meaning* of the original" (GNB).

• ". . . a *thought-for-thought* translation" (NLT).

• ". . . to reclothe *the meaning* of the original in the words and structure of American English" (SEB).

• "The first concern of the translators has been the accuracy of the translation and its fidelity to *the thought* of the biblical writers" (NIV).

The difference between the two philosophies of translation is clear: The first set of translations believes that it is the words of the original text that need to be translated into English, while the second set espouses the view that it is only the thoughts of the original text that need to be translated. It would be possible to read the second set of quotations without realizing that they are in fact speaking a code language in which the terms *meaning* and *thought* denote a dynamic equivalent philosophy of translation. What is implicitly *denied* by those statements is that the very words of Scripture are the priority of the translator.

The context into which I have placed these two philosophies is the biblical doctrine of verbal inspiration—that the very words of the Bible were inspired by God. It is my belief that an essentially literal translation is congruent with the doctrine of verbal or plenary inspiration. Contrariwise, the preoccupation with dynamic equivalent Bibles is with the thoughts of Scripture, with no priority assigned to the words. I come to the unwelcome conclusion that many evangelicals who theoretically espouse the doctrine of verbal or plenary inspiration—who reject the position of theological liberalism that the Bible contains primarily the thoughts of God—are betrayed by their very choice of a dynamic equivalent translation into the position that they claim to reject.

Having reached the foregoing thoughts on my own, I was pleased that my research assured me that I am not a voice crying in the wilderness. Here are others who have raised the issue of verbal and plenary inspiration in connection with translation:

• "The translator's view of the nature of the Bible's inspiration greatly influences his philosophy of translation. . . . The Bible is inspired in such a way that its very words are inspired (i.e., 'verbal' inspiration); and that inspiration extends to all the words of Scripture (i.e., 'plenary' inspiration). . . . An inspiration that extends to the divine choice of the words can only imply that God is concerned with much more than general ideas. . . . The translator must keep in mind that he is dealing with truth exactly expressed."[13]

• "When the Bible is being translated, its own doctrine as to its verbal inspiration imposes limitations on the translators' function. The Scripture teaches us that, as God's word written, its form as well as its thought is inspired. The translator of Scripture has, therefore, above all else, to *follow* the text: it is not his business to interpret it or to explain it."[14]

I can imagine dynamic equivalent translators saying that they accept the doctrine of verbal and plenary inspiration. In that case, my reply is that my understanding of verbal inspiration is different from theirs, that I believe their translation practice to be incongruent with their view of inspiration, and that I do not see a basis for differentiating their emphasis on the thoughts rather than the words of the Bible from the twentieth-century liberal and neoorthodox position that gave rise to a renewed evangelical emphasis on plenary inspiration.

THE ETHICS OF BIBLE TRANSLATION

To get a focus on the ethics of Bible translation, we need to start at the much broader level of the ethics of publishing. What *are* the ethics of publishing? The ethics of publishing are rooted in the assumed and understood contract between publisher and reader. A reader assumes that the book that is ascribed to an author is an accurate version of what the author wrote. For texts published in the author's native language, violations of the contract are almost always inadvertent and a result of error or laxity in quality control.

A whole new level of opportunity for breach of contract enters the picture when translation is involved. The reader is now at the mercy of the translators' expertise and philosophy of translation. The crucial point is this: *Readers who do not know the original biblical languages assume that an English translation reproduces what the Bible really says.* I have witnessed this premise repeatedly in Sunday school classes and Bible studies. People naturally and legitimately appeal to the English translation in their hands as constituting "what the Bible says."

Nor is this premise limited to unsophisticated readers. I have built part of a scholarly career out of the Bible as literature, using the English Bible as my text. Three decades ago a publisher sent me an anthology of essays and reviews occasioned by the appearance of the RSV and NEB. The authors were literary scholars who repeatedly lamented the erosion of the literary excellence of the KJV in modern translations. These literary critics made no attempt to conceal their scorn for modern translations.

I remember being in total agreement with the debunkers, and in fact to this day I think that what they said about the *literary* superiority of the KJV was accurate. After working on a Bible translation project, I now know that virtually all of the KJV passages praised by the literary scholars are today considered inaccurate translations of the original. How should I regard the misguided literary critics who praised the superiority of an inaccurate translation? Should I be critical of them for their foolishness? No. It is their translation that let them down. They thought that the KJV was an accurate translation of the original text in many places where it was not.

I offer this as an example of what happens every day with users of the English Bible. Users of English translations do not read prefaces, and even when they do, they do not follow the intricacies of claims about the translation of meaning rather than words. Readers of English translations operate on the premise that they are reading what the Bible actually says. Surely this is a legitimate assumption for any translation, whether of the Bible or Dante's *Divine Comedy* or Albert Camus's *The Stranger*. Whenever I discover that a translation has violated the assumed contract between translator and reader by giving me something other than what the author wrote, I feel betrayed. To me, the assumption of being taken to the words of an author's original text is nothing less than the ethics of translation and publishing. Even when a given interpretation in a dynamic equivalent translation is accurate, I believe that it is misleading and deceptive to put it before the public with the implied claim that this is what the original text says.

I am not alone in thinking that there is an ethical problem with dynamic equivalent translations. Robert L. Thomas writes, "A closely related ethical question may also be raised: Is it honest to give people what purports to be the closest representation of the inspired text in their own language, yet which is something that intentionally maximizes rather than minimizes the personal interpretations of the translator or translators?"[15]

SUMMARY

This chapter has covered important theological and ethical material. It would be wrong to think that this is merely theoretic, with little practical application. A translation has an obligation first to be accurate as the text on which theology can be accurately based. If it is a theologically impoverished text, it will produce a defective theology, which will in turn undermine the foundation of the church. Secondly, an English Bible translation should be congruent with what we believe theologically *about* the Bible, including its authority that demands reverence before it, its inspiration by the Holy Spirit in such a way that the text of the Bible as we find it is what God intended us to have, and its verbal and plenary inspiration, leading us to believe that the very words (and not just the thoughts) of the Bible are inspired. Finally, a translation is not exempt from the ordinary ethics of publishing, with its cornerstone of putting before the reader what an author wrote as accurately as possible. It hardly needs to be added that this ethical claim has unique weight when the author in question is God.

NOTES

1   D. A. Carson, "The Limits of Dynamic Equivalence in Bible Translation," *Evangelical Review of Theology*, July 3, 1985, 109.

2   James Barr, "Modern English Bible Versions as a Problem for the Church," *Quarterly Review* 14 (1994): 269-273.

3   J. I. Packer, *Fundamentalism and the Word of God* (Grand Rapids, MI: William B. Eerdmans, 1958), 73, 75.

4   All of my Puritan quotations are taken from my book *Worldly Saints: The Puritans as They Really Were* (Grand Rapids, MI: Zondervan, 1986).

5   Clyde S. Kilby, reprinted in *The Christian Imagination: The Practice of Faith in Literature and Writing*, ed. Leland Ryken (Colorado Springs: Harold Shaw, 2002), 105.

6   Raymond C. Van Leeuwen, "We Really Do Need Another Bible Translation," *Christianity Today*, October 22, 2001, 31.

7   Edward J. Young, *Thy Word Is Truth* (London: Banner of Truth, 1957), 49.

8   J. I. Packer, "The Adequacy of Human Language," in *Inerrancy*, ed. Norman L. Geisler (Grand Rapids, MI: Zondervan, 1979), 211.

9   L. Berkhof, *Principles of Biblical Interpretation* (Grand Rapids, MI: Baker, 1950), 45-50.

10 Charles Hodge, *Systematic Theology*, Vol. 1 (London: James Clarke, 1960), 164-165.

11 Martin Luther, as quoted in René Paché, *The Inspiration and Authority of Scripture*, trans. Helen I. Needham (Chicago: Moody, 1969), 75. Paché's chapter on plenary and verbal inspiration is an excellent short treatment.

12 L. Gaussen, *Theopneustia: The Plenary Inspiration of the Holy Scriptures*, trans. David Scott (Chicago: Bible Institute Colportage Association, n.d.), 278.

13 Robert P. Martin, *Accuracy of Translation* (Edinburgh: Banner of Truth, 1989), 13-14.

14 Iain Murray, "Which Version? A Continuing Debate," in *The New Testament Student and Bible Translation*, ed. John H. Skilton (Phillipsburg, NJ: Presbyterian and Reformed, 1978), 132.

15 Robert L. Thomas, *How to Choose a Bible Version* (Ross-shire, UK: Christian Focus, 2000), 189.

8

TRANSLATION AND HERMENEUTICS

HERMENEUTICS IS THE science of interpreting a written text. In this chapter I will draw connections between hermeneutics and Bible translation. The hermeneutical principles that I discuss come directly from the evangelical consensus on what constitutes the right way to interpret the Bible. I will make no attempt to defend the principles themselves, which will have a thoroughly familiar look to them. I believe that for the last fifty years Bible translators have gone about their business in relative isolation from the hermeneutical implications of what they are doing.

The relationship between hermeneutics and translation is a two-way street. Half of the process consists of the ways in which the translation of a given Bible passage affects its interpretation. The crucial question here is how specific translation decisions or translation theories actually determine the shape of what can be done with the interpretation of the biblical text. The other half of the equation is to ask how specific principles of interpretation impact—or *should* impact—the way in which we translate the Bible. Here the premise is that if a principle is right for interpretation, it should be right for translation also.

WHAT IS THE PLACE OF INTERPRETATION?

Before I relate hermeneutics to translation, I need to clarify what I believe the place of interpretation to be. Interpretation presupposes a text that needs to be interpreted. That a text requires interpretation is not a sign of its deficiency. It might be a sign of the text's difficulty, but it is more likely to be an index to the text's richness and depth. A text that lends itself to commentary is likely to be what scholars call a normative text—a text possessing an authority and richness far surpassing the ordinary discourses of life.

Inasmuch as dynamic equivalent translations try to eliminate much of the need for interpretation as it has traditionally been understood, we need to remind ourselves that from the beginning of the Bible's existence the believing community has assumed that the Bible is a book that needs interpretation for its fullest understanding. Here is how biblical scholar Ray Van Leeuwen states the matter:

> *Bible reading and translation without [written and spoken] commentary based on thorough study of Hebrew and Greek is inadequate.* Translation is no substitute for commentary. The church and synagogue have recognized this from their beginnings. Both have continuous traditions of commentary and preaching based on the biblical text. . . . These functions are not accidental but essential.[1]

D. A. Carson is of the same opinion: "Do not the Scriptures themselves encourage us to multiply the number of evangelists, pastors/teachers and other workers, thereby discouraging the notion that the *entire* task depends exclusively on the quality of the Bible translation used?"[2]

From one point of view, dynamic equivalent translators acknowledge the importance of interpretation. They are so zealous for it that they import interpretation right into the process of translation. But in other ways they betray a misunderstanding of hermeneutics. Hermeneutics presupposes that the Bible as it really exists in the original languages is the type of book that requires interpretation, and further that interpretation is separate from translation and no less exalted than it in the functioning of the church. I do not mean to imply that dynamic equivalent translators deny that even *their* translations benefit from further interpretation, but they are so eager to remove difficulties for Bible readers that they end up lowering the stature and scope of Bible interpreters, in effect usurping their position.

How Some Translations Undermine Interpretation

My thesis in regard to the impact of translation on interpretation is simple, and it underlies this entire book: *A good translation preserves the full exegetical or interpretive potential of the original biblical text.* Conversely, a translation is inadequate to the extent to which it diminishes the interpretive potential of the original text.

Here are the leading ways in which dynamic equivalent translations can short-circuit the interpretive process (each of these will receive extended treatment later in the book):

• by making preemptive interpretive decisions, with the result that readers never have a chance to make the interpretive decision themselves;

• by reducing multiple meanings of a biblical statement to a single meaning and offering that meaning as the sole meaning;

• by resolving ambiguous statements in a single direction instead of allowing the ambiguity of the original text to stand;

• by interpreting images and figures of speech instead of allowing them to stand in their original, uninterpreted form.

The root problem here is that the translators have blurred the line between translation and interpretation. What is wrong with such confusion of boundaries? At least three things.

First, blurring the boundary between translation and interpretation misleads and confuses readers. In its effect, it is a case of false advertising. Dynamic equivalent translations do not inform readers that the text that has been placed before them is really a hybrid—a mixture of biblical text and commentary on it. Readers are unaware of this. They operate on the premise that they are reading the original text of the Bible in their own language.

Secondly, blurring the distinction between translation and interpretation sets a limit on the full interpretation of the Bible. To see how this works, we can compare translations of a line from Psalm 24:10:

• "the LORD of hosts" (ESV and other essentially literal translations).

• "our Lord, the All-Powerful" (CEV).

• "the LORD Almighty" (NIV, NLT).

A literal translation reproduces the original with the rendition "LORD of hosts." These "hosts" are the armies or citizens of heaven (or Israel)—created beings who are under God's command. By preserving the image implied in the epithet as we find it in the original and leaving it *open to interpretation* (instead of transforming it *into an interpretation*), the literal rendition allows multiple meanings. To be the leader of hosts requires power, but it implies much besides, just as the epithet "president of the United States" implies much beyond the fact that the president is a powerful figure.

The dynamic equivalent translations remove the literal reference to "hosts" and replace it with an interpretation that stresses God's omnipotence. This is not a bad interpretation, inasmuch as it is a safe inference that any leader of armies or of citizens of a heavenly realm is mighty. Where the translators get the added idea of God's being *all*-powerful is not evident. The problem with the dynamic equivalent translations is that they have cut off additional interpretive options that inhere in the formulation "LORD of hosts." What does it take to be a leader of heavenly hosts? The answers are multiple, and each one of them is cause for exalting the King of glory celebrated in Psalm 24.

By removing the hosts from the reader's sight, moreover, the translations that move beyond translation to interpretation have further limited the range of interpretations open to their reader and expositor. Simply to say that God is all-powerful does not even refer to the heavenly (or earthly) kingdom at all. No angels and saints and followers of the Lamb are in view. Furthermore, some scholars and preachers allow a possible eschatological interpretation of the hosts as believers in heaven, and this option, too, gets lost when the reference to God's hosts is deleted.

My point of departure for considering Psalm 24:10 is that blurring the line between translation and interpretation regularly diminishes the full exegetical potential of the text. More often than not, replacing translation with interpretation limits the reader to just one interpretation of a text and is often guilty of replacing the concreteness of the original with an abstraction. Furthermore, such translations put the reader at the mercy of a translation committee's interpretation of a passage. When we read, "You know everything I do" (Psalm 139:2a, GNB), we have no way of knowing that a preemptive interpretive strike has been made for us, that the actual imagery ("You know when I sit down and when I rise up," ESV) has been bypassed. Someone has correctly said that with dynamic equivalent translations a reader might legitimately "feel that his mind is being made up for him instead of his being presented with the most faithful mirror of the original text . . . so that he may draw his own conclusions."[3]

A third objection to the blurring of the boundary between translation and interpretation is that doing so misunderstands the task of translation. The function of translation is to present the original text as faithfully as possible in the receptor language. Its goal is to be transparent to the original text. It is the means by which readers are able to experience a text written in a language other than their own. Why would a reader read a translation except to be brought into contact with the original text? When translators blur the line between translation and interpretation, they have thrust themselves *between* the reader and the text. Jakob Van Bruggen is correct when he writes that "the proper role of the translator is to give the church an accurate translation upon which it may do exegesis. The work of exegesis . . . may be aids to the translator, but his own role should not be one of exegete for the church"; doing the latter "puts the translator in the wrong position and leaves the church without a reliable translation."[4]

Is there a place for a combined translation and commentary? There is, and it is nearly the opposite of what is usually claimed for easy-reading dynamic equivalent translations that consistently interpret the original text. The real usefulness of these hybrids is paradoxically not as a translation (where they are untrustworthy as a window to the original text) but as a commentary. This is how I use them. Their virtue as commentaries is their thoroughness. There is not a single verse in the Bible that is left untouched. When I am faced with a difficult text, I often consult dynamic equivalent Bibles—not as a translation but as a gloss or commentary on a difficult passage. Of course there are liabilities to these commentaries. They are a rather rudimentary form of commentary, offering just one interpretation of a passage where an avowed commentary often offers more information about possible interpretations. Furthermore, when I consult half a dozen dynamic equivalent translations, I more often than not find that they vary so widely that I end up confused and with a new sense of the unreliability of them as translations.

To sum up this point, biblical interpretation presupposes a text that can be interpreted. Dynamic equivalent translators are so intent on producing a reader-friendly Bible that they are unwilling to accept a division of duties between translation and interpretation. In conflating these two, dynamic equivalent translations have misled Bible readers, frequently concealing the original text from their view without informing readers that this is what they have done. The effect has also been to hamstring the process of interpretation by limiting the meaning of a passage to a single interpretation. In the words of Ray Van Leeuwen, "functional equivalent translations are liable to confuse the complementary tasks of translation and commentary—to the detriment of both."[5]

HERMENEUTICAL PRINCIPLES AND THE TRANSLATOR'S TASK

Thus far I have discussed hermeneutics in principle as it relates to translation. In the remainder of this chapter I propose to look at specific hermeneutical rules and the implications that they hold for translation. In arriving at these principles, I have simply surveyed the time-honored principles of biblical interpretation and selected for discussion the ones that have the greatest carryover to the task of translating the Bible.

The premise underlying my enterprise is that if a hermeneutical principle is the right way to handle the Bible in interpretation, it stands to reason that the same principle should govern Bible translation. Conversely, if a translation of a Bible passage violates an accepted rule of interpretation, this may be a sign that something has gone awry in the translation *process*. If, moreover, a given translation *theory* runs afoul of standard hermeneutical principles, surely the problem needs to be considered a global issue that extends far beyond localized decisions for specific passages.

Listening to the Text

The process of interpretation begins with a reader confronting a text. The text is the starting point. Readers are dependent on the words of the text for all that they eventually experience in their reading of the work. Accordingly, the humility of the reader before the text is the chief "readerly" virtue. Literary scholar Peter Leithart puts it this way in an essay provocatively titled "Authors, Authority, and the Humble Reader":

> As G. K. Chesterton said, humility makes us small, and that means that everything around us becomes large and astounding and magnificent. Humility before the world that the author presents means that we allow him to set the rules. . . . Humility before the text means entering the text and the world that it creates. . . . Having humbled himself before the author, the reader shall, quite properly, be exalted.[6]

Also excellent is C. S. Lewis's viewpoint that "the first demand any work of any art makes upon us is surrender. Look. Listen. Receive. Get yourself out of the way."[7]

Some scholars object to Lewis's theory as applied to ordinary texts because readers have a responsibility to "talk back" to authors and texts—to assess the claims of an author in terms of their own values and worldview. Lewis does not deny this. His point is simply that readers have a moral obligation *first* to hear an author out, free from constant interruption and the impaired listening that always occurs when someone interrupts and immediately asserts one's own viewpoint. Having listened, readers are *then* obliged to be themselves as readers with their own values and viewpoints.

But this scholarly disagreement about how to read extrabiblical texts is actually irrelevant when we come to the Bible. The Bible is an authoritative and normative text. We do not "talk back" to it. We receive and obey it. That is why biblical scholars agree with Lewis's emphasis on receiving the text. Anthony Thiselton writes that

> interpreters conditioned by their own embeddedness in specific times, cultures, and theological or secular traditions need to *listen*, rather than seeking to "master" the Other by netting it within their own prior system of concepts and categories.[8]

As I draw connections between the hermeneutical principle of listening to the text and the process of translating the Bible, I need to clarify that I am not talking about the *attitude* of the translators to the Bible. All evangelical translators have approached their task with reverence toward the Bible. My concern here is what theory of translation most nearly corresponds to the interpretive principle of listening to the text.

My own answer to that question is that an essentially literal translation most nearly approximates the practice of a reader's listening to a text. Translators who strive to reproduce the actual words of the original text are like readers assimilating the words of a text. Translators who strive to give more than the text—to impose an interpretation in place of what the text says—are like readers who have moved beyond their first task to further interpretive activities.

There is nothing inherently wrong with these further activities. Indeed, I have already argued that they are essential. The question that I am addressing is what happens when a dynamic equivalent translation is put into the hands of readers. My conclusion is that readers of a dynamic equivalent translation have been deprived of the possibility of humbly and attentively listening to a text, putting aside as completely as possible anything that would interfere with the reception of what a biblical author has said by means of the text. Dynamic equivalent translations are equivalent to a reader who is busy adding personal interpretations to a text.

What happens in these cases is that readers are deprived of the opportunity fully to listen to the text and receive it in a stance of full surrender. No matter how thoroughly readers might want to receive the text in the form in which the author presented it, they cannot do so because something else has been intermingled with the original text and often also deleted from the original text. In short, the hermeneutical principle of receptivity before the text cannot happen as it should.

If we ask what translation *theory* most closely approximates the act of listening to a text, the answer is obvious. A translation that aims to reproduce the words of the original is most akin to the act of a reader's humility before a text and a reader's desire to receive the text as it really is. By comparison, translators who are not content to translate what the original text says—who incessantly go beyond the actual words of the original text—violate the spirit of what I have termed receiving the text.

Respecting Authorial Intention

The principle that has dominated evangelical hermeneutics for the past half century is the notion that correct interpretation hinges on accurately determining the intention of a biblical author in every statement that the author makes. Determining authorial intention has been regarded as the goal of hermeneutics. Here are four representative statements that suggest how thoroughly the primacy of authorial intention has been embraced in evangelical hermeneutics:

• "With Hirsch and those emphasizing the primacy of the author in interpretation, we can maintain . . . the plausibility of determining a text's normative meaning. . . . The author's meaning is available only in the text, not by making contact with the author's mental patterns."[9]

• "Though one may never completely understand all dimensions and nuances of a specific message, normally the goal of the recipient in communication is to understand what the author/speaker intended."[10]

• "The author's intention is the real causality that alone accounts for why a text is the way it is. . . . A text must be read in light of its intentional context."[11]

• "We have no access to the mind of Jeremiah or Paul except through their recorded words. A fortiori, we have no access to the word of God in the Bible except through the words and the minds of those who claim to speak in his name."[12]

The guru whose book has provided the theoretic foundation for biblical scholars is literary critic E. D. Hirsch. Hirsch's landmark book *Validity in Interpretation* is the most widely quoted source in books on hermeneutics written by evangelical scholars. It is an exhaustive defense of the primacy of authorial intention in interpretation of written texts, along with a proposed methodology for ascertaining an author's intention. Here is an oft-quoted summary statement from Hirsch's book:

> A stable and determinate meaning requires an author's determining will. . . . All valid interpretation of every sort is founded on the re-cognition of what an author meant.[13]

Elsewhere Hirsch states that "the meaning of a text is the author's meaning."[14]

The relevance of the hermeneutical principle of the primacy of determining an author's intention should be obvious: The most reliable index to what authors intended to say is what they *did* say. It is a presupposition of the process of communication of any type that people say what they intend to say. We ourselves do not like having what we have said or written slighted by someone who presumes to know what we "intended to say." What we intend to say is what we *do* say.

If this is true of ordinary verbal communication, how much more should we assume that the writers of the Bible, carried along by the Holy Spirit (2 Peter 1:21), said what they intended to say. It is true that dynamic equivalent translators are very interested in authorial intention. Their translations claim to give us *the meaning* that biblical authors intended to convey. The problem is that dynamic equivalent translations often disregard what is primary and prior and instead focus on what is secondary and subsequent. What biblical authors *primarily* intended to say is what they *did* say, that is, their words. To jump over their words to an inferred meaning during the process of translation is to exchange certainty for inference. As readers of the English Bible, we need an actual text, not an inferred or hypothetical text. In a Bible translation we need reality, not something that approximates "virtual reality."

Respecting the Genre of a Work

Another cornerstone of hermeneutical theory is the need to interpret a text in light of its genre (literary type or kind). According to a literary scholar, genre is nothing less than a "norm or expectation to guide the reader in his encounter with the text."[15] Biblical scholars have come to attach a similar importance to genre. Gordon Fee and Douglas Stuart claim in their book *How to Read the Bible for All Its Worth* that "the basic concern of this book is with the understanding of the different types of literature (the *genres*) that make up the Bible. . . . This generic approach has controlled all that has been done."[16]

Later chapters in this book will explore some ramifications of the importance of literary genres for Bible translation. For purposes of this chapter, I will simply list the ways in which attention to the genres of literature should influence Bible translation. A Bible translation that respects the genres of the Bible does these things:

• In keeping with the principle that meaning is always communicated through a specific form (so that before we can know the meaning of a story or poem or other genre we need to absorb the particulars of the story, poem, etc.), it preserves the particulars of the original text, respecting the very form in which meaning has been embodied.

• In keeping with the literary principle that the subject of literature is human experience, it retains the concrete presentation of human experience in literary parts of the Bible, resisting the impulse to turn the concretions into abstractions.

• It preserves the poetic qualities of poetic discourse, including the interspersed images and figurative language embedded in expository parts of the Bible (such as the epistles).

• Insofar as the translation into English permits, it retains such rhetorical patterns as word patterns, linguistic variety within a passage (e.g., using three different words for sin in Psalm 32:1), consonance (translating the same Hebrew or Greek word the same way in a passage to show the pattern of repetition), rhetorical questions, etc.

• It preserves as much of the artistry of the original as the process of translation allows.

• It reproduces as much of a biblical writer's distinctive style as possible.

As we will see in later chapters of this book, English translations show a wide range of adherence to and deviation from these practices. While the division is not as sharply along the essentially literal vs. dynamic equivalence lines as is true for most of the topics covered in this book, there is nonetheless a general division along these lines, and it is easy to see why. If a translation committee starts its process with a target audience in view, the target audience determines the parameters within which the translation occurs. The lower the abilities of the target audience are assumed to be, the more fully the criteria I have listed drop out of sight. These principles are often regarded as frivolous luxuries at best and obstacles to understanding at worst.

The Unity and Interrelatedness of the Bible

Some principles of biblical interpretation belong to the realm of general hermeneutics—principles that apply to the interpretation of *any* text, whether in the Bible or the Harvard Classics. Other principles apply specifically to the Bible and are known as special or particular hermeneutics. The subject of the unified network of cross-references and foreshadowings and echoes that we find in the Bible is perhaps the preeminent example of special hermeneutics.

As an entry into this complex subject, I would ask you to picture the pages of a Bible with cross-references listed in the margin. I would note first that the Bible is the only book I know where this format regularly appears. Even after we have eliminated the somewhat arbitrary listing of passages that express similar ideas or simply use identical words, we are left with an anthology of diverse writings that are unified by an interlocking and unified system of theological ideas, images, and motifs. Together the diverse elements make up a single composite story and worldview known as salvation history.

Biblical interpretation has legitimately been preoccupied with tracing the intricacies of this system of references. Of particular importance has been the use that New Testament writers make of the Old Testament. Often a New Testament writer will evoke an Old Testament passage in such a way as to show its fulfillment in the New Testament, though many different scenarios also exist. To cite a random example, the poet in Psalm 16 at one point expresses his trust in God's providence and goodness with the claim that "you will not abandon my soul to Sheol, / or let your holy one see corruption" (verse 10, ESV). In the book of Acts we find a sermon of Paul in which he quotes this verse and applies it to Christ (Acts 13:35-39).

The relevance of this to Bible translation is that although biblical interpretation insists on the importance of the network of cross-references, some Bible translations and translation theories do a much better job of retaining the system of cross-references than other translations do. It is easy to see why dynamic equivalent translations have been nervous about the New Testament metaphors and technical theological vocabulary that are rooted in Old Testament religious rituals. The New Testament references are frequently odd and difficult. That modern readers will find such references easy to understand is out of the question. But to remove them from sight violates a leading tenet of biblical hermeneutics.

Many of the New Testament references of which I speak pick up something from the Old Testament system of sacrifices and offerings and turn it to metaphoric use in discussing some aspect of the Christian faith. James 1:18 provides a typical example: "Of his own will he brought us forth by the word of truth, that we should be a kind of firstfruits of his creation" (ESV). The mention of firstfruits is an evocative allusion to one of the three most important annual festivals in Old Testament religion. The firstfruits were the first portions of a crop. It is impossible to overemphasize how evocative the first portion of a crop is in an agrarian society. (From my childhood on a farm I can remember the thrill of seeing the radishes that appeared on the supper table every spring as the first produce from our garden.) In the Old Testament religious rituals, firstfruits were presented to God as part of the annual harvest festival known as the feast of weeks (also called Pentecost).

When New Testament writers refer to believers as God's firstfruits, they are tying into a multilayered set of associations between believers and the firstfruits of Old Testament offerings to God. Believers are set apart and dedicated to God. The first wave of believers were literally first—the first of a long line of subsequent believers. In addition to these metaphoric meanings, by using the Old Testament frame of reference the New Testament writers were participating in the grand drama of unifying images and motifs that thread their way through the Bible. All of this gets lost in the following renditions of James's statement that believers are "a kind of firstfruits of his creation":

- "He wanted us to be his own special people" (CEV).
- "And we, out of all creation, became his choice possession" (NLT).
- ". . . showing us off as the crown of all his creatures" (*The Message*).
- ". . . so that we should have first place among all his creatures" (GNB).

By excising the reference to firstfruits, these translations eliminate the way in which James's statement positions itself in the unifying story

of the Bible as a whole. The scholar who has written on this most inci-
sively is Ray Van Leeuwen, who provides further examples and concludes this about a good translation: "By consistency in rendering
biblical expressions and metaphors, it helps readers see the unity and
coherence of Scripture, how one part echoes or enriches another."[17] And
again,

> The language, imagery, narratives and poetry of Scripture are perva-
> sively cross-referential. Much of the New Testament material consists
> of quotations, paraphrases, or allusions to Old Testament texts. . . .
> My argument is thus that the massive text we call the Bible is itself the
> primary context of meaning within which we must find the meaning
> of each smaller unit of text.[18]

Special hermeneutics tells us to respect the interrelatedness of Old
and New Testament references. Some dynamic equivalent translations
fail to show that respect. Contrariwise, essentially literal translations and
some dynamic equivalent translations preserve the network of cross-references. These translations assume that Bible readers will find the inner
and outer resources to ascertain the meaning of a reference to firstfruits.
Translations that are unwilling to make that assumption and that aim
for immediate comprehension by an uninitiated reader are compelled by
their very theory to abandon a hermeneutical principle that is a central
tenet of evangelical hermeneutics, thereby *obscuring* the meaning of the
original.

The Otherness of the Biblical Text

The most immediate effect of sitting down to read a text is an encounter
with a world that the text evokes in our mind, our awareness, our imagination. When we read, "Once when Jacob was cooking stew" (Genesis
25:29, ESV), we are transported in our imagination to a time and place
remote from our own. When Paul begins an epistle with the salutation,
"Paul, an apostle of Christ Jesus by the will of God, To the saints who
are in Ephesus" (ESV), our minds and imaginations reach backward
across the centuries to the first-century church at Ephesus, with its particular issues and concerns as these emerge from the unfolding epistle.

Biblical hermeneutics has stressed the need of the reader to enter a
foreign world that in many of its details is remote from the reader's contemporary world. Those who theorize about biblical interpretation

accordingly stress the need to enter the world of the original text. As long ago as 1962, biblical scholar Krister Stendahl published a landmark essay on this subject.[19] Stendahl proposed that interpretation of the Bible must be governed by two questions: "what it meant" and "what it means." What this implies is that before we can know what the Bible *means*, we need to understand what it originally *meant*.

This has remained a constant theme in biblical hermeneutics to the present day. Anthony Thiselton writes that "hermeneutics nourishes respect as *respect for the otherness of the Other*."[20] Ray Van Leeuwen speaks of "the basic hermeneutical principle of respect for the other."[21]

There is no need to belabor the point that dynamic equivalent translations consistently violate this hermeneutical principle by obscuring the "otherness" in favor of something contemporary. Indeed, no tenet in the dynamic equivalence platform is more important than that a translation should be slanted to the contemporary experience of a Bible reader. The whole thrust is to find a contemporary *equivalent* to what a biblical author has said whenever the author's statement is foreign to the reader's experience, so that the contemporary reader need not enter the ancient world at all. Here is how Eugene Nida expresses his theory:

> Translating consists in producing in the receptor language the closest natural equivalent to the message of the source language. . . . By "natural" we mean that the equivalent forms should not be "foreign" either in form . . . or meaning.[22]

As Van Leeuwen correctly notes, this theory is guilty of accommodating "the other to *our* pre-understandings and situation" (italics added for emphasis).[23]

SUMMARY

While other hermeneutical principles might have been adduced in this discussion, I chose the ones that have the most far-reaching effect on translation theory and practice. In writing this book, I have been aware throughout that dynamic equivalence devotees are likely to disagree with my conclusions at virtually every point. On the subject of hermeneutics, however, I feel that the case against dynamic equivalence is objectively verifiable. The principles of interpretation that I have covered are not simply my preferences; they are a matter of consensus among evangelical biblical scholars. That dynamic equivalence is on a collision course with these hermeneutical principles is self-evident.

NOTES

1   Raymond C. Van Leeuwen, "On Bible Translation and Hermeneutics," in *After Pentecost: Language and Biblical Interpretation*, ed. Craig Bartholomew et al (Grand Rapids, MI: Zondervan, 2001), 307.

2   D. A. Carson, "The Limits of Dynamic Equivalence in Bible Translation," *Evangelical Review of Theology* 9 (1985): 212.

3   G. Duncan Lowe, as quoted by Iain Murray, "Which Version? A Continuing Debate," in *The New Testament Student and Bible Translation*, ed. John H. Skilton (Phillipsburg, NJ: Presbyterian and Reformed, 1978), 133.

4   Jakob Van Bruggen, *The Future of the Bible* (Nashville: Thomas Nelson, 1978), 106.

5   Van Leeuwen, "On Bible Translation and Hermeneutics," 307-308.

6   Peter J. Leithart, "Authors, Authority, and the Humble Reader," in *The Christian Imagination: The Practice of Faith in Literature and Writing*, ed. Leland Ryken (Colorado Springs: Harold Shaw, 2002), 211, 221, 223.

7   C. S. Lewis, *An Experiment in Criticism* (Cambridge: Cambridge University Press, 1965), 19.

8   Anthony Thiselton, "Communicative Action and Promise in Interdisciplinary, Biblical, and Theological Hermeneutics," in *The Promise of Hermeneutics* (Grand Rapids, MI: William B. Eerdmans, 1999), 134.

9   David S. Dockery, *Biblical Interpretation Then and Now* (Grand Rapids, MI: Baker, 1992), 182.

10   William W. Klein et al, *Introduction to Biblical Interpretation* (Dallas: Word, 1993), 117.

11   Kevin J. Vanhoozer, *Is There a Meaning in This Text?* (Grand Rapids, MI: Zondervan, 1998), 249, 265.

12   G. B. Caird, *The Language and Imagery of the Bible* (Grand Rapids, MI: William B. Eerdmans, 1997), 61.

13   E. D. Hirsch, *Validity in Interpretation* (New Haven, CT: Yale University Press, 1967), 126.

14   Ibid., 25.

15   Jonathan Culler, *Structuralist Poetics* (Ithaca, NY: Cornell University Press, 1975), 136.

16   Gordon D. Fee and Douglas Stuart, *How to Read the Bible for All Its Worth* (Grand Rapids, MI: Zondervan, 1982), 11.

17   Raymond C. Van Leeuwen, "We Really Do Need Another Bible Translation," *Christianity Today*, October 22, 2001, 34.

18   Ibid., 306-307.

19   Krister Stendahl, "Biblical Theology, Contemporary," in *The Interpreter's Dictionary of the Bible*, Vol. 1, ed. George A. Buttrick (Nashville: Abingdon, 1962), 418-432.

20   Thiselton, "Communicative Action and Promise in Interdisciplinary, Biblical, and Theological Hermeneutics," 133.

21   Van Leeuwen, "On Bible Translation and Hermeneutics," 294.

22   Eugene A. Nida, "Principles of Translation as Exemplified by Bible Translating," in *On Translation*, ed. R. A. Brower (Cambridge, MA: Harvard University Press, 1959), 19.

23   Van Leeuwen, "On Bible Translation and Hermeneutics," 296.

PART FOUR

Modern Translations: Problems and Their Solution

9

IGNORING THE LITERARY QUALITIES OF THE BIBLE

UNDERLYING THIS CHAPTER is a conviction that the literary nature of the Bible holds immense importance for Bible translation. Not everyone agrees with that premise. When the NIV translation was first printed, *Christianity Today* carried two reviews of it, one dealing with content and the other with its literary merit. Subsequently a minister wrote a letter to the editor complaining about the frivolity of attaching importance to the style of the Bible. He chastised the magazine for "wast[ing] two pages dealing with the 'literary merit' of a version of Scripture" and expressed his doubt that "literary value is any concern of God's or should be a concern of ours, in his Word."[1]

Even people who do not dismiss literary criteria as crassly as that often pay mere lip service to the importance of the literary quality of an English Bible translation. The clearest evidence is simply modern translations themselves, but other signposts point the same way. As I have read reviews of Bible translations during the past three decades, the only criteria to receive major attention are accuracy of translation and suitability to the assumed abilities of a target audience. And if one reads the prefaces of some modern translations, one gets the impression that the translators were actively demoting literary considerations.

HOW IMPORTANT IS THE IDEA OF THE BIBLE AS LITERATURE FOR TRANSLATION?

In the abstract, I would be inclined to think that literary criteria are a rather small piece of the total picture of Bible translation. After all, how much difference can it make to translation theory and practice to pay close attention to the literary qualities of the Bible?

That is how I thought before I wrote this book. This book began as an essay on criteria for literary excellence in an English Bible translation. Gradually the project grew from the specific topic of literary criteria to a full-scale analysis of translation theory and practice. Here is the revealing thing: Although I have ceased to phrase the issues primarily in literary terms, virtually all of the topics that I cover in this book appeared in the original essay dealing with criteria for literary excellence in an English Bible translation. I have come to the surprising conclusion, therefore, that the main issues of Bible translation are at some level literary in nature or involve literary principles or are issues for which literary considerations provide a lens by which to understand Bible translation as a whole.

LITERATURE AS A GENRE

One of the standard sources on literary genres is a book entitled *Kinds of Literature*.[2] I remember what a moment of epiphany it was for me to see the title of the first chapter of that book: "Literature as a Genre." From the beginning of my teaching career, I had operated on the premise that literature itself—literature en masse—had identifiable traits that make it different from other types of discourse, but I had never viewed the matter in terms of literature as a whole being a genre just as narrative and poetry are genres.

The concept is valid, and I have used it for this chapter. My governing questions in this chapter are these two:

- What qualities make the Bible a literary book?
- How do these traits factor into Bible translation?

IS THE BIBLE LITERATURE?

I need to begin by emphasizing that the Bible is a largely literary book. It comes to us in the form of distinct genres, each with its own conventions and craft. Some of the writers of the Bible refer with technical precision to such genres as complaint, parable, proverb or saying, vision, song, gospel, and apocalypse, showing that the biblical writers wrote in an awareness of literary forms. Beyond that, we can simply look at the works that the biblical writers composed in order to confirm that they were literary craftsmen. Biblical storytellers knew how to shape well-made plots and to paint vivid characters. Biblical poets had mastered the dynamics of metaphor and simile. Modern biblical scholarship has demonstrated conclusively the subtlety of stylistic effects in the Bible. It is obvious from the biblical text itself that its writers did not have something better to do than to be craftsmen of the word. If literary artistry and expression were thus important to the original authors of the Bible—and to the divine Author of it—these things should matter to Bible translators as well.

In addition, we have one biblical writer who tells us flat-out what his theory of composition was. The passage occurs near the end of Ecclesiastes: "Besides being wise, the Preacher also taught the people knowledge, weighing and studying and arranging many proverbs with great care. The Preacher sought to find words of delight, and uprightly he wrote words of truth" (ESV). Here we have the picture of the biblical writer as a self-conscious composer, greatly concerned about structure and style.

Several questions naturally arise at this point. If, as some claim, literary form and style do not matter in the Bible, why did God give us a literary Bible? And if the Bible is a predominantly literary book, why are some translations and translation theories so careless about preserving the literary aspects of the Bible? And if Francis Schaeffer is correct in his claim that "art forms add strength" to an utterance and that "we can count on [it]" that the presence of art will "heighten the impact" of an utterance, why would any lover of the Bible want it to be less than all it can be?[3]

In sum, C. S. Lewis was right when he wrote that "there is a . . . sense in which the Bible, since it is after all literature, cannot properly be read except as literature; and the different parts of it as the different sorts of literature they are."[4] The implications of this for Bible translation will occupy the rest of this chapter.

LITERATURE AS INCARNATION

There is no more foundational literary principle than that the subject of literature is human experience concretely presented. Literature incarnates its meaning and ideas in concrete form. Every writing student knows the cliché about the writer's task being to *show*, not to *tell*. To show means to embody in the form of characters, settings, and action if the text is a story, and in image and figurative language if it is a poem. C. S. Lewis's formula was that literature "is a little incarnation, giving body" to its subject.[5] And in an entirely different discussion, Lewis theorizes that "the most remarkable of the powers of Poetic language" is its ability "to convey to us the quality of experiences."[6]

The chief means by which literature communicates the very quality of experiences is concreteness of expression. In literature we constantly encounter the sights and sounds of real life. For biblical poets, virtually nothing remains abstract. Choosing for or against following Christ is like building a house on either a good or bad foundation (Matthew 7:24-27). To be spiritually pure is pictured as having clean hands (Psalm 24:4). God himself is light and a fortress (Psalm 27:1).

The literary impulse to be concrete rather than abstract is equally true of the Bible's stories. A storyteller cannot be abstract if he or she tries, for the simple reason that stories are comprised of characters doing specific acts in concrete settings. For example: "So when Joseph came to his brothers, they stripped him of his robe, the robe of many colors that he wore. And they took him and cast him into a pit. The pit was empty; there was no water in it" (Genesis 37:23-24, ESV).

Even the most theological of all biblical genres, the epistles, are not as devoid of concrete imagery and actual experience as many people think. Here is the type of passage that is common in the epistles: False prophets "are waterless springs and mists driven by a storm. For them the gloom of utter darkness has been reserved" (2 Peter 2:17, ESV).

What are the implications of the incarnational nature of literature for Bible translation? To respect the literary quality of the Bible partly means to preserve the concrete language of the Bible and to resist the impulse to turn the concretion into abstraction. It means allowing the Bible to be what brain research has taught us to call "right brain" discourse in places where it genuinely is such. There has been a general tendency toward abstractness in modern Bible translations, as I will show later.

Although the record of dynamic equivalent translations has not been as good as one would prefer in this regard, I want to acknowledge that their record is not uniformly bad, especially in the narrative parts of the Bible. Dynamic equivalent translations do show a proclivity to translate poetic imagery and metaphors into abstractions. But the colloquialism of these translations and their urge for everyday realism often results in a text that re-creates the concrete details of the Bible's stories with a nice vigor. As I will show in a later chapter, though, this modern colloquialism commits the literary offense of obscuring the otherness of the ancient text by making it sound modern and contemporary.

ARTISTRY

A notorious non-Christian of the twentieth century called the King James Bible "unquestionably the most beautiful book in the world."[7] It is with regret that I have many times concluded that the beauty of the Bible meant more to this cultured pagan than it does to most modern Bible translators. I refer again to the credo of the writer of Ecclesiastes, who claims to have arranged his material "with great care" and who "sought to find words of delight" (12:9-10). He was a self-conscious artist, as were the other writers of the Bible.

Beauty and *artistry* are wide and elusive terms, but aesthetic theorists through the years have established certain criteria by which to identify beauty of form. At the level of arrangement, for example, the elements of beauty include unity, progression, balance, symmetry, contrast, repetition or recurrence, and pattern or design. At the level of language, beauty includes eloquence, exaltation, vividness, and harmony of sound. Syntax can be a source of beauty, with such elements as the tight control of language that produces a proverb or aphorism and the elaboration of syntax that leads to eloquently parallel and balanced clauses—the rise and fall of phrases. And then there are the rhetorical patterns of repetition, balance, and progression that characterize formal discourse.

Here is a passage that illustrates some of the range of literary beauty and artistry in the Bible (Psalm 103:1-2, ESV):

Bless the LORD, O my soul,
and all that is within me,
bless his holy name!
Bless the LORD, O my soul,
and forget not all his benefits.

The patterning of the passage is impressive and beautiful. The poet begins his poem with a threefold call to bless. The utterance adheres to the verse form known as parallelism. It also displays a rhetorical form known as chiasmus ("crossing"), in which the second half of a construction repeats what appeared in the first half in reverse order. In

Psalm 103:1, two pairs of items are arranged in the pattern a-b-b-a: "bless . . . my soul: all that is within me [= my soul], bless." The language of the passage, too, is exalted: "O my soul," "all that is within me," "his holy name."

It is not my purpose in this theoretic part of my book to assess specific English translations or their literary merits at length. My aim here is to assert at the level of theory that if the Bible is a literary book, a translation of it needs to preserve the artistry of the original text. It is my considered opinion that tributes to the literary excellence of the Bible by translators and readers are today (though not in previous centuries) largely lip service. I believe that the decline in literary standards of English translations is traceable in both the prefaces and translations.

The trend perhaps started with the Revised Version (1881-1885). The story of the deliberations of the committee yields a picture of biblical scholars repeatedly outvoting the concerns of literary scholars on the committee. B. F. Westcott, the leading exponent of the primacy of extreme literalism (not to be confused with the essentially-literal ideal that I advocate in this book) over elegance, congratulated himself for his triumphs in a book that he subsequently published on the RV:

> This endeavour after faithfulness was indeed the ruling principle of the whole work. From first to last, the single object of the Revisers was to allow the written words to speak for themselves to Englishmen, without any . . . suppression of roughness. Faithfulness must, indeed, be the supreme aim of the Biblical translator.[8]

Westcott saved his sharpest barb for the very last page of his book, where he paid his final disrespects to "scholars who appear to find nothing better than solemn music in the English version of words of life."[9] The result of this triumph of strict literalism over aesthetic considerations is a notoriously unliterary translation that Charles Spurgeon said was "strong in Greek, but weak in English."[10]

The priority that the RV translators gave to meaning over literary qualities has a counterpart in dynamic equivalent theory. In the words of Nida and Taber, "Meaning must be given priority," and "style is secondary to content."[11] Meaning, in turn, is conceived in modern colloquial translations in terms of a target audience generally assumed to have limited rather than high abilities. The marvelous poetry of the opening verses of Psalm 103 quoted earlier ends up thoroughly prosaic, stripped of its artistic beauty and power:

> *With all my heart*
> *I praise the Lord,*
> *and with all that I am*
> *I praise his holy name!*
> *With all my heart*
> *I praise the Lord!*
> *I will never forget how kind he has been. (CEV)*

> *Praise the Lord, I tell myself;*
> *with my whole heart, I will praise his holy name.*
> *Praise the Lord, I tell myself,*
> *and never forget the good things he does for me. (NLT)*

Literary authors and literary scholars overwhelmingly regard the KJV as being the supremely literary English translation, and others in its tradition as being superior to dynamic equivalent Bibles. Allen Tate called modern translations "dull and vulgar," W. H. Auden considered the KJV "immeasurably superior," Thornton Wilder said that he was "never . . . able to read long in any other version" than the KJV, and T. S. Eliot considered modern translations to be "an active agent of decadence."[12]

I want to remind you of my line of argument at this point in my book: *All* that I am saying in this section of a chapter that discusses how literature works is that beauty and artistry of expression are important to literature. The verdict of literary experts does not cover all that is important in a Bible translation; for example, it does not speak directly to accuracy and fidelity to the original. On the other hand, authors and literary critics *are* people whose literary intuitions can be trusted, and if they almost uniformly dislike modern colloquial translations, this is surely an index to the literary deficiency of these translations.

How does the presence of artistry in the Bible affect translation? It stands to reason that a translation committee that self-consciously elevates literary criteria to a high position will do a better job of capturing the artistry of the original text than a committee that gives priority to immediate ease of comprehension by a target audience perceived to have low literary and linguistic abilities.

SUBTLETY AND INDIRECTION

Because literature is inherently incarnational, it frequently (though not uniformly) conveys its meanings by a technique of indirection. Literature gives the example rather than the precept. Even when it states the precept along with the example (a relative rarity), it is up to the reader to determine *how* the example embodies the stated theme. The story of Cain (Genesis 4:1-16), for example, never states outright such themes as that human life is sacred, murder is wrong, uncontrolled sin destroys a person, and God is both just and merciful. The story embodies these themes indirectly.

Poetry also works by indirection. Figurative language is the chief illustration. "They eat the bread of wickedness / and drink the wine of violence," Proverbs 4:17 (ESV) states about violent people. There *is* no literal bread of wickedness and wine of violence. These are metaphors for wickedness and violence, and metaphors always require that we "carry over" (the literal meaning of *metaphor*) the meaning from level A to level B. In a word, they are *indirect* in their very method of proceeding.

Accompanying this indirectness is a prevailing subtlety—a refusal to Spell It Out, putting on the reader the burden of figuring things out. "He leads me beside still waters," the poet tells us in Psalm 23:2 (ESV). Psalm 23 is a pastoral poem built around the daily provision of a shepherd for his sheep. The opening picture of green pastures and still waters evokes a familiar detail of shepherding in ancient Palestine—the resting of the sheep for several hours at midday in a type of oasis (the woman in the Song of Solomon asks where her beloved pastures his flock and makes it "lie down at noon"—1:7, ESV). The poet expects the reader to figure out what human provisions from God are expressed by the picture of sheep resting contentedly at midday in lush surroundings.

The subtlety that often inheres in a literary text is on a collision course with the dynamic equivalent theory that a Bible translation must "use language that is natural, clear, simple, and unambiguous."[13] Not content with the statement in the original text that the shepherd leads his sheep "beside still waters," the urge to Spell It Out yields the translation, "He leads me to water *where I may rest*" (REB; italics added to highlight what has been added to the original). Even turning a metaphor into a simile is a move toward dampening down the subtlety and indirection of the original, as when the statement that "the LORD

God is a sun and shield" (Psalm 84:11, ESV) is rendered explicit in the translation,

> *Our Lord and our God,*
> *you are like the sun*
>   *and also like a shield. (CEV)*

This practice of Spelling It Out almost always results in a loss of the aphoristic succinctness; in the example just cited, eight words have become a clunky fifteen.

I hope that none of my readers will raise what in our culture has become a knee-jerk reaction to good literary taste by making a charge of literary elitism. I am not the one who wants to make the Bible literary. It is the biblical writers, moved by the Spirit of God, who gave us a literary Bible. I am only asking for a translation theory that preserves what God gave us.

Dynamic equivalent translators incessantly feel an obligation to help modern readers by in effect "correcting" biblical authors, as though both are deficient. The basic impulse is to fix interpretive problems, real and imagined. One of the truly evocative assertions in the Psalms is the poet's claim that "the lines have fallen for me in pleasant places" (Psalm 16:6, ESV). From childhood, this has been one of my favorite verses. I knew from early years that at one level this was an allusion to the division of the land after the Israelites entered the Promised Land. Pictures of surveyors' measurements and drawings entered my mind, along with maps and fences. The unidentified "lines" reached beyond that to imagined metaphoric lines of God's providence reaching down to me. At the most latent level of meaning, I have intuitively also thought that the lines might be pathways that stretch in front of a person, with an accompanying picture of walking down the paths of God's providence. In short, I have never felt a need for help with the evocative and crisp formulation of the psalmist.

Modern translations that want to help the reader do so by rendering it in an amazing variety of ways, arranged below on a scale of increasing movement away from the original text:

* "The boundary lines have fallen for me in pleasant places" (NIV, NRSV).
* "The land you have given me is a pleasant land" (NLT).

- "You make my life pleasant" (CEV).
- "How wonderful are your gifts to me, / how good they are!" (GNB).

As we move down the line, we lose a great deal more than indirection and subtlety. We eventually lose the original text entirely. This is the inevitable result when translators operate on the premise that the original text of the Bible is faulty by virtue of its obscurity and needs the translator's salvage job. Ray Van Leeuwen's criticism of the whole venture is surely valid—namely, that dynamic equivalent translators consistently run the risk of having "replaced God's word with their own."[14]

MULTILAYERED DISCOURSE

Some literature (though by no means all) possesses the quality of being multilayered. When literature possesses this quality, it allows and perhaps even invites readers to assimilate the text in multiple ways and at the level(s) at which readers' experiences (including previous contact with literature) equips them to experience the text. T. S. Eliot has provided a good framework by which to understand this quality of literature:

> In a play of Shakespeare you get several levels of significance. For the simplest auditor there is the plot, for the more thoughtful the character and the conflict of character, for the more literary the words and phrasing, for the more musically sensitive the rhythm, and for auditors of greater sensitiveness and understanding a meaning which reveals itself gradually.[15]

Eliot's scheme has narrative and drama in view, but poetry and prophetic visions and even epistles have their specific layers of meaning akin to the narrative strata that Eliot delineates.

Lifelong readers of the Bible can trace their chronological progress through these levels of meaning in many biblical texts. My own childhood experience of Lot's rescue from Sodom was solidly entrenched at the level of plot. My attention was riveted on the question of whether Lot and his family would make it out of Sodom in time. Later I saw the subtlety of characterization in Lot—the divided soul who lived in an evil city with a bad conscience. As my experience of life grew, I came to see in the story the appeals of worldly-mindedness and the success ethic that afflict me in my own social situation. Still later I came to wrestle with the interpretive question of how the character who in Genesis 19 comes off so poorly can possibly correspond to the picture that 2 Peter 2:7-8 paints of Lot as a "righteous man" who was tormented in his righteous soul by the lawless deeds prevalent in his society.

The implications of literary multilayeredness for Bible translation are twofold. First, while much of the multilayered quality of the Bible remains even in a free translation, the general orientation of dynamic equivalence is to pare down the multiplicity of the text in the direction of simplicity. In the words of Nida and Taber, "We should assume that [the writers of the Bible] intended one meaning and not several."[16] Virtually any scholarly commentary on the Bible will at once reveal that readers have found many legitimate meanings in many statements in the Bible.

Secondly, the idea of multilayered discourse provides an illuminating analogy or model for the rival translation theories. The whole thrust of dynamic equivalence is to keep readers at the level of plot summary— the simple, obvious level of meaning, a level of meaning, say the prefaces, that can be immediately grasped by relatively uneducated readers. The very quest for a simplified vocabulary and syntax insures that the translation will keep readers at a rudimentary level. By contrast, an essentially literal translation seeks to preserve the full range of meanings in the original text. It is not a matter of putting complexity into the text; it is a matter of preserving the multilayered nature of the Bible. There is obviously a night-and-day difference between Shakespeare's plays and Charles and Mary Lamb's children's classic *Tales from Shakespeare*. We can find the same basic dichotomy in English Bible translations. "The Bible," writes Van Leeuwen, "is a book that communicates on multiple levels, to readers of varying levels of sophistication and competence."[17] The problem with dynamic equivalent translations is that they conspire to keep everyone down at the surface level.

DOES LITERATURE SOUND JUST LIKE EVERYDAY CONVERSATION?

There is a final trait of literature that is on a collision course with modern translation theories. Only a tiny slice of the total body of literature aims to sound like everyday discourse. Literature virtually *never* sounds like everyday conversation. Surely it is obvious that poetry, replete with verse form and meter, makes no pretense of sounding like everyday discourse. Neither do formal orations and sermons. Neither do the formal "open letters" represented by the New Testament epistles. For example:

> Paul and Timothy, servants of Christ Jesus, To all the saints in Christ Jesus who are at Philippi, with the overseers and deacons: Grace to you and peace from God our Father and the Lord Jesus Christ. (Philippians 1:1-2, ESV)

This is emphatically not how we begin an informal letter today. It is almost always this way with literature. Modern poetry is, indeed, closer to the everyday idiom than poetry in previous centuries tended to be, but even modern poetry advertises its difference from everyday discourse. For illustration, we can take a specimen passage from an eminently "folksy" poet—a poet of the common person—Robert Frost:

> Two roads diverged in a yellow wood,
> And sorry I could not travel both
> And be one traveler, long I stood
> And looked down one as far as I could
> To where it bent in the undergrowth. . . .

The vocabulary is relatively (though not wholly) common, but there is much about the stanza that elevates it above the idiom of the dormitory and bus stop—the long syntax, the rhyme, the rhythm, the word order. A dynamic equivalent translator would set about at once to tamper with the passage, and this underscores a main complaint that I have already made—namely, that dynamic equivalent translators do things with the Bible that we would never tolerate in the handling of native-language texts.

What about prose narrative? The use of everyday colloquial prose as the medium for storytelling is a very recent arrival on the literary scene. Until the rise of the novel in the middle of the eighteenth century, verse rather than prose was the preferred way in which to tell stories (even long stories) and compose dramas. And even when novels were written in prose, they did not sound much like everyday conversation. The father of modern fiction is James Joyce, and here is the opening of his most famous short story ("Araby"):

> North Richmond Street, being blind, was a quiet street except at the hour when the Christian Brothers' School set the boys free. An unin-

habited house of two storeys stood at the blind end, detached from its neighbours in a square ground. The other houses of the street, conscious of decent lives within them, gazed at one another with brown imperturbable faces.

This is not the idiom of the grocery store or waiting room. At the very heart of the literary enterprise is the impulse to do something special with language—to overcome the cliché effect of ordinary discourse.

I have raised the question of modern realism, with its preference for colloquial speech patterns, only because it has been put on the table by dynamic equivalent translation theory. The topic is actually an irrelevance when we are talking about the Bible. The Bible preceded by two and three millennia the advent of modern realism. My concern has been to suggest that even modern realistic literature does not regularly follow the degree of colloquialism that we find in some dynamic equivalent Bibles.

Dynamic equivalence has sometimes tried to perpetuate the image of the barely literate biblical author, but this stereotype is easily refuted. Moses received the best education that his day afforded in the court of Pharaoh. The Old Testament chroniclers were court figures, not everyday laborers in the field or village. Nor should we make a priori assumptions about the educational and literary ability of New Testament writers. Paul was a towering intellectual figure and public speaker who had mastered the forms of classical rhetoric. Luke was an educated physician writing in an excellent literary style to "Theophilus," who was probably a Roman official or a person of high position or wealth. And even if we regard the other Gospels as folk literature, that does not prejudge anything, since folk literature tends to be highly stylized, conventionalized, and artistic.

I have raised the contextual issue of what we can infer about the biblical authors only because that is the direction in which dynamic equivalent theory and biblical prefaces have often taken the discussion. But the proof of the pudding is the texts that the biblical authors actually wrote. We might possibly reach a clearer picture if we looked at specimen New Testament passages as if they were anonymous, unclouded by presuppositions about the educational and literary level of its authors. We do not need to know anything about the author of the following passage to sense that this is the very touchstone of poetic and rhetorical refinement:

Blessed are the poor in spirit,
for theirs is the kingdom of heaven.
Blessed are those who mourn,
for they shall be comforted.
Blessed are the meek,
for they shall inherit the earth.

Or consider the beginning of the Christ hymn that opens John's Gospel, a poem that in its totality parodies (echoes with inverted effect) a Greek "Hymn to Zeus" and is a virtual mosaic of biblical allusions:

In the beginning was the Word,
and the Word was with God,
* and the Word was God.*
He was in the beginning with God.

Or consider this passage from Romans 5:3-5, based on *gradatio* ("gradation"), a stair-step design in which the last key word of a phrase becomes the first key word of the next phrase:

We rejoice in our sufferings, knowing that suffering produces
endurance, and endurance produces character, and character pro-
duces hope, and hope does not put us to shame. (ESV)

We need to put to rest the image foisted on us by modern translations of unsophisticated and unliterary writers of the Bible.

THE PROBLEM OF THE UNLITERARY BIBLE

It is not my purpose here to attempt to prove *that* the Bible is literature, something that I have discussed in half a dozen books.[18] Today everyone who is knowledgeable about the Bible should know that the Bible is a very literary book. It has been my purpose to expose fallacies about literature as they relate to Bible translation.

I have laid out five characteristics of literature as it has always existed and as we find it in the Bible. Literature prefers the concrete over the abstract. It values artistry and often gains its effects by indirection and subtlety. Literature often possesses a multilayered quality, and it ordinarily aims to be different from everyday informal conversation.

The context in which I have raised these literary issues is problems and solutions in modern English translations of the Bible. Some modern translations—and virtually all the old ones—have been attuned to the principles that I have articulated, and they have accordingly given us a literary Bible that corresponds to the literary nature of the original text. In an increasing trajectory, though, most translations that have sailed under the banner of dynamic equivalence have by both their avowed theory and their actual practice violated essential principles of literature. We might say that they have sinned against the heart and soul of literature. The result is an emaciated Bible that on the score of literary qualities has fallen far short of a standard of excellence. Most dynamic equivalent translations have actually flaunted their allegiance to theories that directly contradict what we know about literature. If *The Norton Anthology of English Literature* were subjected to the transformations that modern translation theories espouse, it would cease to exist as an anthology of literature.

What is bad about an unliterary Bible? It distorts the kind of book that the Bible is (mainly an anthology of literary genres). It robs the Bible of the power that literature conveys. And it changes the nature of the writing that God by his Holy Spirit moved the biblical authors to produce.

I have entitled this section of my book "Problems and Their Solution." What is the antidote to the problem of an unliterary Bible and the translation practices that produce it? All that translators need to do is give us what the original text says. They should make the Bible neither more literary nor less literary than what the original authors gave us. This means, insofar as possible, retaining the concreteness, artistry, indirectness, subtlety, multilayeredness, and language patterns of the original. It is as simple as that.

NOTES

1   Letter to editor, *Christianity Today*, December 1, 1978, 6.
2   Alastair Fowler, *Kinds of Literature: An Introduction to the Theory of Genres and Modes* (Cambridge, MA: Harvard University Press, 1982).
3   Francis A. Schaeffer, *Art and the Bible* (Downers Grove, IL: InterVarsity, 1973), 38, 41.
4   C. S. Lewis, *Reflections on the Psalms* (New York: Harcourt, Brace and World, 1958), 3.
5   Ibid., 5.
6   C. S. Lewis, "The Language of Religion," in *Christian Reflections*, ed. Walter Hooper (Grand Rapids, MI: William B. Eerdmans, 1967), 133.
7   H. L. Mencken, *Treatise on the Gods* (New York: Alfred A. Knopf, 1946), 286.
8   Brooke Foss Westcott, *Some Lessons of the Revised Version of the New Testament* (New York: James Pott, 1897), 5.
9   Ibid., 222.

10   Charles Spurgeon, quoted in Jack P. Lewis, *The English Bible from the KJV to NIV: A History and Evaluation* (Grand Rapids, MI: Baker, 1981), 76.

11   Eugene A. Nida and Charles R. Taber, *The Theory and Practice of Translation* (Leiden: E. J. Brill, 1969), 13.

12   All of these quotations come from *Literary Style of the Old Bible and the New*, ed. D. G. Kehl (Indianapolis: Bobbs-Merrill, 1970), 7, 56. This anthology documents comprehensively the negative stance of literary experts toward modern translations and their high regard for the KJV.

13   Preface to the *Good News Bible*.

14   Raymond C. Van Leeuwen, "On Bible Translation and Hermeneutics," in *After Pentecost: Language and Biblical Interpretation*, ed. Craig Bartholomew et al (Grand Rapids, MI: Zondervan, 2001), 302.

15   T. S. Eliot, *The Use of Poetry and the Use of Criticism* (London: Faber and Faber, 1933, 1980), 153.

16   Nida and Taber, *The Theory and Practice of Translation*, 7.

17   Van Leeuwen, "On Bible Translation and Hermeneutics," 308.

18   Leland Ryken, *The Literature of the Bible* (Grand Rapids, MI: Zondervan, 1974); *How to Read the Bible as Literature* (Grand Rapids, MI: Zondervan, 1984); *The New Testament in Literary Criticism* (New York: Frederick Ungar, 1984); *Words of Delight: A Literary Introduction to the Bible* (Grand Rapids, MI: Baker, 1987; rev. ed., 1992); *Words of Life: A Literary Introduction to the New Testament* (Grand Rapids, MI: Baker, 1987); *A Complete Literary Guide to the Bible*, co-editor (Grand Rapids, MI: Zondervan, 1993); *Dictionary of Biblical Imagery*, co-editor (Downers Grove, IL: InterVarsity, 1998).

10

Obscuring the World of the Original Text

ANOTHER MAJOR PROBLEM with modern translations is their tendency to obscure the world of the original text. This is a somewhat technical point with huge practical repercussions. It will repay us to exercise the patience required to understand the issues.

This chapter will follow a simple plan. I will begin by explaining the idea known as "the world of the text." Then I will explore what is at stake when translations obscure the world of the text. I will end by applying this theory to actual translation practices. As an epigraph for the chapter, I offer the following excerpt, which was written as a comment on interpretation of the Bible but which is equally relevant to the translation of the Bible:

> There is today a general religious bias toward a galloping subjectivity. But our first obligation to a text is to let it hang there in celestial objectivity—not to ask what it means *to us*. . . . There's something in the mood of our culture that hates that. . . . The text had a particular meaning before I saw it, and it will continue to mean that after I have seen it. It expresses an intention that is meant to be heard by all, not interpreted according to any one individual's preferences or biases.[1]

At the level of translation, too, there is a galloping subjectivity—an impatience to understand what the text originally said and a hurry to make the Bible a modern book.

The Concept of the "World" of a Text

One of the best ways of understanding what happens when we read a text is the concept that every text transports us in mind and imagination to an implied world. This is most evident with stories, where we are at once confronted with characters doing specific things within particular settings. We enter a whole world the moment we begin to read. A New Testament scholar claims that stories achieve their effects by "plucking [a reader] out of his time and place . . . and setting him down in another time and place."[2] But even a poem, prophetic oracle, or epistle asks us to enter its implied world. A literary scholar has explained the concept of a textual "world" this way:

> In a work of art . . . there is presented to us a special world, with its own space and time, its own ideological system, and its own standards of behavior. In relation to that world, we assume (at least in our first perceptions of it) the position of an alien spectator, which is necessarily external. Gradually, we enter into it, becoming more familiar with its standards, accustoming ourselves to it, until we begin to perceive this world as if from within.[3]

This idea of a "world" of the text not only explains the reading process—it is also crucial to our interpreting the meaning of a text. Novelist Flannery O'Connor asserted that "it is from the kind of world the writer creates, from the kind of character and detail he invests it with, that a reader can find *the intellectual meaning* of a book" (italics added).[4] As a literary scholar, I have never doubted that one of the best and simplest ways to understand what a work is telling me about the real world is to note the features of the imagined world that I enter when I read.

If literary authors and critics thus emphasize the importance of the world of the text to the literary transaction, the counterpart in biblical studies is the way in which respect for the otherness of the world of the biblical text has been elevated to the status of a major hermeneutical principle. Ray Van Leeuwen writes that "for us moderns to understand the Bible, we have to learn a lot about the world of the Bible and the world *in* the Bible."[5] Anthony Thiselton similarly speaks of the otherness of the biblical text, writing that "hermeneutics nourishes respect . . . *for the otherness of the Other*."[6]

Applying this hermeneutical principle to Bible translation yields the principle that "we need a translation that allows the Bible to say what it says, even if that seems strange and odd to readers at first glance. If God is 'other' than we are, we should be willing to work at the 'otherness' of the Bible, in order to understand what the Lord is saying through his Word."[7] Anthony H. Nichols, in his dissertation-length critique of Eugene Nida's dynamic equivalence translation theory, agrees: "A good translation of the NT will preserve a sense of historical and cultural distance. It will take the reader back into the alien milieu of first century Judaism where the Christian movement began. It will show him how the gospel of Jesus appeared to a Jew, and not how that Jew would have thought had he been a British or American."[8]

WHAT HAPPENS WHEN THE WORLD OF THE TEXT IS OBSCURED?

Proper interpretation of the Bible entails a two-way journey. First we journey to the world of the biblical text and enter its very being. Then we make a return journey to our own world and apply the principles and experiences of the biblical text to our lives. The proper role of Bible translation is to facilitate the first leg of this two-way journey. Some translations live up to this obligation, while others do not. Before I explore the ways in which this is true, I want to lay out theoretically why it is detrimental to our experience of the Bible when a translation short-circuits the journey to the world of the biblical text.

The first negative effect is that we simply lose sight of the literal facts of the matter. To speak of Jesus as sitting at a table when he actually followed the ancient practice of eating while reclining hardly undermines one's theology, but it does evoke an incorrect picture of how people in the Greco-Roman world behaved at meals. To change Paul's command to "greet one another with a holy kiss" (1 Corinthians 16:20, ESV) to "shake hands all round as a sign of Christian love" (Phillips) is to obscure the practices that prevailed in the New Testament world, while translations that transform the greeting into an abstraction equally remove the original world from sight: "give each other a warm greeting" (CEV); "greet each other in Christian love" (NLT).

A second negative effect of obscuring the world of the biblical text is that it violates the historical nature of biblical revelation by fostering what Van Leeuwen correctly calls "an implicitly a-historical theory of understanding."[9] This is more serious than simply evoking a slightly anomalous picture that violates the literal facts of the matter or dissipating a concrete depiction into an abstraction. Here we are dealing with something principial—namely, that the Bible portrays an actual historical world into which God entered and performed historical, space-time events. To remove that historical world from sight gradually, by a process of accumulation, undermines the historicity of the biblical revelation. John Skilton has expressed the matter thus:

> It is . . . not in the translator's province to lift the Bible out of its milieu. He should not try to dehistoricize it, reset it, or deculturize it. God chose to give His revelation in history at certain times and places.[10]

Thirdly and most importantly, to remove the original world of the biblical text has the effect of assimilating the world of the Bible to our own modern viewpoint, thereby preventing the Bible from having its confrontational function of standing over against our own worldview and informing it, perhaps even transforming it. Here is how four biblical scholars describe the threat:

• "Interpreters conditioned by their own embeddedness in specific times, cultures, and theological or secular traditions need to *listen*, rather than seeking to 'master' the Other by netting it within their own prior system of concepts and categories."[11]

• Dynamic equivalent "translations focus on the reader's subjectivity *as it exists before it encounters the biblical text*. They seem to assume that the text itself has little role in 'creating' its reader."[12]

• "God has revealed himself to men in time-space history—to particular men and women, spatially and temporally and linguistically located. If we are not very cautious about the way we treat the historical particulars, we may introduce such substantive anachronisms that the story becomes intrinsically unbelievable."[13]

• "The determinative role given to receptor response [in Eugene Nida's translation theory] constantly jeopardizes the historical and cultural 'otherness' of the Biblical text [and] guarantees that indigenous receptors must approach Scripture through a Western grid and denies them direct access to the Biblical universe of discourse."[14]

There is no need to belabor the way in which these statements are on a collision course with dynamic equivalence theory. The very word *equivalence* shows that, in the words of Eugene Nida, "The translator must strive for equivalence rather than identity" in the process of translation.[15] It is the consequences of this theory to which I now turn.

THE PASTNESS OF THE PAST

It is a literary principle that the world evoked by a text that comes to us from the past must retain its flavor of pastness and even antiquity. We should expect an ancient text to *sound* like an ancient text in the sense of preserving the references to customs, idioms, literary style, and mindsets of the past era from which the text comes. We do, indeed, need to bridge the gap between the biblical world and our own world, but this is the domain of exposition, not of translation. When we read Chaucer, we do not expect to find the fact camouflaged that the Canterbury pilgrims rode on horses rather than in cars, that they stayed in inns instead of motels, and that they contended with mire on the road rather than with traffic jams.

I will note in passing that the principle that I am here urging is not limited to the Bible but extends to other ancient texts that I teach in translation. There is much in the world of Homer, for example, that is totally foreign to my own modern American lifestyle. My sensibilities are shocked every time I read that at the court of Odysseus, where the best of the best is served at mealtimes, there "are a lot of black puddings by the fire, stuffed with blood and fat, ready for supper." Why is it important to know that the characters in the world of *The Odyssey* loved black puddings stuffed with blood and fat, as opposed to a dynamic equivalent that either removes the specificity of the picture from sight and renders it "a very special meal" or transposes ancient tastes into modern ones with the rendition "pot roast and potatoes"? It is important because a modern reader needs to experience the world of Homer's epic as an ancient and primitive world. Without that awareness, the story does not come close to being the story that Homer told.

The Bible abounds in ancient customs, idioms, and viewpoints. Except where they are totally undecipherable by a modern reader, such as the ancient view that the kidneys were the seat of the emotions, we should expect to see the remnants of the ancient world visible in the text. To make Psalm 84:10 read "the homes of the wicked" (CEV) rather than "the tents of wickedness" (ESV) might seem to be a small matter, but the cumulative effect of such cultural adjustments is to conceal the world of the text and replace it with a familiar suburban world that finally misleads a reader.

THE BIBLICAL MIND-SET AND WORLDVIEW

One dimension of the world of the biblical text is the mind-set and worldview of the original author and audience. While there is much that is universal in the Bible, there is also much that differs from our own outlook. For example, the ancient world, with its subsistence economy, had a view of fat that is the opposite of that of most Westerners. Whereas to us fatness is feared as something unhealthy, for people living in a subsistence economy fatness is a status symbol, signaling that a person is prosperous enough to eat in such a way as to become fat. (Incidentally, the Lewis and Clark chronicles reveal that the explorers got very tired of lean meat and were overjoyed when they finally got their teeth into some fat-laden beaver tails and buffalo tongues.)

Literature from the ancient world freely uses fat as the literal image for abundance. The picture of God-sent human prosperity that Elihu paints in Job 36 includes the detail that "what was set on your table was full of fatness" (36:16, RSV, NRSV, ESV; similar in KJV). As readers of an ancient text, we need the world of the text retained in such a detail. Quite apart from meeting the literary criterion of concrete and vivid expression, it alerts us to the kind of world that the ancient world was, with its relative impoverishment by modern Western standards.

Being kept conscious of the subsistence economy of the biblical world makes a lot fall into place, including the ethical commands of the Bible (such as the command not to keep a poor person's coat overnight because it was the only coat he or she owned). But some translations conceal the actual world of the biblical text from their readers. Instead of reading about a table full of fatness, we get such vague renditions as "you have prospered" (NLT), "a generous table" (REB), "your table laden with choice food" (NIV), "your table with your favorite food" (CEV), or "rich food piled high on your table" (Jerusalem). Some of these translations encourage a modern reader to fill in the picture of what a choice meal looks like in a modern setting, and imperceptibly the biblical world thus becomes the modern affluent West. The problem with excising the ancient aura from the Bible and translating as much as possible into a contemporary counterpart is that translators—and readers after them—impose their own worldview on the Bible instead of allowing the Bible to shape the reader's worldview.

Did the Old Testament Kings Die or Sleep with Their Fathers?

Three dozen times we read in the Old Testament court chronicles that a king "slept with his fathers" (e.g., 1 Kings 2:10). Stop to consider what all is contained in this evocative formula to record a person's death. The continuity of generations is present in the idiom, along with the idea of death as the common human fate. Perhaps the covenant is hinted at in the patriarchal reference to fathers who preceded a person. The mystery of death is captured in the metaphor of death as a sleep. So is the thought of cessation from labor. A whole view of death is encapsulated in the ancient idiom.

All of these resonances get wiped out in modern translations that tell us simply that a given king "died" (NLT, CEV). One of the translations that renders it thus claims in its preface that it is the "only" translation that "clearly translates the real meaning of the Hebrew idiom . . . into contemporary English" (NLT). On the contrary, it has precisely *not* translated the real meaning of the Hebrew idiom; it has instead given us an emaciated version of the original, and in fact it has replaced the ancient attitude toward death with the utilitarian modern view that death is only an abstraction.

City or Village?

The preface to one modern Bible (NLT) argues that the biblical word *city* should often be rendered *town* or *village* in keeping with what a modern reader would call it. The preface claims that this is what the original author "intended." I believe that the relevant question is not what *we* would call it but what the original author *did* call it. The ancient world of the text is a simplified and primitive world in which the basic dichotomy is between country and city, the open landscape and the community of houses that stands in contrast to the open countryside. To use the undifferentiated term *city* to cover a wide range of actual sizes of the community of houses reflects a mind-set that is different from the modern, and to change the word to fit our outlook conceals the nature of the world of the text. Ancient customs and idioms often gesture toward an understanding of God, people, and the world that is different from our own and is of value to us for that very reason, setting something up against our natural tendency to think that our own way of thinking is the only plausible one.

WHAT ABOUT THE GREEK WORD *SARX*?

Sooner or later the discussion of this topic winds its way to the New Testament word *sarx*, which literally means "flesh." This is, in fact, a good test case, regardless of where one comes down on the issue of whether or not to retain the original idiom and mind-set of the biblical authors and their audience. Let me say forthrightly that there are no easy solutions to some of the key words in the original text of the Bible. There is no doubt that the uninterpreted translation of *sarx* as "flesh" opens the door to misinterpreting some passages, such as Romans 7:18, which reads, "For I know that nothing good dwells in me, that is, in my flesh" (ESV and other literal translations). With verses like this, it would indeed be possible for modern readers to misinterpret Paul as locating evil in the physicality of the human body.

But consider the problems that arise if we do *not* translate *sarx* consistently as "flesh." The NIV translates Romans 7:18, "I know that nothing good lives in me, that is, in my sinful nature." Other dynamic equivalent translations are similar: "sinful nature" (NLT), "selfish desires" (CEV), "human nature" (GNB). It is a pointless statement to say that nothing good lives in our sinful nature. *Of course* there is nothing good in a sinful nature. Paul is not wasting our time by stating the obvious. What the verse means is that sin is rooted in our entire entity as a human individual. Our way of saying this would not be to use the word "flesh," but modern attempts to find the right term have probably not improved on the technical theological and anthropological term used throughout the New Testament.

First Corinthians 5:5 reinforces this point. In commanding the Corinthian church to expel a notorious sinner from its congregation, Paul tells the church to "deliver this man to Satan for the destruction of the flesh, so that his spirit may be saved in the day of the Lord" (ESV). Dynamic equivalent translations substitute such formulas as "sinful nature" (NIV, NLT) for "flesh." But is this what Paul is saying? Do people even *have* a separate part of them that we can label a "sinful nature" that can be isolated and turned over to Satan for destruction? Surely Paul envisions that the sinful person in his entire earthly life and endeavors will be exiled from the congregation in the hope that as his earthly existence crumbles around him, he will be brought to his spiritual senses and come to repentance.

As with other aspects of the biblical world that seem strange to the uninitiated modern reader, our best course of action is to translate literally, wrestle with the meaning, teach that meaning to the uninitiated, and become so familiar with the Bible that the references will become second nature to us. The dynamic equivalent solution, as Van Leeuwen notes, "prevents us from finding out why Paul used the Greek word for 'flesh.'"[16] Furthermore, in the words of Robert Martin, "Paul uses *sarx* in a very precise manner. . . . When Paul uses *sarx* to describe man's sinfulness, he is not speaking of a distinct 'nature' in man but of a moral reality at work in man by virtue of the fall," adding that while it is important not to equate the physical body with inherent sinfulness, "we must likewise be careful that the reader not conclude that *sarx* and 'body' have no relation at all."[17]

THE STYLISTICS OF THE BIBLICAL WRITERS

Another aspect of the world of the biblical text is stylistics. Literary styles vary drastically from one age or culture to another. The ancients did not tell a story the way a modern novelist does, nor did the ancient poets write in the idiom and verse forms of contemporary English or American poetry. In narrative, for example, we might recall the Hebrew fondness for beginning sentences with the coordinate usually translated as *and*: "And God said, 'Let there be light,' and there was light. And God saw that the light was good" (Genesis 1:3, ESV). "But we no longer speak in that style," some will say. Precisely, which is the very reason why it is important to retain the ancient feel of the original.

In addition to reminding us that the world of the Bible was, *in fact*, an ancient world, the writers' fondness for tying statements together with the word *and* may once again hint at a mind-set different from the modern, and it certainly adds a quaint artistry to the account. The repeated and formulaic *and* creates a tremendous momentum of onward movement as one thing is piled on another in a never-ending flow. As for the mind-set that is expressed in this style, it surely hints at a conscious sense of continuity and coherence in one's view of history and even daily events. By contrast, when I read some contemporary translations with their endless series of short, self-contained sentences, I am reminded of the effect of reading Albert Camus's novel *The Stranger*, where the world dies and is reborn from one sentence to the next, in keeping with Camus's absurdist view of the world. Two literary critics have rightly said that "the use of the word *and* at the beginning of sentences gives a sense of continuity to narratives, but it also conveys a feeling of the endlessness of existence, the rise and fall of life."[18]

Ancient expressions and formulas undoubtedly seem foreign to the modern ear, but in fact they often contain embedded meanings that get lost when the idiom is dropped. The formula that Jesus "opened his mouth" and began to speak (ESV, RSV, NASB) signaled to the ancient listener something like, "Now this is really important." Translations that dispense with the formula flatten out the original meaning: "[Jesus] began to speak" (NRSV; NIV similar).

What about Archaisms?

Before I leave the criterion of retaining the ancient feel of the biblical text, let me forthrightly raise the issue of archaism in Bible translation. I believe there is an appropriate archaism in an English Bible translation. I am *not* advocating the use of English words that have become obsolete, or even words that are definitely out of usage, though there may be such a thing as the Lord's Prayer principle with very famous passages, especially if they appear in traditional liturgy or Handel's *Messiah*. The biblical world was in fact an ancient world, not the world of contemporary England or America. Someone has correctly observed that "the Hebrew Old Testament is an archaic document, far more primitive even than Homer, and the old usage seems more appropriate" than a thoroughly modern idiom.[19] I believe that it is correct for an English translation to preserve an appropriate archaic flavor as a way of preserving the distance between us and the biblical world. Joseph Wood Krutch used an evocative formula in connection with the King James Bible when he spoke of "an appropriate flavor of a past time."[20]

If archaisms can mislead a reader, so can rendering the original in a modern colloquial idiom. I recall sitting in a Bible study in which someone stressed that those who honor their parents will not simply live long but will "*enjoy* long life on the earth" (Ephesians 6:3, NIV; italics added to capture the person's inflection). But the original does not, in fact, stress the idea of enjoying life. By phrasing the matter in the terms of our own colloquial expression in which "to enjoy" means "to experience," this translation actually misled a modern reader.

We should note in passing that a decisive difference exists between archaic English vocabulary and *ancient institutions* that are now archaic. Not all archaisms in some English translations are examples of the retention of outmoded language. The word *kinsmen* does a better job of denoting the ancient institution of clans and extended families than the modern word *relative* does, since the latter does not generally have associations of the close ties that clans possess in some cultures. To use the word *slave(s)* in the epistles is misleading because it evokes the picture of slavery as it has existed in modern times. Paul actually refers to bonded or indentured servants who often had rights and limited terms of service quite alien to the way in which slaves were treated in antebellum America.

Lessons from Literature

It is not only with the Bible that these issues of translation surface. Whenever I teach Homer or Virgil or Dante, I face the need to choose a translation. I assemble examination copies from various publishers and pore over them. I do not want a colloquial translation that sounds like the idiom of the dormitory. When a translation of the Greek play *Antigone* has the king speak the following, I know that I do not want it as my text:

> *Be quiet, before you make me lose my temper.*
> *Do you want to look like fools when you get old?*
> *What you say is ridiculous.*

What is wrong here? It violates what I know about the world of the original text. On public occasions, ancient kings spoke formally, not in colloquial style. Furthermore, ancient Greek drama enacted ritual action, not everyday action. Finally, I want a text whose style will keep alive in my imagination my awareness that the action is taking place long ago in a courtly setting, not in the local grocery store today.

In the wake of my work on Bible translation, I recently watched a modern translation video version of the Greek play *Antigone* with a new awareness of what was happening. Everything was prsented in modern dress and modern idiom. The world evoked was remote from Greek antiquity. The messenger who arrived to inform the king of Antigone's crime was dressed and spoke like a British cockney. He ended his major speech to the king with the colloquial line, "You gotta look out for number one, that's what I always say." Here in heightened form is dynamic equivalence: Details from the ancient world of the original have been transformed into a modern *equivalent*. The same thing happens when Shakespeare's plays are situated in a contemporary milieu. The result is something that we can repeatedly find in dynamic equivalent Bibles—the eclipse of the world of the original text.

In regard to archaisms, we need to be clear about the degree of license that occurs in the translation process. Translators do things with texts that we would never do with a text written in our own language. When we find archaisms in Shakespeare or Milton or Dickens, we do not rewrite the text to make it sound contemporary. We educate readers into what the difficult words mean. The fixedness of the text is a literary principle. To rewrite Macbeth's question to the cleric who has observed Lady Macbeth's sleepwalking, "Canst thou not minister to a mind diseased?" (5.4.10) as "Aren't you a psychiatrist?" is something from which we recoil.

My mention of Shakespeare leads me to observe that we can see the translation principles that are my concern in this book highlighted in a publisher's series of Shakespearean plays printed in "parallel text" editions. Shakespeare's text appears on the left page and a "modern English" version on the right page. The introduction to the edition of *Hamlet* reads like a primer on modern Bible translations.[21] The purpose "is to make Shakespeare fully intelligible to the modern reader." The Shakespearean text "has become remote and difficult to understand," with the result that the text needs to be rewritten in such a way as "to make it immediately understandable for the reader." The modernizing produces approximately what modern translations do with the Bible. "The slings and arrows of outrageous fortune" become "the trials and tribulations that unjust fate sends." "The law's delay" becomes "the law's frustrating slowness." One thing is clear: The person who reads the updated version is not reading Shakespeare, and someone who thinks it *is* Shakespeare is badly misled.

I need to guard against misunderstanding by saying that I do not want a Bible translation to use obscure or totally obsolete words. I am only saying that it is appropriate for a Bible translation to have a slightly archaic feel to it in situations where there are good reasons to retain old-fashioned or quaint language. Let me add that although I do not use the King James Version for my regular Bible reading, I do read it occasionally. One of several reasons for doing so is that when it comes to transporting us from our own time and place to another time and place, one cannot beat the King James translation. As a result, reading the KJV has the salutary effect of reminding us that the world of the biblical text is, in fact, a world in which much is strange.

SUMMARY

When we read a text that comes to us from the past, the relevant question is not how *we* would say it, or how we think the writer would say it if he were living today (something we can never know with certainty), but how the author *did* say it in terms appropriate to his own time and place.

The solution to the problems I have outlined in this chapter is simple—to produce a Bible that is transparent to the world of the original text (not transparent to the reader's world). Van Leeuwen expresses it thus:

> My concern has been that the dominance of [functional equivalent] translations has made it more difficult for English readers to know what the Bible actually said. We need an up-to-date translation that is more transparent to the original languages. . . . I am pleading for a type of translation that is more consistently transparent, so that the original shines through it to the extent permitted by the target language.[22]

In order to be transparent to the original text, a translation must be essentially literal. Such a translation will by its very nature evoke the world of the original authors and the audience of the Bible, which has been the subject of this chapter.

NOTES

1 Joseph Sittler, "Provocations on the Church and the Arts," *Christian Century*, March 19, 1986, 294.

2 Norman R. Peterson, "Point of View in Mark's Narrative," *Semeia* 12 (1978): 99.

3 Boris Uspensky, *A Poetics of Composition*, trans. V. Zavarin and S. Wittig (Berkeley, CA: University of California, 1973), 137.

4 Flannery O'Connor, *Mystery and Manners* (New York: Farrar, Straus and Giroux, 1963, 1969), 75.

5 Raymond C. Van Leeuwen, "We Really Do Need Another Bible Translation, *Christianity Today*, October 22, 2001, 33.

6 Anthony Thiselton, "Communicative Action and Promise in Interdisciplinary, Biblical, and Theological Hermeneutics," in *The Promise of Hermeneutics* (Grand Rapids, MI: William B. Eerdmans, 1999), 133.

7 Van Leeuwen, "We Really Do Need Another Bible Translation," 30.

8 Anthony Howard Nichols, "Translating the Bible: A Critical Analysis of E. A. Nida's

Theory of Dynamic Equivalence and Its Impact Upon Recent Bible Translations," dissertation, University of Sheffield, 1996, 301-302.

9   Raymond C. Van Leeuwen, "On Bible Translation and Hermeneutics," in *After Pentecost: Language and Biblical Interpretation*, ed. Craig Bartholomew et al (Grand Rapids, MI: Zondervan, 2001), 296.

10 John H. Skilton, "Future English Versions of the Bible and the Past," *The New Testament Student and Bible Translation*, ed. John H. Skilton (Phillipsburg, NJ: Presbyterian and Reformed, 1978), 190.

11 Thiselton, "Communicative Action and Promise in Interdisciplinary, Biblical, and Theological Hermeneutics," 133-134.

12 Van Leeuwen, "On Bible Translation and Hermeneutics," 292.

13 D. A. Carson, "The Limits of Dynamic Equivalence in Bible Translation," *Evangelical Review of Theology* 9 (1985): 209.

14 Nichols, "Translating the Bible: A Critical Analysis of E. A. Nida's Theory of Dynamic Equivalence and Its Impact Upon Recent Bible Translations," 2.

15 Eugene A. Nida and Charles R. Taber, *The Theory and Practice of Translation* (Leiden: E. J. Brill, 1969), 12.

16 Van Leeuwen, "We Really Do Need Another Bible Translation," 32.

17 Robert P. Martin, *Accuracy of Translation* (Edinburgh: Banner of Truth, 1989), 33-34.

18 Bergen Evans and Cornelia Evans, "Biblical English," in *Literary Style of the Old Bible and the New*, ed. D. G. Kehl (Indianapolis: Bobbs-Merrill, 1970), 30.

19 Dwight Macdonald, "The Bible in Modern Undress," in *Literary Style of the Old Bible and the New*, ed. D. G. Kehl, 38.

20 Quoted by D. G. Kehl, *Literary Style of the Old Bible and the New*, ed. D. G. Kehl, 4.

21 *Hamlet*, ed. John Richetti (New York: Simon and Schuster, 1975).

22 Van Leeuwen, "We Really Do Need Another Bible Translation," 34.

11

DESTABILIZATION OF THE BIBLICAL TEXT

THIS CHAPTER IS simple in its design. My topic is the way in which developments in Bible translation during the past half century have seriously undermined people's confidence in the reliability of the Bible. Translators, of course, did not set out to do this. Their intentions were the opposite—to put people in possession of the Bible as never before. The dream has not become a reality. It is time to count the cost and soberly lament much of what has happened.

HAVE YOU READ A NEW TRANSLATION LATELY?

I begin with the sheer proliferation of Bible translations. Whatever the positive effects of this are (and they are probably overrated), the negative effects are in plain view. With English Bible translations now appearing almost as regularly as new car models, how can the Bible reading public possibly *not* come to look upon new Bible translations as something as changeable and subject to fashion as new cars and clothes styles? The effect has been to destabilize the biblical text—to render it ever-changing instead of permanent.

With this succession of new translations (and their constant revision), people have lost confidence in the reliability of English translations. If every year brings a new translation, apparently the existing ones must not be good enough. And if the previous ones were inadequate, what reason is there to believe that the current ones will be better? After all, they will be succeeded by new translations and their revisions with predictable regularity.

We can contrast this to the situation that prevailed for over three centuries when the King James Version was the dominant English Bible, starting two or three decades after its first publication and continuing to the middle of the twentieth century. During those centuries, English-speaking people could accurately speak of "the Bible." The King James Version was *the* Bible—the common property of Bible readers in England and America. Compared to the current situation, the unity that rested like a benediction on the Christian and literary communities during those centuries was breathtaking. There is obviously no way to turn back the clock, but we should frankly acknowledge what a toll has been exacted by the decline of the King James Bible and the loss of a common English Bible.

The loss is double. One is the loss of a common Bible. In the centuries when the KJV dominated the scene, when Christians and literary authors and musicians spoke of "the Bible," everyone had the same translation in view. The other loss is the literary excellence represented by the King James translation, which is matchless in its literary qualities among all English translations. While the first loss is irremediable, the second is not. It is entirely possible to perpetuate the King James *tradition* of literary excellence, as the NKJV, RSV, and ESV have done. It spoke volumes when Calvin Linton, the literary stylist for the NIV, pictured the KJV as a menacing foe to be dismissed. A modern translation, wrote Linton, "must start from scratch . . . and not be intimidated by the King James Version peering over its shoulder."[1] Modern translators would do much better to regard the King James Bible as a venerable guide whose effects (though not its archaisms) should be followed wherever possible.

COUNTING THE COST

What have been the results of the proliferation of English Bible translations? Earl Radmacher and Zane Hodges name five "present-day problems" in regard to the English Bible in Christian circles. While these cannot be absolutely proven, they agree completely with what I have observed for a long time. The problems are these:[2]

- decreasing confidence in the inspired text;
- decreasing basis for correct interpretation;
- decreasing use of Scripture in the worship service;
- decreasing expository preaching from the Bible;
- decreasing memorization of Scripture.

To these I would add a decrease in biblical literacy, by which I mean a knowledge of the content of the Bible by the cross section of the believing community.[3] While it is impossible to determine what is cause and what is effect between these features of the contemporary landscape and the proliferation of Bible translations, I suspect that the influence of the latter has been profound.

I have experienced the problem of variant versions of a once-familiar text on a small scale in regard to the Apostles' Creed and the Lord's Prayer. In the circles in which I move, at least two versions of each of these exist, one in the old language, the other in modernized form. Not only do I wonder whenever one of these starts to be recited or stated in unison whether I will get it right for the occasion at hand, but I hesitate to pray the Lord's Prayer in *any* group setting because I have lost confidence in my ability not to be confused.

ARE ALL TRANSLATIONS EQUALLY RESPONSIBLE FOR DESTABILIZING THE BIBLE?

While the proliferation of English Bible translations has undermined the idea of a stable text, I do not believe that proliferation itself is the major problem. The remainder of this chapter will document a very simple point: It is the dynamic equivalent translations that have primarily destabilized the biblical text. By contrast, the range of variation among essentially literal translations does not threaten the stability of the biblical text. For the most part, the variations among these latter translations represent only a small linguistic range. The main culprit is the principle of dynamic equivalence. Once that principle was adopted, the floodgates were opened, as the following specimens demonstrate.

John 6:27

Here is how three modern translations that belong to the "essentially literal" camp have translated the conclusion of John 6:27:

- "... for on Him the Father, *even* God, has set His seal" (NASB).
- "... because God the Father has set His seal on Him" (NKJV).
- "For on him God the Father has set his seal" (ESV).

These are slightly different, and all have departed from the KJV. But no one would be unsettled by the variation that exists here. The text remains stable.

Here is how dynamic equivalent translations have rendered the statement:

- "On him God the Father has placed his seal of approval" (NIV, TNIV).
- ". . . for on him God the Father has set the seal of his authority" (REB).
- ". . . because God the Father has given him the right to do so" (CEV).
- "For God the Father has sent me for that very purpose" (NLT).
- "He and what he does are guaranteed by God the Father to last" (*The Message*).

This is a destabilized text. I myself have no confidence in the reliability of what the family of dynamic equivalent translations offer me with this verse. How could I when the meaning varies so widely? The variation is so great that as I was compiling the list, I had to double check to make sure I had the right verse with some of the translations.

If it is true, as Eugene Nida claims, that "the average reader is usually much less capable of making correct judgments about . . . alternative meanings than is the translator, who can make use of the best scholarly judgments on ambiguous passages,"[4] how is it that these translators with their allegedly superior knowledge cannot agree among themselves? In many instances, the experts produce more potential meanings among themselves than the average readers would produce on their own.

Psalm 73:7

Here is a cluster of translations of Psalm 73:7:
- "Their eyes stand out with fatness: / they have more than heart could wish" (KJV).
- "Their eye bulges from fatness; / The imaginations of their heart run riot" (NASB).
- "Their eyes swell out through fatness; / their hearts overflow with follies" (ESV).

These translations are not as consonant as I would expect from essentially literal translations, suggesting that it is a difficult text in the original manuscripts; but the range is nothing compared with the range introduced by these translations:
- "From their callous hearts comes iniquity; / the evil conceits of their minds know no limits" (NIV).

• "These fat cats have everything / their hearts could ever wish for!" (NLT).

• "their hearts pour out evil, / and their minds are busy with wicked schemes" (GNB).

• "their spite oozes like fat, / their hearts drip with slyness" (Jerusalem).

• "Pampered and overfed, / decked out in silk bows of silliness" (*The Message*).

To any of my readers who might object to my including *The Message*, my reply is that it simply represents the logical extension of a spirit of license that settled in with the acceptance of dynamic equivalence. I note in this regard that *The Message* is viewed by most people as just another translation, and that its dust jacket claims that it is a "unique rendering from the original Hebrew" that "breathes new life into the enduring wisdom of the ancient biblical texts."

1 Timothy 1:16

Modern translations that strive to retain the original language of 1 Timothy 1:16 give us these versions of the central clause in the verse:

• ". . . in order that in me as the foremost, Jesus Christ might demonstrate His perfect patience" (NASB).

• ". . . that in me, as the foremost, Jesus Christ might display his perfect patience" (RSV, ESV).

• ". . . that in me, as the foremost, Jesus Christ might display the utmost patience" (NRSV).

The range here is the normal linguistic variation that naturally arises among translators who have slightly different understandings of which English words best capture the meaning of the original. The text remains stable.

Here is the range that sets in when translators think the original needs "fixing":

• ". . . so that in me . . . Christ Jesus might display his unlimited patience" (NIV).

• ". . . of the endless patience of Christ Jesus" (CEV).

• ". . . his inexhaustible patience" (REB, Jerusalem).

"Unlimited," "endless," "inexhaustible": The range is not unsettling, but it renders a less stable text than the translations that say "perfect." The theological problems of these translations are also troubling:

God's patience is not unlimited, endless, and inexhaustible, as a host of biblical characters from the citizens of Sodom and Gomorrah to Ananias and Sapphira will attest. That a dynamic equivalent translation *can* get this verse right is nicely illustrated by the NLT: ". . . so that Christ Jesus could use me as a prime example of his great patience."

1 Corinthians 4:9

In one of Paul's striking statements about the unfashionableness of Christian commitment by the world's standards, the apostle paints this picture, as rendered by essentially literal translations:

• "For, I think, God has exhibited us apostles last of all, as men condemned to death; because we have become a spectacle to the world, both to angels and to men" (NASB).

• "For I think that God has exhibited us apostles as last of all, like men sentenced to death, because we have become a spectacle to the world, to angels, and to men" (ESV).

• "For I think that God has displayed us, the apostles, last, as men condemned to death; for we have been made a spectacle to the world, both to angels and to men" (NKJV).

This is a stable text because the translators simply strove to translate into English what the original says.

Dynamic equivalent translators, intrigued by the word translated as "spectacle," want to enrich the literal translation, so they produce these versions:

• "For it seems to me that God has put us apostles on display at the end of the procession, like men condemned to die in the arena. We have been made a spectacle to the whole universe, to angels as well as to men" (NIV).

• "For it seems to me God has made us apostles the last act in the show, like men condemned to death in the arena, a spectacle to the whole universe—to angels as well as men" (REB).

• "It seems to me that God has put us apostles in the worst possible place. We are like prisoners on their way to death. Angels and the people of this world just laugh as us" (CEV).

• "But sometimes I think God has put us apostles on display, like prisoners of war at the end of a victor's parade, condemned to die. We have become a spectacle to the entire world—to people and angels alike" (NLT).

• "For it seems to me that God has put us apostles on display at the end of the procession, like those condemned to die in the arena. We have been made a spectacle to the whole universe, to angels as well as to human beings" (TNIV).

Since these translations are fairly similar, wherein lies the instability that I am claiming? The instability is not primarily disagreement among the dynamic equivalent translations themselves but consists instead of the incongruity between these translations and the original text. Although most recent commentators think that there is an implied *allusion* to the Roman practice of marching condemned prisoners into an arena to face death, there is nothing *in the original text* about a procession, an arena, a parade, an act in a play, or a gladiatorial death in the Colosseum. The entire interpretive edifice has been built on the simple word *spectacle* (from the Greek word *theatron*). While it is true that the English word *theater* comes from this root, the most customary meaning of the word in Greek is simply "that which is observed or seen." The translations preserve this meaning of the word *theatrum* but use it as the occasion to add words extravagantly elsewhere in the verse.

To English readers who do not know the slender basis of the interpretive translation (really a commentary), there is no problem. To those who know how adventuresome the translation is, the biblical text has been rendered unstable in comparison with a literal translation. In other words, the uncertainty of knowing where translation ends and commentary or exposition begins in a dynamic equivalent Bible introduces a whole additional level of uncertainty. To repeat a point I made early in this book, playing fast and loose with a text by introducing interpretive elements into it is a license that we do not tolerate with untranslated texts in their original language. There is no good reason to waive ordinary standards of accuracy and the integrity of texts for translators.

Will the Real Romans 1:5 Please Stand up?

To get a handle on how the unidentified mixture of translation and interpretation destabilizes a text, I list below a range of how modern translations have rendered Romans 1:5. The question I would ask my readers to ponder as they read through the list is how they can differentiate what the original actually says from interpretation by a translation committee. In each case I have italicized the key phrase for purposes of the comparison.

• "Through him I received the privilege of an apostolic commission to bring people of all nations *to faith and obedience in his name*" (REB).

• "Through him and for his name's sake, we received grace and apostleship to call people from among all the Gentiles *to the obedience that comes from faith*" (NIV).

• "Through him we received grace and apostleship to call all the Gentiles *to faith and obedience* for his name's sake" (TNIV).

• "Jesus was kind to me and chose me to be an apostle, so that people of all nations *would obey and have faith*" (CEV).

• "Through Christ, God has given us privilege and authority to tell Gentiles everywhere what God has done for them, *so that they will believe and obey him*, bringing glory to his name" (NLT).

• ". . . through whom we have received grace and apostleship to bring about *the obedience of faith* for the sake of his name among all the nations" (ESV).

Which of these translations reproduces what the original actually says? To answer that, one would need to know Greek, someone will protest. Exactly. But the reader of an English translation *should* be able to have confidence that a translation has not tampered with the original. The fact that English readers do not know where translation has left off and interpretation is superimposed shows how destabilized the text has become, and the sheer range shows the same thing.

The last translation in the list reproduces the phrase "the obedience of faith" as it appears in the original text. The other translations have added an interpretive slant to this phrase, and we should note that they do not agree among themselves as to what the correct interpretation is. Are faith and obedience on the same plane, equals in the condition that Christian conversion bestows on a believer (REB, CEV, NLT, TNIV)? Is obedience something that follows from faith (NIV)? The original does not answer that question. The simplest meaning is to take the statement literally: The phrase "the obedience of faith" might simply mean that faith itself is an act of obedience, along the lines of an identical grammatical formulation, "the virtue of love."

I do not want my preferred reading to obscure the main points. Readers of an English Bible should not be at the mercy of a translation committee's interpretation of a passage. They have a right to make up their own minds regarding what a passage means. Furthermore, a translation should preserve the full exegetical potential of the original text. Finally, the more literary a text is, the more regularly it employs ambiguity in the sense of multiple meanings, so that it is entirely possible that the phrase "the obedience of faith" can legitimately embrace some of the suggested interpretations.

The more that translations intermingle commentary with translation, the more they destabilize the biblical text, partly because a reader has no way of knowing where a translation committee's interpretation has entered the English text and partly because the dynamic equivalent interpretations introduce a bewildering set of contradictions into the mix. The only way readers of a dynamic equivalent translation can have confidence in a given translation is to remain ignorant of two things that, if confronted, *should* undermine their confidence in their chosen translation. (1) They need to stick to just one translation, because the moment they start reading other dynamic equivalent translations they will frequently see how consistently these translations contradict each other. (2) Readers of a dynamic equivalent translation had also better not compare their translation to a literal translation, because when they do, they *should*, at least, be unsettled by all that has been added and changed from what the original text actually contains.

Dynamic equivalence became the entrenched philosophy of translation because it claimed to give the English reader a more understandable Bible. The goal was a noble one—to produce a translation that people could both understand and trust. The former ideal has been realized, but not the second one. Dynamic equivalence contains within itself a fatal flaw—namely, a lack of adequate curbs on translation. To defend dynamic equivalence on the ground that it is the right kind of translation if it is done *correctly* is a frivolous position, since translators who take this view equate a "correct" translation with one that agrees with their own interpretation of a passage. As we all know, interpreters of the biblical text do *not* agree among themselves. To introduce the resulting range of variability into the translation itself has produced an increasingly unstable biblical text. People have rightly become skeptical of the reliability of the English Bible. The dynamic equivalent experiment aimed for clarity and has produced confusion.

An analogy from literature will confirm my critique of dynamic equivalence. When Shakespeare's Romeo kisses Juliet for the first time in the play, Juliet says, "You kiss by the book." That is what

Shakespeare wrote. Suppose I consult an edition (purely hypothetical) of the play and find that the line has been changed to read, "You kiss by the book of etiquette." Knowing that this is not how I remember the line, I consult another modern edition and find that there the line reads, "You kiss expertly." And suppose by accident I run across yet another edition in which the line has been changed to read, "You kiss perfunctorily instead of passionately." What has happened here? All three of the changed lines are possible interpretations of the meaning of Shakespeare's line, but no editor would dare to infuse an interpretation in place of the original text. Yet the three versions that I have offered are exactly the kind of thing that dynamic equivalent translations do with the Bible. It is no wonder that the biblical text has become destabilized.

WHAT TO DO?

Given the current instability of the English translation scene, what solution exists? We cannot do anything about the proliferation of English Bible translations. They will keep coming. This is something to lament, not to celebrate. People are not more biblically literate as more and more English translations are available. On the contrary, they know less and less about the content of the Bible.

My proposal is for the Christian world to acknowledge that dynamic equivalence has not produced a reliable Bible. The best that can be said for it is that it established a tradition of contemporary translation freed from the archaisms of the King James Version. It should be increasingly clear that dynamic equivalent translations have begun to produce major problems, for reasons that I outline in this book, including the undermining of people's confidence in English translations. Contemporary Christians also take the Bible less seriously than earlier generations did, and this is nowhere more evident than in the disappearance of the Bible from sermons.

The solution is to return to the principle of essentially literal translation as the only sure foundation of reliability for an English translation. Within the essentially literal family of translations, individual readers and communities of readers should choose the translation that is literarily superior to the others—the one that has the most accurate language, the most affective power, the best rhythm, and the most beauty and memorability. In my view it is as simple as that.

NOTES

1 Calvin Linton, "The Importance of Literary Style," in *The Making of the NIV*, ed. Kenneth L. Barker (Grand Rapids, MI: Baker, 1991), 26.

2 Earl D. Radmacher and Zane C. Hodges, *The NIV Reconsidered* (Dallas: Redención Viva, 1990), 12-15.

3 For some evidence of biblical illiteracy among evangelical Christians, see Gary Burge, "The Greatest Story Never Read," *Christianity Today*, August 9, 1999, 45-49.

4 Jan de Waard and Eugene A. Nida, *From One Language to Another: Functional Equivalence in Bible Translating* (Nashville: Thomas Nelson, 1986), 39.

12

REDUCTIONISM

THIS CHAPTER SUMS UP much of what this book is about. In brief, I am opposed to the range of ways in which a majority of modern translations have whittled away at standards that were once the norm and expectation in English Bible translation. The specific forms of this erosion are variations on the theme of reductionism, by which I mean a diminishing of the fullness that the Bible possesses in its original form.

THE IDEAL: THE FULL RICHNESS OF THE BIBLICAL TEXT

Since I will be ringing the changes on what has been taken away in modern translations, it is salutary to begin by positing the ideal to which any good translation should aspire. If reductionism is the problem, the solution is obvious. It is nothing less than to present the full richness of the biblical text in its original form. Above all, this means preserving the complete exegetical and affective potential of the original. The specific things that make up this ideal are these:

- using language as beautiful and sophisticated as the original itself possesses;
- preserving as many levels of meaning as the original contains;
- retaining poetry in its original, literal expression;
- passing on the stylistic range of the original;
- preserving theological terminology as complex as the original contains;
- remaining transparent to the original text.

Fullness is the ideal. Reductionism has become the norm in dynamic equivalent translations.

REDUCED EXPECTATIONS OF BIBLE READERS

One of the most obvious developments in Bible translation during the past fifty years is the reduced expectations that translators have of their assumed readers. The King James Version that dominated the scene for more than three and a half centuries emphatically refused to patronize its readers. Although the KJV preface claims that the translation "may be understood even of the very vulgar [common person]," it is obvious from the book that the translators produced that their estimate of the abilities of "the vulgar" was very high indeed. The King James Bible is, in the words of a literary scholar, a work of "high art, which will always demand more from the reader, for it makes its appeal on so many planes."[1]

It is, of course, ironic that the common reader through the centuries was regarded as capable of rising to the demands of the King James Version, while modern readers, with more formal education than their forebears, are assumed to have ever-decreasing ability to read. When the NEB appeared, one of its translators said in a television interview that "the new Bible was intended . . . for people who do not go to church" and "for a rising generation less well educated than formerly in classical and literary traditions."[2]

Since I have already devoted a chapter to exploring assumptions that dynamic equivalent translations make about their readers, I will simply list those assumptions here, phrased in keeping with my claim that the most widely used modern translations have reduced the expectations that once prevailed for readers of the Bible:

• Bible readers today have a more limited vocabulary than Bible readers were assumed to have until the middle of the twentieth century; modern translations should therefore use a simplified vocabulary.

• Contemporary Bible readers can understand only a simple sentence structure, with the result that the syntax of a modern translation should consist of short sentences only.

• Because modern readers find it difficult to sustain a line of thought for anything more than a short time, paragraphs should be conspicuously shorter than those that were once the norm in English Bibles.

• Because modern readers are unaccustomed to reading poetry, translations should help readers with the interpretive difficulties posed by poetry, often to the extent of interpreting figurative language in the actual translation.

• Because modern readers cannot be trusted to interpret multilayered statements, translations today must make interpretive decisions for them, in contrast to earlier translations that passed on the interpretive options to their readers.

• Because readers today dislike formality, the style of translations should be close to the everyday conversational idiom of relatively uneducated people.

• Modern readers find the ancient world of the biblical text so foreign that a translation should prevent their needing to enter the strange world of the original text whenever doing so will be difficult for them.

All of these principles represent a scaling down of expectations from the earlier tradition of English Bible translation.

WHAT PAUL WAS *TRYING* TO SAY WAS . . .: DIMINISHED RESPECT FOR BIBLICAL AUTHORS

I co-teach a course on the use of the Bible in ministry. A main component of the course is the methods of inductive Bible study, including practice in writing inductive Bible study questions. One of the formulas that my colleague and I need regularly to combat is the question, "What was the writer *trying to say* in this verse?" We have no reason to be surprised at our students' use of this formula, for the simple reason that they hear it from the pulpit and read it in the commentaries.

What is implied by the formula "what the author was *trying to say*"? The implication is that the author expressed his content obscurely, and further that the contemporary reader needs to function like a midwife, bringing the biblical author's problematical statements to clarity. The interpreter is a prison breaker, freeing the biblical author's fettered thought from its shackles of inept expression. The natural result of this way of thinking is diminished respect for the biblical text, which is perceived as a repository of important meaning struggling to find expression.

It should not surprise us that the "trying to say" fallacy has become commonplace. The seeds of this attitude are right there in the dynamic equivalent prefaces. Here is a sampling:

• "Because for most readers today the phrases 'the LORD of hosts' and 'God of hosts' have little meaning, this version renders them 'the LORD Almighty' and 'God Almighty'" (NIV).

• "*Ancient customs* are often unfamiliar to modern readers. . . . Where there was potential for confusion, *rhetorical questions* have been stated according to their implied answer. . . . *Figures of speech* have been translated according to their meanings. . . . *Idiomatic expressions* of the biblical languages are translated to communicate the same meaning to today's reader that would have been understood by the original audience" (*New Century Version*).

• "Some traditional 'religious' words (e.g. saints, baptism, church, justification, redemption, etc.) . . . [have been translated] into expressions which can be understood by everyone, especially those who have never read the Bible" (SEB).

• "We are also concerned about historical and cultural barriers to understanding the Bible, and we have sought to translate terms shrouded in history or culture in ways that can be immediately understood by the contemporary reader. . . . Metaphorical language is often difficult for contemporary readers to understand, so at times we have chosen to translate or illuminate the metaphor" (NLT).

What are the general impressions that a reader would carry away from repeated exposure to statements like these? At least three: (1) the original text of the Bible is filled with difficulties; (2) contemporary readers are especially subject to being victimized by these difficulties; (3) modern translators must therefore resort to special methods to overcome the problems that the ancient text poses for today's readers.

In short, the ancient text needs a lot of help if modern readers are going to understand it. While no condescension toward biblical authors is *intended*, I do believe that the biblical writers have suffered from a diminution in their stature. Many contemporary readers of the Bible no longer have confidence that the biblical authors *said* thus and so; often they are perceived as *trying to say* something. Dynamic equivalent translations have not consciously encouraged readers to doubt the ability of biblical authors to express definite and clear meaning, but there is, in my view, an incipient skepticism at the heart of dynamic equivalence theory regarding the ability of the ancient text to communicate its stated meanings clearly to a modern reader unless the person in charge of the text (either the translator or the Bible expositor) helps the biblical author communicate his meaning. I would note in passing the irony involved when the allegedly handicapped reader portrayed in dynamic equivalent Bible prefaces adopts a condescending stance toward biblical writers who are pictured as "trying to say" what the reader confidently claims to know.

THE REDUCED AUTHORITY OF THE BIBLE

It is an easy step from such preoccupation with the difficulty of the original text and its acute need of help from the modern translator to a de facto reduction in the authority that the Bible holds for today's reader. As already elaborated in an earlier chapter devoted to the destabilization of the biblical text, the reduced stature of the Bible includes these salient points:

• The sheer proliferation of English Bible translations, accompanied by the constant process of revision among existing translations, has brought a skepticism that any translation is worthy of complete trust.

• The large number of available translations has resulted in a smorgasbord approach to choosing an English Bible translation, with readers shopping among Bible translations the way they shop for clothes or an automobile.

• The widely varying renditions of the same texts by dynamic equivalent translations have further undermined the confidence of a reader that a given translation of a passage is fully trustworthy.

• The mingling of translation and interpretation has reduced a reader's confidence that what is forwarded in a translation is actually what the original text says.

The net result has been a reduced sense of the authority of the Bible. The symptoms are plain to view: a relative scarcity of expository preaching from the Bible in deference to topical preaching, a decline in biblical literacy, and a loss of confidence in the reliability/infallibility of the Bible.

IMPOVERISHMENT OF LANGUAGE

People with literary sensitivities have long been troubled by the impoverishment of language in modern Bible translations. So I want to begin with representative statements by them:

• [On biblical renditions in a modernized Prayer Book:] "What has been gained in strength of structure has been lost in poverty of language. . . . We're told that the new Prayer Book is meant to be in 'the language of the people.' But which people? And in language which is left after a century of war, all dwindled and shrivelled? Are we supposed to bring our language down to the lowest common denominator in order to be 'meaningful'? . . . In restricting the language in the new translation we have lost that depth and breadth which can give us the kind of *knowing* which is our heritage."[3]

• "We ask in alarm, 'What is happening to the English language [in modern Bible translations]?' . . . It does not seem to have occurred to the mind of the anonymous author of this Introduction [to the NEB] that change can sometimes be for the worse, and that it is as much our business to attempt to arrest deterioration and combat corruption of our language, as to accept change. . . . So long as 'The New English Bible' was used only for private reading, it would be merely a symptom of the decay of the English language in the middle of the 20th century. But the more it is adopted for religious services the more it will become an active agent of decadence."[4]

• "I believe the Christian Church has a profound responsibility towards a people's language, and I cannot see an awareness of this responsibility in this translation [NEB]. . . . It is as serious a matter to corrupt a people's language as it is to corrupt a people's behaviour. . . . Far from canonizing, or exploiting, the flaccid, vague language of our time, the Bible should be constantly showing it up, directing an arc-light upon it, cauterizing its impurities."[5]

• Modern translators "have done wrong to our language, by not stretching it at any point; the richest of all the world's languages, treated as post-office savings."[6]

Before I explore the effects of this diminishment of language in some modern translations, we should pause simply to note what it is that these protestors have in view. We can compare the following versions of the same passage (Matthew 6:31-33):

• "Therefore take no thought, saying, What shall we eat? or, What shall we drink? or, Wherewithal shall we be clothed? (For after all these things do the Gentiles seek:) for your heavenly Father knoweth that ye have need of all these things. But seek ye first the kingdom of God, and his righteousness; and all these things shall be added unto you" (KJV).

• "So don't worry about having enough food or drink or clothing. Why be like the pagans who are so deeply concerned about these things? Your heavenly Father already knows all your needs, and he will give you all you need from day to day if you live for him and make the Kingdom of God your primary concern" (NLT).

• "Don't worry and ask yourselves, 'Will we have anything to eat? Will we have anything to drink? Will we have any clothes to wear?' Only people who don't know God are always worrying about such things. Your Father in heaven knows that you need all of these. But more than anything else, put God's work first and do what he wants. Then the other things will be yours as well" (CEV).

• "What I'm trying to do here is to get you to relax, to not be so preoccupied with *getting*, so you can respond to God's *giving*. People who don't know God and the way he works fuss over these things, but you know both God and how he works. Steep your life in God-reality, God-initiative, God-provisions. Don't worry about missing out. You'll find all your everyday human concerns will be met" (*The Message*).

What is lost as we move down the continuum from the exalted to the colloquial? The first thing that is lost is the dignity of the Word of God. If we scale down the stateliness and, where appropriate, the eloquence of the Bible into a flat, prosaic format, the Bible ceases to be anything special. A critic of modern colloquial translations has rightly said that this "kind of familiarity, too, can breed contempt."[7] This may sound excessive, but it is appropriate.

Here is the King James version of Psalm 32:1-2: "Blessed is he whose transgression is forgiven, whose sin is covered. Blessed is the man unto whom the Lord imputeth not iniquity, and in whose spirit there is no guile." Here are the same two verses in a translation (*The Message*) whose dust jacket claims that it is a "unique rendering from the original Hebrew":

> *Count yourself lucky, how happy you must be—*
> *you get a fresh start,*
> *your slate's wiped clean.*
> *Count yourself lucky—*
> *God holds nothing against you*
> *and you're holding nothing back from him.*

Forgiveness of sins has degenerated into getting lucky with God.

I can imagine someone saying that the latter is an extreme version of dynamic equivalency and does not represent the mainstream of that tradition. My reply is that it shows in heightened form a tendency that is woven into the very fabric of dynamic equivalent Bibles. Once Bible translation was set in the direction of abandoning the very words of the Bible for its thoughts, a spirit of license was set into motion that has gotten progressively accentuated.

A second effect of the diminishment of language is the loss of the affective power of which the King James Bible was once the very touchstone. A reviewer of a modern translation comments on a quoted passage with the statement, "Almost everything has been lost [from the KJV]: not only the rhythm, but the sense of authority that goes with it— that bracing sense that we aren't appealing to ideas or vague hopes of our own but to firm promises and facts. It has become weak."[8] To cite a random example, the exuberant "abounding in the work of the Lord" (1 Corinthians 15:58, KJV, NASB, ESV) becomes "enthusiastic about the Lord's work" (NLT) or "busy always in your work for the Lord" (GNB) or "work for the Lord always, work without limit" (REB) or "give yourselves fully to the work of the Lord" (NIV). To cite another example, the evocative formula "blessed are" of the Beatitudes has become reduced to the shallow "happy are" in some dynamic equivalent translations.

Thirdly, simplifying the language of the Bible simultaneously diminishes its ideas. Someone who laments how in modern translations "words begin to decay [and] rhythms begin to go loose and soggy" defends his distress on the ground that "how men's minds work is revealed in what their words say."[9] A literary scholar writes in a similar vein that "a limited, poverty-stricken vocabulary works toward an equally limited use of ideas and imagination."[10] The Greek playwright Aristophanes claimed that "high words must have high language." Modern colloquial translations have proven the accuracy of the statement by negative example, which brings me to my next major point.

EMACIATED THEOLOGY

No single thing accounts for the diminishment of theological precision in some modern translations. Two influences at least have been coercive. Impoverished vocabulary—the studied avoidance of "big words"—is a leading ingredient. But anxiety over the use of technical theological vocabulary has been equally destructive of theological precision. Someone has rightly objected that "the simple translation makes the Bible easy to understand at the expense of there being a lot less to understand, a lot less of that which forces the reader to stop and reevaluate his concepts and categories."[11]

The evidences of this impoverishment of religious meaning are plentiful in modern easy-read translations. The theologically charged "grace and truth" of John 1:14 becomes "unfailing love and faithfulness" (NLT) or "kindness . . . and . . . truth" (CEV) or "generous inside and out, true from start to finish" (*The Message*). Christ's crucial question to the disciples, "What do you think about the Christ?" (Matthew 22:42, NASB, NIV, ESV), designed to evoke a confession of faith, becomes reduced in one version to the question, "What is your opinion about the Messiah?" (REB). Translations that want to avoid the theological term *justification* reduce its range of meanings by rendering it "make us right with God" (SEB, NLT) or "put us right with God" (GNB) or "made acceptable to God" (CEV), none of which conveys as many meanings as the word *justification* does.

Some of the theological terms of the Bible are doubtless technical and difficult for modern readers. The perennial hot potato is the New Testament word *propitiation*. Readers who encounter this word can look it up in the dictionary, and when they do, they will find that "to propitiate" means "to appease anger through the offering of a sacrifice." The advantage of a translation's retaining the difficult word *propitiation* is that it gives readers the right material with which to work. Readers can grasp and eventually memorize the technical meaning "to appease wrath by means of a sacrifice."

Translations that opt for an easy way out end up confusing their readers because what they offer as a substitute does not contain within itself the potential for getting the right definition. Attempted evasions include these: "sacrifice of atonement" (NIV), "sacrifice" (CEV), "the means by which people's sins are forgiven" (GNB). In scaling back a difficult theological term, these translations also make it impossible by ordinary lexical means to get the idea of a sacrifice that appeases divine wrath. To show that a dynamic equivalent translation *can* get the meaning right, though only at the cost of losing the succinctness of the single word *propitiation*, I note that the NLT translates the word as "satisfy God's anger against us."

It is a commonplace that at the very start of English Bible translation, William Tyndale found it necessary to coin words like *intercession* and *atonement* in order to adequately express the theological content of the Bible. It stands to reason that when modern translations remove these terms, they impoverish the theological content of the Bible.

THE PROBLEM OF THE ONE-DIMENSIONAL BIBLE

One of the most serious forms of reductionism in some modern translations is the narrowing of the range of interpretive options that the original text possesses. In a later chapter I will extol the literary virtue known as ambiguity, defined as multiple levels of meaning and a degree of mystery that inheres in some words and statements. Here I am concerned with what happens when the range of meanings is limited by preemptive interpretive strikes that translation committees make and hide from view.

Before considering how this plays out with the Bible, I want to look at the principle of the matter as we find it in literature beyond the Bible. John Milton's famous sonnet written on the occasion of his becoming blind in his early forties begins with the line, "When I consider how my light is spent." The light image here is ambiguous in the sense of having multiple meanings. It refers to eyesight, first of all. The argument of the sonnet makes it clear, secondly, that "light" means "daylight" and by extension active service for God, as based on Jesus' parable of the workers in the vineyard and his aphorism about the need to "work the works of him that sent me, while it is day: the night cometh, when no man can work" (John 9:4, KJV). Thirdly, based on customary Renaissance symbolism, light means knowledge in general and the poetic gift and influence in particular.

The concluding line of Milton's poem is the famous aphorism, "They also serve who only stand and wait." Who are "they"? It is an ambiguous word, referring both to people, who lack the powers of transport that have just been ascribed to active angels "who post o'er land and ocean without rest," and to contemplative angels, who remain always in God's heavenly court. And what kind of waiting is in view in the last word of Milton's poem? If we trace the image of waiting on God through the Bible, it turns out to be a richly ambiguous or multiple image, encompassing such meanings as submission to God's providence, contentment with what God has sent, patience, expectation, and hope, including the eschatological hope of waiting for a new heaven and new earth.

No lover of literature would tolerate a change in the text to make it read, "When I consider how my sight is gone." That would be reductionistic, offering just one meaning among several legitimate meanings to the reader. No one who values literature would accept as adequate a copy of Milton's poem where the last line reads, "People also serve who submit patiently to God's providence." That would not be Milton's poem, and it would represent a severe reduction of the meanings in Milton's glorious line about standing and waiting.

The Bible is a book replete with ambiguity in the original. That ambiguity extends to small as well as large elements. The Hebrew and Greek genitive could yield a chapter by itself. "The love of Christ" constrains us, says 2 Corinthians 5:14 (RSV, NASB, REB, Jerusalem, ESV). Does this mean our love of Christ or Christ's love of us? The original does not resolve the ambiguity. Probably both are in view. But translations that are unwilling to pass the ambiguity on to their readers do not retain that ambiguity. "Christ's love," they render it (NIV, CEV, NLT).

In 1 John 2:5 we read regarding believers who keep God's Word that "the love of God" is perfected in them (KJV, NASB, ESV). In the original "the love of God" could be either God's love for the believer or the believer's love for God, or both. Translations that are unwilling to pass the ambiguity on to modern readers that John passed on to his original audience resolve the ambiguity in the direction of either human love or divine love, rendering it either "love for God" (RSV, GNB) or "God's love" (NIV). In both cases, the translations have reduced the potential range of meanings.

In the opening verse of his Gospel, Mark announces that his theme is the Gospel "of Jesus Christ" (KJV, RSV, NASB, REB, ESV). This is an ambiguous statement in the original, referring both to the Gospel *about* Jesus Christ and the Gospel *of* Jesus Christ—that is, the message that Jesus declared about himself. Translations that are anxious about multiple meanings resolve the meaning in a single direction, translating it "about Jesus Christ [or the Messiah]" (NIV, NLT, CEV, GNB). Dynamic equivalent Bibles repeatedly give us a one-dimensional Bible in places where the original is multidimensional. The result is a loss of the richness of meaning that the original embodies and an organized movement that keeps English readers from what the original actually says.

Examples of such reductionism abound in dynamic equivalent translations. The first of Jesus' famous beatitudes speaks of those who are "poor in spirit" (Matthew 5:3). This encompasses at least two meanings—the spiritual bankruptcy that sinners feel about their condition when they look within and their consequent need to be forgiven by God (an outward-looking dimension). Some dynamic equivalent translations narrow the meaning to just one option: "God blesses those who realize their need for him" (NLT); "God blesses those people who depend only on him" (CEV); "you're blessed when you're at the end of your rope" (*The Message*). The last example illustrates something that I encountered repeatedly while doing the research for this book— namely, the practice among the more radical dynamic equivalent trans- lations to introduce or substitute metaphors that are not even present in the original text.

Sometimes the linguistic quality of ambiguity also lends a sense of mystery to a word or statement. Consider the quaint term (not necessar- ily a euphemism) *know* or *knew* for sexual intimacy and union. The King James translation established this as the standard term, as in Genesis 4:1 ("and Adam knew Eve his wife, and she conceived"). There is something metaphoric and mysterious about this word for sexual intimacy, which in a context of wedded love implies multiple kinds of knowledge that a husband and wife have toward their spouse. The mystery gets dissipated, and the multiple levels of meaning get reduced, in some modern transla- tions: "Adam lay with his wife Eve, and she became pregnant" (NIV); "Adam and Eve had a son" (CEV); "then Adam had intercourse with his wife, and she became pregnant" (GNB); "now Adam slept with his wife, Eve, and she became pregnant" (NLT). A. H. Nichols observes that the writer had terminology at his disposal by which to give a version as crude as the colloquial English translations give us but did not use it, leading Nichols to conclude that the colloquial English rendering "underesti- mates the readers and loses the force and delicacy of the original."[12]

One of the problems with such a translation practice is that it does not present the reader and interpreter with the full exegetical potential of the original text. In a word, the procedure is reductionistic. The peti- tion that God will "establish the work of our hands upon us" (Psalm 90:17, ESV; NIV virtually identical) invites us to ponder the statement. What does it mean to "establish" our work? Why choose the specific picture of "hands"? What are the metaphoric carryovers of this image? Translations that are uneasy with open-ended statements narrow the meaning to just one: "let all go well for us" (CEV); "give us success in all we do" (GNB); "make our efforts successful" (NLT); "make all we do succeed" (Jerusalem).

Biblical scholar Ray Van Leeuwen calls dynamic equivalent trans- lations "'closed' rather than 'open' because they shut down the process of wrestling with what God has said. . . . By choosing one meaning and rejecting another, they close the door to reflection and new insight."[13]

The solution to the problem, of course, is to translate the original text as it stands instead of interpreting it.

LOWERED LITERARY STANDARDS

At several points in this book I stress the literary nature of the Bible. When this principle is ignored, the literary excellence of the Bible—in fact, its very nature as literature—consistently gets lost in the translation process. For my purposes here, I will only illustrate the types of reductionism that occur.

One of the most obvious forms of literary reductionism is the transposing of poetry into prose. Sometimes this takes the form of removing figurative language from sight and substituting direct statement in its place. Thus the metaphoric statement "Oh, taste and see that the LORD is good!" (Psalm 34:8, ESV) becomes "find out for yourself how good the Lord is" (GNB). Psalm 34:7 uses a metaphor to picture how "the angel of the LORD encamps around those who fear him" (NIV, ESV); some dynamic equivalent translations remove the metaphor from sight: "his angel will protect you" (CEV); "the angel of the Lord guards all who fear him" (NLT; GNB similar). Even more common in easy-read translations is the reduction of the stateliness and artistry of poetry into colloquial prose such as poets never use: "I was a nobody, but I prayed" (Psalm 34:6, CEV); "work hard at living in peace with others" (Psalm 34:14, NLT); "they invent all kinds of lies about peace-loving people" (Psalm 35:20, GNB).

A second form of literary reductionism is flattening out the style of the Bible as a whole, thereby reducing the stylistic range of the original text. This inevitably happens when a translation committee gives priority to a target audience instead of to the contours of the original text. A uniform sentence length at once descends on the translation, quite contrary to the rich diversity of the original. If the vocabulary of the target audience is assumed to be limited, the language of the original becomes narrowed from its actual richness and variety.

A third type of literary reductionism is the transforming of the concreteness of the original text into a prevailing abstractness. This is not to say that the Bible does not have grand abstractions; it certainly does, and this is also one of the literary glories of the Bible. But the language of literature is the language of concretion in the service of capturing the very texture of lived human experience. Dynamic equivalent translations tend to reduce this language of the imagination (our image-making and image-perceiving capacity) in the direction of abstraction.

To illustrate, one of the great brief narratives in the Bible is the story of the exchanged birthright (Genesis 25:29-34). Despite its brevity, the story is filled with vivid touches. To clinch the impact of the story, the narrative concludes with what one commentator calls "a staccato succession of five verbal forms . . . calculated to point up Esau's lack of manners and judgment."[14] Here is a translation that maintains the punchiness of the action: Esau "ate and drank and rose and went his way. Thus Esau despised his birthright" (Genesis 25:34, ESV; NASB virtually identical). Here is how a range of translations flatten the vividness of the succession of verbs by resorting to explanation instead of simply recording the action:

• "He ate and drank and then got up and left. That was all Esau cared about his rights as the first-born son" (GNB).

• "When Esau had finished eating and drinking, he just got up and left, showing how little he thought of his rights as the first-born" (CEV).

• "And he ate and drank and went his way. Esau showed by this how little he valued his birthright" (REB).

• "Esau ate and drank and went on about his business, indifferent to the fact that he had given up his birthright" (NLT).

The literary quality of the Bible can also be reduced by the impulse to Spell It Out. Literature is inherently subtle and indirect. Students in creative writing courses are encouraged to "show rather than tell." Anyone who has been tracking with me thus far in this book can predict what I am about to say: Dynamic equivalent translations consistently jettison the subtlety of the Bible by making the text explicit where the original leaves things implicit.

For example, in the prophecy of Amos the description of the famine that God visited on the nation of Israel is couched in the vivid, shocking, and surrealistic picture of God's giving the nation "cleanness of teeth in all your cities" (Amos 4:6, NASB, RSV, ESV). This is typically literary in its subtlety; it leaves readers to make the connection between clean teeth and lack of food (though the next line virtually editorializes the meaning with its parallel phrase "lack of bread in all your places"). Translations that assume their readers cannot come to an understanding of what the literal picture of clean teeth means in this context find ways to Spell It Out. Cleanness of teeth variously becomes "empty stomachs" (NIV; note that a new image, not in the original, has been added), "took away . . . food" (CEV), "brought starvation" (REB), "brought famine" (GNB), and "brought hunger" (NLT).

A final way in which many modern translations reduce the literary quality of the Bible consists of stepping down the exaltation of passages that in the original are elevated and that sweep us upward with their sheer exhilaration. This by no means accounts for the whole Bible, which especially in its narrative parts is often couched in a simple, even matter-of-fact prose style. But the Bible is frequently and perhaps most often eloquent and elevating, as in a passage like this (Psalm 139:1-3, ESV):

> O LORD, *you have searched me and known me!*
> *You know when I sit down and when I rise up;*
>   *you discern my thoughts from afar.*
> *You search out my path and my lying down*
>   *and are acquainted with all my ways.*

This is elevating and affective, with the effect achieved partly by the stately artistry of the poetry. This literary exaltation gets deflated in a dynamic equivalent translation like the following (CEV):

> *You have looked deep into my heart, Lord,*
>   *and you know all about me.*
> *You know when I am resting*
>   *or when I am working,*
> *and from heaven*
>   *you discover my thoughts.*
> *You notice everything I do*
>   *and everywhere I go.*

It is obvious that contemporary translation theory has not been friendly to the literary power of the Bible. For those of my readers who want to write off my concern as a trivial concern of a few literati, let me say firmly that it is not my taste that is at issue but the nature of the Bible. It is the biblical authors and the divine Author who inspired them who produced a thoroughly (though not completely) literary book. The quarrel of those who prefer colloquial translations is not with me but with the authors and ultimately with the God who gave us the Bible.

THE GREAT CHOICE: FULLNESS VS. REDUCTIONISM

Dynamic equivalence has resulted in translations that regularly reduce the Bible from what it is in the original. Such reductionism takes a variety of forms, including lowered expectations of readers, reduced respect for biblical authors and the authority of the Bible, impoverishment of language, theological diminution, one-dimensional translation, and loss of the Bible's literary dimension.

Because dynamic equivalence has dominated the scene for the past half century, it is easy to get the impression that the entire translation scene has succumbed to reductionism. I need to guard against leaving a false impression on this point. What I call the great tradition has always had its representatives in print, right to the present day. Modern translations in the King James tradition—NASB, RSV, NKJV, ESV—have given readers the full richness of the biblical text. They have not patronized their readers or bemoaned how difficult the biblical text is for modern readers. They have used ordinary, standard English language and style and have preserved the theological vocabulary of the Bible. They have also retained multiple meanings in the original text and the literary integrity of the Bible.

NOTES

1   Dwight Macdonald, "The Bible in Modern Undress," in *Literary Style of the Old Bible and the New*, ed. D. G. Kehl (Indianapolis: Bobbs-Merrill, 1970), 42.

2   C. H. Dodd, quoted in T. S. Eliot, review of the NEB, in *The New English Bible Reviewed*, ed. Dennis Nineham (London: Epworth, 1965), 100.

3   Madeleine L'Engle, *Walking on Water* (Wheaton, IL: Harold Shaw, 1980), 40, 42.

4   T. S. Eliot, review of the NEB, in *The New English Bible Reviewed*, 96, 100-101.

5   Martin Jarrett-Kerr, "Old Wine: New Bottles," in *The New English Bible Reviewed*, 128.

6   Henry Gifford, review of the NEB, in *The New English Bible Reviewed*, 111.

7   F. L. Lucas, "The Greek 'Word' Was Different," in *Literary Style of the Old Bible and the New*, ed. D. G. Kehl (Indianapolis: Bobbs-Merrill, 1970), 52.

8   Jarrett-Kerr, "Old Wine: New Bottles," 124.

9   Ibid., 128.

10 Ruth Sawyer, *The Way of the Storyteller* (New York: Viking, 1962), 139.

11 Noel K. Weeks, "Questions for Translators," in *The New Testament Student and Bible Translation*, ed. John H. Skilton (Phillipsburg, NJ: Presbyterian and Reformed, 1978), 107.

12 Anthony Howard Nichols, "Translating the Bible: A Critical Analysis of E. A. Nida's Theory of Dynamic Equivalence and Its Impact Upon Recent Bible Translations," dissertation, University of Sheffield, 1996, 285.

13 Raymond C. Van Leeuwen, "We Really Do Need Another Bible Translation," *Christianity Today*, October 22, 2002, 32.

14 E. A. Speiser, *The Anchor Bible: Genesis* (Garden City, NJ: Doubleday, 1964), 195.

PART FIVE

*Criteria for Excellence in
an English Bible*

13

FIDELITY TO THE WORDS OF THE ORIGINAL

THE IMPLIED THESIS of this entire book is that an English Bible translation must be faithful to the original text of the Bible. In this chapter I want to make that argument explicit. I will (a) restate the case for conceiving of faithfulness as a matter of words rather than ideas, (b) examine what this means in actual translation, and (c) explore the often overlooked matter of preserving the stylistic variety found within the original texts of the Bible.

FIDELITY TO THE WORDS OF THE ORIGINAL

There is no more basic literary principle than that meaning is communicated through form. We can never quote too often Cleanth Brooks's famous dictum that "form is meaning" or Marshall McLuhan's even more famous formula that "the medium is the message."[1] The most basic of all forms through which meaning is conveyed is surely *words*. As I argued in a chapter on fallacies about translation, it is illogical to claim that one can translate the thought of a biblical text rather than its words. There is no such thing as disembodied thought. As one translation theorist has accurately said, "Not just ideas, but words are important."[2]

Not only does a translation that reproduces the very words of the original text have logic on its side (translation of ideas *rather than* words being an illogical notion); it is also the only type of translation that respects and obeys other important principles regarding the Bible. Since I have already discussed these further principles at length in earlier chapters, I will only list them here:

• Translating the words of the original takes seriously the doctrines of verbal inspiration and plenary inspiration, whereas "thought for thought" translators, no matter how reverential they are toward the Bible, operate as though they do not believe that the *very words themselves* are inspired by God and therefore something to be retained in translation.

• An essentially literal translation is transparent to *the world* of the original text, whereas a translation that phrases matters in modern equivalents often prevents a reader from ever making the journey *to* the world of the original text.

• Translating the words of the original minimizes blurring the line between translation and interpretation, whereas dynamic equivalent translations continually mingle translation and interpretation, often depriving readers of the freedom to reach their own conclusions about the correct interpretation of a passage.

• Taking the biblical authors' very words seriously retains respect for the authors and their intentions, whereas elevating the reader to the role of determiner of what is put forward as the biblical text usurps the role of the authors.

• Translating the very *words* of the original allows readers to be confident that they have before them what the Bible actually says, whereas dispensing with the words of the original sets readers afloat in a hypothetical Bible that may or may not be what the Bible actually says.

• Finally, an essentially literal translation meets the literary expectation that the words set forth in the translation are, within the limits of translation, an uncorrupted text on which an interpretation can be confidently constructed.

"NOW, CONGREGATION, WHAT THIS VERSE SAYS IN THE ORIGINAL IS . . ."

How often have you listened to a sermon in which the preacher evoked the formula, "What this verse says in the original is. . ."? Church attenders who attend churches where topical preaching reigns hear it rarely, but that is a whole different problem. In churches where expository preaching is the norm, the formula is common, depending on the translation that the preacher uses. I recently listened to a sermon on Psalm 24 where the preacher (using the NIV because it was in the pew) three times said, "Now what the original actually says is . . ." (I was later told that if he had used a literal translation like the NASB or ESV, he would not have had to evoke the formula at all.)

A translation is inadequate if an expositor needs continually to correct it. It is the preacher's task to explain a biblical text, but not to correct it. This is where dynamic equivalent translations let us down, and correspondingly where essentially literal translations show their worth. Except on those rare occasions where a completely literal translation would make no sense and where therefore even an essentially literal translation has changed the original, an expositor using a literal translation does not need to explain what the original "really says."

THE PRACTICAL IMPLICATIONS OF THIS THEORY

It is time to turn to some actual examples that will show how important fidelity to the words of the original is, and how impossible it is to translate just the ideas of a text. The last line of Psalm 88 proves instructive. "The darkness is my closest friend," one translation renders the line (NIV). "Darkness is now my only companion," says another translation (REB). This is catchy, aphoristic, clever, memorable—something to excite a literary critic. But before we can legitimately unleash our literary raptures, we need to know if the translation is what the original says. Our interpretation is only as good as the text in front of us. It so happens that the translations I have quoted are not a faithful rendition of the original, which says, "My companions have become darkness" (the ESV renders this correctly), or, even more literally, "My acquaintances—darkness!"[3] A translation that substitutes an interpretation for what the original actually says (in some of the specimens by reversing the word order) removes the foundation on which to build a trustworthy interpretation of a text.

The very passage in which the writer of Ecclesiastes articulates the importance of words in the process of composition illustrates how words determine meaning. The Preacher tells us that he "sought to find words of delight" (Ecclesiastes 12:10, ESV; KJV margin). Words obviously mattered to this author, who was a writer of words before he was a writer of ideas. English translations vary on their rendition of the phrase "words of delight": "pleasing words" (RSV), "acceptable words" (KJV, NKJV), "comforting words" (GNB), "just the right words" (NIV), "accurate" words (CEV), "an attractive style" (Jerusalem), and "delightful words" (NASB). The variability of translations proves that one cannot just translate the *meaning* of a passage, as thought-for-thought translation theory claims. Meaning is communicated through words, and the specific words that one chooses determine the meaning.

To abandon the actual words of the Bible typically leads to a loss of both the specificity and richness of the biblical text. Psalm 32 begins with a threefold reference to the forgiveness of sins, and the original uses three separate words for *sin*. Translations committed to remaining faithful to the original preserve the nuances and specificity of the three different words: "transgression," "sin," "iniquity" (NASB, NRSV, RSV, ESV). To reduce the three terms for sin to two (NIV, NLT) or one (CEV) is reductionistic and fails to do justice to the specificity of the text.

I do not wish to be understood as saying that I am opposed to a degree of dynamic equivalence if a literal translation makes no sense in English, but my verdict after four years of work on a Bible translation committee is that the number of such instances is very small indeed, probably even statistically insignificant. The issue is not whether in a tiny number of instances we need to "go dynamic" but rather whether *in principle* a translation intends to translate the actual words of the Bible or take liberties with them.

PRESERVING THE CONCORDANCE OF THE ORIGINAL

Literary texts tend to contain word patterns and image patterns; that is, the author consciously repeats the same image or word throughout a text. The effect is always artistic. But often the intended effect extends beyond artistry to meaning. When a translation is careful to retain the word pattern of the original, the result is called *concordance*, in implied contrast to the criterion of *variation*.

Translations vary widely in regard to the translators' interest in maintaining concordance. The King James translators regularly made a choice to suppress concordance in favor of a variety of synonyms for the same original word. By their own testimony, the translators claimed that they "have not tied ourselves to an uniformity of phrasing or to an identity of words. . . . Why should we be in bondage to [words or syllables] if we may be free, use one precisely when we may use another no less fit, as commodiously?" This was in every way a Renaissance decision, in keeping with the Baroque exuberance of the sixteenth- and early seventeenth-century spirit. To dip widely into what the Old English poets quaintly called "the word hoard" yields one type of artistry—an artistry of variety and color. I myself prefer a rich and varied vocabulary to a limited one.

But when we come to translate a text, it is not up to our preference as to what type of artistry a text exhibits. The translator is not an author or editor but (as John Skilton expresses it) "a steward of the work of another" and someone who should "view his task as reportorial in character, as holding up the mirror to the nature of his original."[4] Literal translations beginning with the Revised Version of 1885 have generally chosen to translate the same Hebrew or Greek word the same way throughout a text, thereby preserving the concordance of the original. This, too, yields a kind of artistry—the simple as a form of beauty. More to the point, fidelity to the words of the biblical original *prescribes* that an English translation strive for concordance, for the simple reason that the author used concordance. The effect may or may not be artistic, but it almost certainly brings out nuances of meaning.

A particularly striking example occurs in the story of Ruth. On the occasion of the first meeting of Ruth and Boaz, Boaz courteously extends a wish, phrased in religious terms, that Ruth will find her needs met by God: "a full reward be given you by the LORD . . . under whose wings you have come to take refuge" (2:12, ESV). There is irony in the statement, inasmuch as Boaz at this point has no inkling of the role that he himself will play in God's blessing of Ruth. When Boaz wakes up at midnight on the threshing floor and finds Ruth at his feet, Ruth in effect asks Boaz to propose marriage: "Spread your wings over your servant, for you are a redeemer" (3:9, ESV). This is beautiful. The very same word, here translated as "wings," appears in both speeches. A literary critic comments:

> [In the first exchange] Boaz attempts to evade his responsibility by placing the whole burden upon the LORD. It is true that the LORD will recompense Ruth fully on one level, yet it is Boaz who will recompense her fully on the human level. . . . [In the second exchange, Ruth's statement] triggers a memory, recalls to [Boaz] his previous words. . . . Once this correspondence has been made, the full meaning and implications of his previous words flood in upon him.[5]

Of course, before we can relish this bit of artistry and its implications for the providential theme of the story, we need a translation that believes in the principle of fidelity to the words of the original and the concordance that flows from this principle. This is where translations that are indifferent to retaining the words of the original let us down.

They translate the word for "wings" in the second exchange as "corner of your garment" (NIV) or "edge of your cover" (CEV) or "corner of your covering" (NLT) or "skirt of your cloak" (REB).

The book of Genesis yields examples of how concordance can be important. A key parallel between similar events occurs in Genesis 3:17, where Adam "listened to the voice" of his wife (ESV, NASB), and Genesis 16:2, where Abraham, too, brings ignominy on himself when he "listened to the voice" of his wife (ESV, NASB). This is the kind of parallel that literary critics and theologians regard as important. A new cycle of wrong priority and wrong choice unfolds when Abraham repeats Adam's mistake. The original text calls our attention to the situation, but dynamic equivalent translations, with a nonchalant attitude toward the actual words of the original, apparently have no incentive to maintain the concordance of the original. They almost uniformly (NIV, CEV, GNB, NLT) use the verb "listen to" for Adam and "agreed with" for Abraham, thereby missing the parallel between the two actions and blunting the force of what actually took place between Abram and Sarai.

Often concordance stretches across books of the Bible. The mysterious "sons of God" that we read about in Genesis 6:2 and Job 2:1 are sufficiently mysterious and sparsely mentioned within the Bible that it is important to translate the original word used in both contexts in an identical way. Essentially literal translations do so (KJV, ESV, NASB). Translations with a casual attitude toward concordance translate the two passages differently (NIV, CEV, NLT).

RETAINING THE STYLISTIC VARIETY OF THE ORIGINAL

A commitment to translate the actual words of the original also has ramifications for the literary criterion of preserving the variety of styles that we find in the original text of the Bible. A survey of prefaces shows that most translators pay lip service to the ideal of preserving stylistic variety, but with dynamic equivalent translations the claims are generally false. There is reason to believe that when translation committees do their work, they consciously decide whether to keep their eye primarily on the actual text of the Bible or on a target audience. If they begin with a target audience, of whatever type, they will naturally slant everything toward it, and the various books of the Bible naturally end up in a uniform style—a veritable monotone in which every hill is made low and every rough place a plain.

Dynamic equivalent Bibles tend overwhelmingly to reduce the entire Bible to a uniform style because (a) most of these translations begin with assumptions about the audience they wish to reach instead of a commitment to the actual texture of Scripture, and (b) if the concern is to convey the thought rather than the literal words of a biblical text, there is little scope for paying attention to the contours of a biblical writer's style. In the words of Eugene Nida, "Style is secondary to content."[6]

VARIETY VS. UNIFORMITY IN PROSE STYLE

Some of the prose of the New Testament epistles is famous for its long, flowing sentences, rising to a climax of eloquence. Ephesians 5:19-21 is a good example. In the original, it consists of four participial clauses, flowing in stately parallelism to a climax of eloquence. Here is how the ESV renders the passage:

> . . . *addressing one another in psalms and hymns and spiritual songs, singing and making melody to the Lord with all your heart, giving thanks always and for everything to God the Father in the name of our Lord Jesus Christ, submitting to one another out of reverence for Christ.*

The prose style here is deliberative, meditative, consciously rhetorical, and exalted. In a literal translation, no one would mistake the epistolary style of Ephesians for the fast-paced narrative prose of Mark's Gospel:

> *And they went into Capernaum, and immediately on the Sabbath he entered the synagogue and was teaching. And they were astonished at his teaching, for he taught them as one who had authority, and not as the scribes. And immediately there was in their synagogue a man with an unclean spirit. (Mark 1:21-23, ESV)*

This is a narrative style of a particular type—fast-moving, atomistic, almost kaleidoscopic in the rapid shifts in what we see as we read. The effect is the opposite of what we find in the passage from Ephesians.

As we might predict, the dynamic equivalent and colloquial translations are in their element with a passage like the one from Mark's Gospel. The sign of their failure to reproduce the range of styles found in the original text of the Bible is how they handle the passage from Ephesians 5:19-21. Here are three specimens:

Speak to one another with the words of psalms, hymns, and sacred
songs; sing hymns and psalms to the Lord with praise in your hearts.
In the name of our Lord Jesus Christ, always give thanks for every-
thing to God the Father. Submit yourselves to one another because of
your reverence for Christ (GNB).

 Speak to one another with psalms, hymns and spiritual songs.
Sing and make music in your heart to the Lord, always giving thanks
to God the Father for everything, in the name of our Lord Jesus Christ.
Submit to one another out of reverence for Christ (NIV).

 . . . speak to one another in psalms, hymns, and songs; sing and
make music from your heart to the Lord; and in the name of our Lord
Jesus Christ give thanks every day for everything to our God and
Father. Be subject to one another out of reverence for Christ (REB).

The general tendency here, slightly mitigated in the second passage,
is to chop up the stately flow of thought that we find in the original into
a series of short independent clauses. It is not my concern here to weigh
the merits of this tendency in itself; my point is that when a translation
committee begins with a grid of rules based on its assumptions about its
target audience, it tends to flatten out the range of distinctive styles in
the original into a monotone style—a style in which the prose of an epistle reads like the prose of a fast-moving narrative.

POETRY VS. PROSE-LIKE POETRY

When we turn to poetry, the crucial element is not primarily syntax but
vocabulary. Poetry aims for an effect that is distinctly different from the
effect of prose. This sometimes results in unfamiliar syntactical effects,
but it is much more likely to consist of the *idiom* or vocabulary in which
a poet writes. The question for the present discussion, therefore, is
whether the poetry in a given translation sounds like poetry or prose.
Here are four versions of Psalm 36:11:

Let not the foot of arrogance come upon me,
 nor the hand of the wicked drive me away. (ESV)

May the foot of the proud not come against me,
 nor the hand of the wicked drive me away. (NIV)

Don't let the proud trample me;
 don't let the wicked push me around. (NLT)

Don't let those proud and merciless people
  kick me around or chase me away. (CEV)

The first two preserve the poetic distinctives of the verse, while the second pair makes the verse read like the colloquial prose that prevails throughout the respective translations.

The ideal of any translation that purports to be faithful to the original is to preserve the stylistic range of the original. Much of the time, moving from one book of the Bible to another should jolt us into sensing that we have entered an entirely different stylistic world. Conversely, when we move from one book to another we should *not* be lulled into a familiar feeling that we have "more of the same."

THE IDEAL: STYLISTIC VARIETY COMMENSURATE WITH THE ORIGINAL

Fidelity to the original will produce its own stylistic variety commensurate with what the original texts actually say and how they say it. If translators simply follow the contours of the original, the results will resemble the original text. I have a lot of sympathy for the position that "in the end it is the Bible itself which will teach us how the Bible is to be rendered."[7]

A good translation, therefore, will reproduce the brooding quality of the mood pieces of Ecclesiastes. For example:

All things are full of weariness;
  a man cannot utter it;
the eye is not satisfied with seeing,
  nor the ear filled with hearing. (1:8, ESV)

A good translation will capture the matter-of-fact journalistic reportage of the Bible's historical chronicles, aware, however, that the account was probably written by a court scribe and not uttered by someone in the barber's chair.

So they took two horsemen, and the king sent them after the army of the Syrians, saying, "Go and see." So they went after them as far as the Jordan, and behold, all the way was littered with garments and equipment that the Syrians had thrown away in their haste. And the messengers returned and told the king. Then the

*people went out and plundered the camp of the Syrians. (2 Kings
7:14-16, ESV)*

If a translation simply follows the path laid down by the original, it
will have no difficulty in capturing the golden style of love poetry found
in the Song of Solomon:

Behold, you are beautiful, my love;
  behold, you are beautiful;
  your eyes are doves.
Behold, you are beautiful, my beloved,
  truly delightful. (1:15-16, ESV)

If fidelity to the original is construed as faithfulness to the *thought*
of the Bible rather than its words, and if a further determinant is the
assumed reading ability of a target audience, the result will be a Bible in
which the stylistic variety of the original has been flattened out to a uniform style. But if fidelity is taken to mean faithfulness to the words and
stylistic distinctives of the original, a translation will strive to capture the
stateliness, the poetic quality, and the mystical overtones of (for example) John's Gospel. A good English translation will manage to capture
the visionary quality of prophetic and apocalyptic writing. A psalm of
lament will have a tone of distress and protest, and a praise psalm the
quality of exaltation. The theological weightiness of Romans cannot be
captured in short sentences and nontheological vocabulary, and a translation committed to faithfulness to the original will accordingly give us
a book of Romans that reads unlike anything else we have ever read.

If the goal is to be faithful to the original, as even dynamic equivalent translations claim, a translation will retain even the quirks of a given
biblical author, something that dynamic equivalent translations tend not
to do. Some of these quirks and distinctive traits do, indeed, strike readers as odd, but (a) they did the same thing for the original audience, and
(b) they are an inherent part of the text, not something that the process
of translation introduces into the mix. They are present for someone
reading the original and should be present for the reader of a translation. They are not something that a translator needs to correct or fix.

Thus if one of Ezekiel's unusual features is the interspersed formula,
"And you, son of man," a translation that claims to be faithful to the
original text will retain it, even if it seems far removed from common

usage. One of Mark's favorite techniques in his Gospel is to use the connectives *kai* ("and") or *euthys* ("immediately") to begin a new train of thought. This is one of the stylistic traits that helps lend the aura of things happening and at an energetic, fast, and furious pace in his Gospel. When Eugene Nida complains that to translate *kai* produces "a kind of style completely contrary to good English usage" and "gives the impression of being 'childish,'"[8] his complaint is not against a given English translation but against Mark as author. In doing this, Nida misses the point that Mark is entitled to his own stylistic effects and that an English translation, if it aims to achieve the same effect in the receptor language that it had in the source language, will pass the formula on to its modern readers.

Since among devotees of modern translations the King James Bible is somewhat disparaged, viewed as being used by readers who do not "know better," I want to note in passing that when it comes to stylistic range and flexibility, the King James Bible is peerless. I am not urging a return to it; I am urging a respect for a monument of excellence that can still serve as an inspiration and model. The flexibility of the King James is such that it can give us this exaltation of style:

> *And let the beauty of the* LORD *our God be upon us: and establish thou the work of our hands upon us; yea, the work of our hands establish thou it. (Psalm 90:17)*

But the King James translation is equally adept at the racy realism that we find in a passage like this:

> *And Ehud put forth his left hand, and took the dagger from his right thigh, and thrust it into his belly: And the haft also went in after the blade; and the fat closed upon the blade, so that he could not draw the dagger out of his belly; and the dirt came out. (Judges 3:21-22)*

Instead of scoffing at the King James Version, we should lament what has been lost with its disappearance from currency, learning from it as much as we can.

SUMMARY

Even dynamic equivalent translations claim faithfulness to the original as their goal. But in fact only an essentially literal translation that claims fidelity to the language of the original achieves a consistently credible degree of faithfulness. Such a translation is as transparent to the original text as the process of translation allows. It also retains the verbal effects, the consonance, and the stylistic variety of the original.

NOTES

1   Cleanth Brooks, "The Formalist Critic," in *The Modern Critical Spectrum*, eds. Gerald Jay Goldberg and Nancy Marmer Goldberg (Englewood Cliffs, NJ: Prentice-Hall, 1962); Marshall McLuhan, *The Medium Is the Message* (New York: Random House, 1967).

2   Francis R. Steele, "Translation or Paraphrase," in *The New Testament Student and Bible Translation*, ed. John Skilton (Phillipsburg, NJ: Presbyterian and Reformed, 1978), 69.

3   Artur Weiser, *The Psalms: A Commentary* (Philadelphia: Westminster, 1962), 585.

4   John H. Skilton, "Future English Versions and the Past," in *The New Testament Student and Bible Translation*, 190-191.

5   D. F. Rauber, "The Book of Ruth," in *Literary Interpretations of Biblical Narratives*, ed. Kenneth R. R. Gros Louis (Nashville: Abingdon, 1974), 169, 171.

6   Eugene A. Nida and Charles R. Taber, *The Theory and Practice of Translation* (Leiden: E. J. Brill, 1969), 13. Although Nida states that "though style is secondary to content, it is nevertheless important," in dynamic equivalent translations the retention of the stylistic distinctives of the original is decidedly secondary and often nonexistent.

7   Martin Jarrett-Kerr, review of NEB reprinted in *The New English Bible Reviewed*, ed. Dennis Nineham (London: Epworth, 1965), 129.

8   Nida and Taber, *The Theory and Practice of Translation*, 14.

14

EFFECTIVE DICTION:
CLARITY, VIVIDNESS,
CONNOTATION, AMBIGUITY

EFFECTIVE DICTION IS a priority with all translation committees, regardless of their philosophy of translation. But a look at translations shows at once that translators do not agree among themselves regarding the criteria for the kind of language required in an English Bible translation.

In this chapter I will delineate what I regard as the four primary criteria for effective diction in an English Bible. These criteria are clarity, vividness of expression, correctness of connotation, and retention of the ambiguity that the original text of the Bible possesses. With each of these criteria, I will clarify the principle and compare translations regarding the degree to which they achieve or deviate from that criterion.

CLARITY

When I speak of clarity as a criterion of a good translation, I do not mean that every statement is immediately clear. As I argue at various points in this book, much of the Bible, including Jesus' ostensibly simple parables and sayings, requires pondering and analysis before we know exactly what a statement means. Jesus' own explanation of why he told parables (Matthew 13:10-17; Mark 4:10-12; Luke 8:9-10) confirms that the Bible does not communicate all of its meaning to everyone immediately. When I praise clarity as a criterion of translation, I mean that the English words and syntax are clear.

Every good translation has been clear in its own generation and when judged by the audience for which it was intended. Certainly most modern translations have met this criterion. The superior clarity of the KJV over its predecessors in the sixteenth century was one of its most obvious virtues, a point that the archaic baggage of the KJV four centuries later should not be allowed to obscure. Compare the KJV's "a man of sorrows, and acquainted with grief" with two forerunners: "a man as hath good experience of sorrows and infirmities" (Bishops' Bible); "a man full of sorrows and hath experience of infirmities" (Geneva).

In claiming that most translations rank high in clarity at the moment of their appearance, I am not saying that there have not been translations that had lapses in clarity from the moment they appeared in print. Surely the Rheims Bible rendition "give us today our supersubstantial bread" had a problem of clarity from the beginning. Likewise the Rheims phrase "the profundities of God" for the phrase that the King James eventually rendered as "the deep things of God" (1 Corinthians 2:10). And surely, too, the Rheims formulation "beneficence and communication do not forget, for with such . . . God is promerited" would give the plowboy difficulty. Tyndale's translation is legitimately praised to this day, but as successive translations built upon his remarkable achievement, gains in clarity were predictably made. We can compare the Tyndale and KJV translations of Matthew 11:28: "All ye that travail, and be charged, come to me, and I shall fulfill you"; "Come unto me, all ye that labour and are heavy laden, and I will give you rest."

Modern translations, too, can have their lapses. How many late twentieth-century readers, I wonder, would have found the statement "our bed is verdant" clear to them (Song of Solomon, 1:16, NIV)? How many modern readers would get the picture when told that the beloved "browses among the lilies" (6:3, NIV)? How many readers in the second half of the twentieth century would find "hind" (Psalm 42:1, NEB) any clearer than the archaic "hart" (KJV, RSV) for the deer mentioned in Psalm 42:1? How many people, when reading the haunting picture of the physical decline of old age in the last chapter of Ecclesiastes, would get much meaning out of the statement of a modern translation that "the caperberry is ineffective" (Ecclesiastes 12:5, NASB)? One might well long nostalgically for the good old days when people knew what it meant to "go circumspectly when you visit the house of God" (Ecclesiastes 5:1, REB), but there is reason to doubt that most people today know what it means.

Why Clarity Is Elusive

Clarity is closely tied to the evolution of the English language, which is changing at a more rapid rate in our day than ever before. No modern English Bible in its current form, including ongoing revisions, remains fully clear as language changes. Until recently, readers would get the right picture when they read that God gave Moses the law on "tables" of stone, but today they almost certainly would get a wrong picture. Renditions that were perfectly clear and appropriate when a translation appeared can become "howlers" almost overnight. One translation has Paul say that "Tychicus will tell you all about my affairs" (Colossians 4:7, RSV) and has the psalmist say that "I will accept no bull from your house" (Psalm 50:9, RSV).

Another variable in regard to clarity is the difference in national and cultural usage, even among nations whose primary language is English. Anyone who has served on a translation committee can attest the difference in usage between British and American English. No English translation is fully clear to both British and American readers. British readers apparently can handle the statement that "a cudgel is but a reed" (Job 41:29, REB), and they apparently will know what Jesus meant when he castigated the Pharisees because they "strain off a midge" (Matthew 23:24, REB); but American readers will choke on these curiosities. The Revised English Bible includes the quaint phraseology "evening or midnight, cock-crow or early dawn" (Mark 13:35), and I have been told by a Britisher that Brits will know what to do with a cock crowing in the story of Peter's denial, while the mention of a rooster will make them scratch their heads in perplexity. I enjoy reading the New English Bible and the Revised English Bible for a quality that I relish in British literature—namely, the sheer quaintness and otherness of its expressions. But in terms of understanding what the biblical text really says, this is a great distraction that undermines the clarity of the translation for an American reader.

On the criterion of clarity, then, two principles are noteworthy. First, the language of every translation becomes progressively less clear the further it is removed from the point of its original publication. It is a melancholy principle for translation committees to confront, but every English Bible is a venture in planned obsolescence. Secondly, the clarity of a translation is also variable with specific audiences and readers. Another unwelcome reality for translation committees, therefore, is that they cannot achieve maximum clarity with more than one nation or even subculture.

CORRECT CONNOTATIONS FOR WORDS

The issue of correct connotations for words falls into two complementary categories. On the one side, clarity means choosing vocabulary that has the best possible connotations for a given idea or expression of the original. On the other side, it means avoiding *incorrect* connotations.

Avoiding incorrect connotations is particularly difficult in a day of rapid changes in usage. To render Song of Solomon 6:3 as "I am my lover's, and my lover is mine" (NIV) would have been appropriate until fairly recently, though the rendition lacks the evocative splendor of most other translations' preference of "I am my beloved's, and my beloved is mine" (KJV, RSV, ESV, NASB, NKJV, NEB, REB). But the use of the word *lover* today conveys the incorrect connotation of illicit sexual relations, as suggested by a recent television interview dealing with sexual relations in which a person used the formula "husbands, lovers, and boyfriends."

Among the numerous sordid sexual scenes in Ezekiel is the one in which Israel is said to have played the whore in Egypt, where "their breasts were pressed and their virgin bosoms [actually nipples] handled" (23:3, ESV, RSV, NASB). This is not a scene of genuine affection but of mechanical sexual contact. The verbs *pressed* and *handled* get the connotations right. Some translations, though, use verbs that connote affection rather than crude sexual handling; for example, "their breasts were fondled and their virgin bosoms caressed" (NIV), and in another translation, "they allowed themselves to be fondled and caressed" (NLT).

The formulation "wicked way" at the end of Psalm 139 (KJV, RSV, NKJV) signals that the behavior in view is evil in principle—morally (as directed toward fellow humans), spiritually (as directed toward God), and personally (as self-destructive to oneself). It is the quintessential *wicked way*. The rendering "grievous way" (ESV), while different in meaning, similarly allows for a multiple reference. To render the phrase "Any path that grieves thee" (NEB, REB) retains the gravity of the evil but (a) lacks the succinctness, alliteration, and aphoristic punch of "wicked way" and (b) limits the action to something directed against God. "Offensive way" (NIV) reduces the behavior to a level of social obnoxiousness (as in "your behavior of the moment is offensive to me"), while "any hurtful way" (NASB) (a) reduces the evil to the pragmatic level of its effects, (b) seems to limit the effect to the evildoer, and (c) even if the "hurt" includes others as well as the doer, makes the evil moral rather than spiritual.

Connotations depend on context and current usage, and every translation is sooner or later blindsided by the vagaries of unexpected idioms that appear with increasing frequency in a culture addicted to jargon and fads. We catch a sense of the extraordinary worth and attractiveness of the beloved when he is said to be "fairer than the children of men" (Psalm 45:2, KJV) or "the fairest of the sons of men" (RSV). But when we read that he is "the most excellent of men" (NIV) we get the impression that the beloved has topped out on a performance test. In turn, the evocative "fairer than the children of men" has become obsolete because fairness now implies complexion only, whereas it once conveyed a general commendation of beauty and worth.

Translations of Philippians 4:3 show how hard it is to avoid incorrect connotations. Here is how various translations handle the epithet by which Paul addresses someone who has aided him in his work:

• "yokefellow" (KJV, RSV, NIV). This communicates nothing to a modern reader except a vague sense of bondage. The fact that *yoke* is a major biblical metaphor does nothing to salvage "yokefellow."

• "comrade" (NEB, REB, NASB). It is a fact that modern communism has made this word synonymous in modern parlance with a fellow communist; in fact, we can still get a laugh by addressing someone as "comrade."

• "partner" (CEV). The most common current connotations of partner are a business partner or a sexual partner.

• "teammate" (NLT). The connotations of *teammate* are solidly athletic.

• "companion" (NRSV, Jerusalem, NKJV, ESV). Only this rendition among those cited is devoid of inaccurate connotative baggage.

VIVIDNESS OF EXPRESSION

Effective diction also requires vivid and concrete expression wherever possible. I am not asking for concretion when the original has an abstraction. I am only taking my stand against the tendency of recent translations to substitute abstract vocabulary for concrete vocabulary with abandon. The Hebrew of the Old Testament, in particular, is noteworthy for its relative scarcity of abstract terms, and words that in our vocabulary are abstract are likely to have denoted a physical action or concrete image.[1]

If we turn to specimens, a huge divergence at once appears between translations that retain the concreteness of the original and those that are eager to turn concretions into abstractions. Since this point will resurface when I turn to poetry in the Bible, I will confine myself at this point to prose. "Vapor of vapors," Ecclesiastes 1:2 says in the original. We can chart the movement away from the concretion of the original almost on a chronological time chart, with the more recent being the most abstract: "vanity of vanities" (KJV, RSV, NASB, NKJV, Jerusalem, ESV), "emptiness, emptiness" (NEB), "Meaningless! Meaningless!" (NIV), "futility, utter futility" (REB), "nothing makes sense" (CEV).

A major New Testament test of whether a translation prefers the concretion of the original or an abstraction that dissipates the metaphor of the original is the verb *walk* in contexts where it metaphorically refers to a person's way of life. For example, in 1 Thessalonians 2:12 Paul claims that he encouraged believers to "walk in a manner worthy of God" (NASB, ESV; KJV, NKJV, "walk worthy of God"). The image of walking, or its variant of the path or way, is a master image of the Bible for the conduct of a person's life. The image of walking down a path is a richly evocative image, embodying the meanings of long-term and continuous motion, a sense of purpose, direction toward and eventual arrival at a goal or destination. All of this gets lost when the image *walk* is dropped in favor of the abstraction *live* (NIV, NLT, REB, Jerusalem, TNIV).

Ezekiel 3:7 claims that the house of Israel had "a hard forehead and a stubborn heart" (ESV). Translations that begin with the premise that modern readers cannot understand metaphor drop the concretion in favor of abstraction, and the hard forehead and stubborn heart become reduced to the adjective "hardened and obstinate" (NIV) or "stubborn and obstinate" (NASB) or "stubborn and defiant" (GNB). Retaining the references to forehead and heart locates the evil in a person's very being, while adjectives like "obstinate" and "defiant" push the interpretation in the direction of behavior.

Vividness is sometimes a matter of particularity as opposed to vagueness. "House of bondage" (KJV, RSV, NKJV) or its variant "house of slavery" (NASB, ESV, NRSV) is more particularized than the vaguer "land of slavery" (NIV, NEB, REB). The edict that Adam will die "in the day" that he eats the forbidden fruit (KJV, RSV, NASB, ESV) is more particularized than the vague "when you eat of it" (NIV). When a translation pictures the landscape in which Ehud decided to turn back and confront Eglon at the place of "sculptured stones" (Judges 3:19, RSV, NRSV) or "carved stones" (REB, GNB) or "stone carvings" (NLT), the reader can actually picture the landscape. Much of the particularity gets lost in the rendition "idols" (NASB, NIV, ESV). To speak of "put[ting] . . . to the sword" (Jeremiah 50:27, REB, NASB) is more vivid than the undifferentiated "kill" (NIV, CEV, ESV) or "destroy" (NLT).

To read that Samuel "hewed Agag in pieces" (1 Samuel 15:33, KJV, RSV, REB; NLT similar) forces us to experience the shock of dismemberment; the rendition "Samuel put Agag to death" (NIV) conceals what happened. Regarding the latter translation, I recall an exchange that I had with an editor regarding an essay in an anthology that I had compiled. One of my writers had adduced the verse about Agag as an instance of dismemberment in the Bible. My editor theorized that the scriptural reference was wrong. I wrote back to her, as I have often written to my correspondence school students, to the effect that it was her translation that had let her down.

LITERARY AMBIGUITY

While transparency and lack of ambiguity are virtues of expository writing, where words ideally mean one thing only, the same is not true of literary writing. Literature possesses a quality of discourse that is customarily rendered by the word *ambiguity*. Ambiguity here encompasses such qualities as multiplicity of meaning, a refusal to limit an utterance to just one meaning when the experience entails more than that, open-endedness of meaning or application, and preservation of a degree of mystery. A literary scholar once wrote a book entitled *Seven Types of Ambiguity*,[2] hinting at how much literary critics value this quality of literary discourse.

I can imagine some of my readers easily dismissing ambiguity as a quirk of literary people. What this betrays is an inadequate respect for how much of the Bible *is* literary in nature. The Bible is a *classic* text. It is, moreover, a *sacred* text. The Bible is not like the daily newspaper. It consistently possesses the quality of ambiguity as literary scholars and practitioners understand that quality of discourse. A biblical scholar has written that

> ambiguity that is generally avoided in scientific language, and tolerated in conventional language, is an essential ingredient in literary language systems and is a major device for evoking feeling. We have drawn attention to such expressions in the teaching of Jesus.[3]

How do literary scholars and writers understand ambiguity? Its primary quality is multiple meanings, referring to the way in which a single utterance possesses more than one legitimate and intended meaning. A second meaning of ambiguity as a literary quality is a quality of utterance that is elusive and mysterious, not conveying all of its meaning on the surface. The "hard sayings" of Jesus, for example, are evocative and awe-inspiring even when we may not be completely sure of what they mean.

In regard to this whole general subject, a literary scholar named Stephen Prickett has written a landmark essay entitled "The Problem of the Transparent Text."[4] Taking issue with the translation theory stated in the preface to the *Good News Bible* that an English translation should be rendered in English that is "natural, clear, simple, and unambiguous," Prickett argues that such a theory consistently gives us a reductionistic Bible. Prickett's main specimen is the "still small voice," or "voice of thin silence," of 1 Kings 19:12. Surveying a wide range of post-Renaissance translations and commentaries, Prickett shows that the overwhelming tendency has been to resolve the question of whether the voice is a natural phenomenon, to be explained by scientific means, or a spiritual phenomenon, to be explained as a miracle. The consistent tendency is to resolve ambiguity and eliminate the possibility that what Elijah encountered was both physical and spiritual.

Prickett's final conclusion is that paradoxically those who attempt to render the biblical text fully transparent—that is, devoid of ambiguity—see *least* in the text, while those who preserve the ambiguity of the original see *most*. Prickett writes, "For the former, the text has become evermore transparent—revealing nothing behind; for the latter, the text's apparent opacity has become evermore richly revealing."[5]

It is hardly an exaggeration to say that advocates of dynamic equivalence have undertaken a sustained campaign to rid the Bible of its ambiguity. Here are specimen statements:

• "Every effort has been made to use language that is natural, clear, simple, and unambiguous" (GNB preface).

• "It is unfair to the original writer and to the receptors to reproduce as ambiguities all those passages which may be interpreted in more than one way."[6]

• "Avoid ambiguity. We translate/paraphrase dynamically when a literal/formal translation would be *ambiguous*."[7]

The whole premise here is faulty. The preface to the *Good News Bible* claims that the first step in translation is "to understand correctly the meaning of the original" and then to render it in "language that is natural, clear, simple, and unambiguous." But when the meaning of the original is multiple, ambiguous, and complicated, to render it "simple and unambiguous" is precisely *not* to "understand correctly the meaning of the original."

A member of the American Bible Society claimed that the *Good News Bible* was designed for the "unsophisticated" or "average" reader who would be grateful for "being delivered from theological subtleties," and further that since God "stooped to the level of human language to communicate with his people," it was the translators' task to render the Bible in language as "simple as possible."[8] We need to scrutinize what is affirmed in such a formulation: Average people cannot handle theological subtlety and exaltation of language, God did not communicate his truth in elevated language, and the theology of the Bible does not require sophistication of thought and language. Furthermore, if an English translation consistently chooses a possible interpretation from among available options, we end up not with a reliable text but with a text of possible interpretations—a hypothetical text based on what a given translation committee decided to dole out to its readers from among available options.

Psalm 88:18 as a Test Case

The last line of Psalm 88 clarifies the issues nicely. The original states, "my companions have become darkness" (ESV), or "my acquaintances—darkness" (Weiser).[9] Certainly the line requires pondering. Several readings are simultaneously possible: (1) the speaker's friends have vanished and are as absent or invisible as darkness is; (2) the ignominious desertion by the speaker's friends makes them morally dark— people with a dark stain on them because of their behavior; (3) the speaker's experience of misery occasioned by his friends' desertion is emotional and psychic pain and darkness to the speaker; (4) darkness is the speaker's friend or acquaintance. Since biblical scholars and translators have considered the original to be problematical, I should add that as a literary critic I find the line rich in ambiguity of the type I regularly encounter in poetry.

Translators who dislike ambiguity have done a number of things with the line, which already signals the problems that arise when literary ambiguity is compromised. Three translations choose the meaning that the speaker's companions are "in darkness" (RSV, NASB, NRSV). This would seem to make the friends the victims of ignorance, which does not fit with the rest of the psalm. "Only darkness remains," says another translation (NLT), which removes the friends from the utterance even though they are present in the original and which narrows the range of possible meanings to one. Other translations reverse the word order of the sentence and change the plural reference to singular: "Darkness is now my only companion" (REB), or "The darkness is my closest friend" (NIV). This is a possible reading, but (a) it is only one of several options, and (b) because it reverses the word order of the original and changes the number from plural to singular, it is the least likely of the legitimate options.

What the translators' toils over the last line of Psalm 88 show is that uneasiness over ambiguity, accompanied by the impulse to Spell It Out, is usually both unnecessary and impoverishing to the meaning of the text. All of the translations that smooth out the last line of Psalm 88 are more immediately understandable than the unretouched line, but they are also reductionistic and lose the multidimensional evocativeness and mystery of the original. One of the points elaborated in A. H. Nichols's critique of dynamic equivalent translations is that "the commitment to explicitness means that the metaphor and the motifs of the Bible had to be reprocessed and replaced by the explicit, analytical language with which Westerners feel more comfortable," a process that "always involves loss of meaning."[10]

PRESERVING MULTIPLE MEANINGS AND MYSTERY

"Everyone will be salted with fire," Jesus is recorded as saying in Mark 9:49 (most English translations). "Everyone will be purified with fire," reads a translation (NLT) that wants to eliminate the ambiguity from the statement. To eliminate the ambiguity of Jesus' saying not only violates a literary principle but also ignores one of the most characteristic features of Jesus' rhetoric—namely, its frequently elusive and mysterious quality. Contrary to the prefaces of some contemporary translations that are fearful of retaining any statement whose meaning is not immediately clear, Jesus' own theory of communication rested on what I call delayed-action insight. We know from Jesus' explanation of why he spoke in parables that he did *not* intend that everyone would immediately understand his sayings and parables (Mark 4:10-23). If we then look at the actual sayings and parables that Jesus uttered, it is obvious that they do *not* carry all of their meaning on the surface. They require pondering and interpretation and mulling over. They are close relatives of the riddle. They yield their meanings only to those who, metaphorically speaking, "have ears to hear," that is, take the time to ponder them. Nichols rightly observes, in his criticism of dynamic equivalent translations, that "ambiguity, arresting imagery, and the evocation of multiple associations pervade the Bible. Jesus himself often used such language to shock or puzzle the hearer, to force him to introspect, or to look at things in a completely new way."[11]

Eugene Nida reveals how profoundly he misunderstands the nature of ambiguity when he equates a writer's use of ambiguity with playing language games instead of communicating a message.[12] In reality, the qualities of multiple meanings and mystery are inherent in texts that are literary, and also in texts that we regard as classic and sacred texts. We should note that Nida and other dynamic equivalent theorists generally do not deny that ambiguities exist in the original text. They simply want to interpose their preferred interpretation and shield their readers from the ambiguities or mysteries of the original.

For purposes of bringing the issue into focus, Mark 9:24 can suffice as a final example. The father who requests that Jesus heal his son blurts out, "I believe; help my unbelief!" (REB, ESV; KJV similar). This is not how *we* might express the thought, but it is how the father expressed it. In writing his Gospel, Mark did not find it necessary to clarify what the father had said. He preserved the mystery of the utterance. "Help my unbelief" is a difficult saying, but its compensating virtue is that it permits multiple meanings at the same time. It might mean, "Enable me to find pardon (help) for my unbelief." It might mean, "Enable me to find relief (help) from my unbelief." It might mean, "Grant improvement (help) in those areas where I am guilty of unbelief." Or again, "Give me power (help) against my unbelief."

Translations that are skittish about ambiguity narrow the range of possible meanings to one, though they do not agree which meaning is right: "help *me in* my unbelief" (NASB); "I do have faith! Please help me to have even more" (CEV); "help me overcome my unbelief" (NIV, TNIV); "help me not to doubt" (NLT); "help me when I don't believe enough" (SEB). It is often the aphoristic statement that is mysterious, and such a saying stays in the memory precisely because it is not transparent or easy. Each of the proposed explanations of the father's statement is eminently forgettable, while "help my unbelief" remains in the memory, teasing us into contemplating its meaning.

SUMMARY

Regardless of one's translation philosophy, it is impossible to escape the requirements of effective diction. The only question is what constitutes the operative principles that should govern the choice of language in an English Bible translation. The criteria for the Bible are no different from the criteria that govern effective writing and speaking everywhere. Particularly with a sacred text that is at the same time a predominantly literary document, the virtues of diction include clarity of English vocabulary, vividness, correct connotations, and ambiguity understood as intended multiple meanings and mysteriousness.

NOTES

1 For brief commentary with examples, see J. C. L. Gibson, *Language and Imagery in the Old Testament* (Peabody, MA: Hendrickson, 1998), 4-6; and Roland Meynet, *Rhetorical Analysis: An Introduction to Biblical Rhetoric* (Sheffield: Sheffield Academic Press, 1998), 173-174. Claus Westermann, *Praise and Lament in the Psalms*, trans. Keith R. Crim and Richard N. Soulen (Atlanta: John Knox, 1981) similarly notes that "in primitive language all the force and intensity of linguistic formations is found in concrete expressions" (25-26).

2 William Empson, *Seven Types of Ambiguity* (Cleveland: Meridian, 1955).

3 Anthony Howard Nichols, "Translating the Bible: A Critical Analysis of E. A. Nida's Theory of Dynamic Equivalence and Its Impact Upon Recent Bible Translations," dissertation, University of Sheffield, 1996, 297.

4 "The Problem of the Transparent Text," in *Words and the Word: Language, Poetics and Biblical Interpretation* (Cambridge: Cambridge University Press, 1986), 4-36.

5 Ibid., 36.

6 Jan de Waard and Eugene A. Nida, *From One Language to Another: Functional Equivalence in Bible Translating* (Nashville: Thomas Nelson, 1986), 39.

7 Eugene H. Glassman, *The Translation Debate* (Downers Grove, IL: InterVarsity, 1981), 101.

8   Quoted by Prickett, "The Problem of the Transparent Text," 6.

9   Artur Weiser, *The Psalms: A Commentary* (Philadelphia: Westminster, 1962), 585.

10   Nichols, "Translating the Bible: A Critical Analysis of E. A. Nida's Theory of Dynamic Equivalence and Its Impact Upon Recent Bible Translations," 300.

11   Ibid.

12   Nida's equation of ambiguity with language games that, if left to themselves, will undermine people's belief in the integrity of the Bible surfaces repeatedly in his writings, including these: de Waard and Nida, *From One Language to Another: Functional Equivalence in Bible Translating*, 39; Eugene A. Nida and Charles R. Taber, *The Theory and Practice of Translation* (Leiden: E. J. Brill, 1969), 8.

15

RESPECT FOR THE PRINCIPLES OF POETRY

IT IS NO MYSTERY why poetry has fared poorly in modern translations of the Bible. Poetry is demanding to read, and the modern mentality wants what is easy. Dynamic equivalent translations have generally indulged this impulse. As poetry is read less and less, people have come to regard it as extraneous to their lives.

We need to remind ourselves at the outset, therefore, how much of the Bible is poetic in form. Whole books of the Bible are poetry—not simply the books of Psalms and Song of Solomon, but a majority of the prophetic books as well. Wisdom literature is likewise poetic in format. Furthermore, the poetic techniques of image, symbol, metaphor, and simile pervade virtually all parts of the Bible, and Jesus himself might well be the world's most famous poet. By the time we factor in all of this data, it is probably accurate to say that one-third of the Bible is poetic in form.

For this very reason, when I come to the first unit on poetry in my literature courses, I begin the class session by asking my students how they know that God intends for them to understand and enjoy poetry. When this question elicits blank looks, I ask the question in a more menacing tone: How do you *know* that God intends for you to understand and enjoy poetry? By this point the brighter students realize that I am serious about the matter, and it is always delightful to see how quickly they produce the right answer.

Before we can rightly value biblical poetry, we need to understand poetry itself. I have chosen to approach the topic by refuting five common fallacies about poetry.

FALLACIES ABOUT POETRY

Fallacy #1: Poetry is an abnormal use of language. It comes as quite a surprise to most people to learn that in most cultures poetry has preceded prose as a form of discourse (especially literary discourse), giving the lie to the claim that ordinary people cannot understand poetry. In fact, Northrop Frye observed that "in the history of literature we notice that developed techniques of verse normally precede, sometimes by centuries, developed techniques of prose," adding, "How could this happen if prose were really the language of ordinary speech?"[1] Genuinely oral cultures seem, in fact, to gravitate toward poetry in their literary texts (though not in everyday discourse). I recall in my study of Old English literature how much more fluent poetry was compared to prose of the same era. The case can be made that ancient poetry is a form of folk literature.

Fallacy #2: Children cannot understand poetry. Poetry consists of two things—a special language or idiom (consisting of images and figures of speech) and verse form (regular rhythm and, in some languages, rhyme). In regard to the rhythmic dimension of verse, children have a natural aptitude for it. Northrop Frye went so far as to claim that our literary education should be rooted in the natural aptitude that children show for rhythmic verse:

> Ideally, our literary education should begin, not with prose, but with such things as "this little pig went to market"—with verse rhythm reinforced by physical assault. The infant who gets bounced on somebody's knee to the rhythm of "Ride a cock horse" . . . is beginning to develop a response to poetry in the place where it ought to start. For verse is closely . . . related to the child's own speech, which is full of chanting and singing.[2]

It is undoubtedly true that children cannot understand complex poetic language. But it is untrue that they have *no* understanding of poetry. Just look at our nursery rhymes: They possess not only the enchantment of regular rhythm and rhyme, but also a fairly heavy incidence of figurative language and poetic license:

> *Twinkle, twinkle, little star,*
> *How I wonder what you are.*
> *Up above the world so high,*

Like a diamond in the sky.
Twinkle, twinkle, little star,
How I wonder what you are.

The poetry of the Bible is many times over more difficult than this, and children naturally struggle with most of it, though decreasingly so as they move into their high school years. My point is that from their earliest years children have contact with poetry, even when they do not think of it as poetry. High schoolers' obsession with lyric music discredits any claim that they have no aptitude for poetry.

Fallacy #3: Poetry is beyond the grasp of most adults. We need to remind ourselves first that poetry pervades our everyday discourse. We speak of the sun rising, our hearts sinking, and our hopes soaring. Even people who do not sit down to read poetry thus have continuous contact with it.

I noted in an earlier chapter that someone who wrote a dissertation on the use of metaphor in preaching found in a survey that a majority of sermon listeners rated metaphor as not only more beautiful and affective but also clearer than abstract propositions.[3] This is not to deny that in our own culture, which is the inheritor of a centuries-old tradition of prose as the most common form of discourse, poetry is a difficult form of discourse. It is only to counter the easy assumption of many modern Bible translations that people cannot handle poetry. They *can* handle it if they are expected to master it and are educated in Sunday school and from the pulpit to understand and eventually relish it.

Fallacy #4: Poetry does not deal with recognizable human experience. Because *the idiom* of poetry is unusual for many people, the misconception has arisen that *the subject* of poetry is likewise far removed from daily life. On the surface level, poetry, because it consists so thoroughly of imagery, is actually closer to lived experience than the typical prose essay is. A poet has written:

> Too often poetry is thought to be impossibly far apart from ordinary human existence. . . . We all know the taste of things sweet or bland or sour, we all have known rage. . . . A rich confusion of awareness underlies all human feeling, and the language for it surges all around us. The poet reaches into that rich confusion. . . .[4]

Poetry is not removed from life but springs from it.

Fallacy #5: Poetry should sound like everyday discourse. If I need to argue against the bias of some Bible translations that poetry is inaccessible to people and therefore requires some type of surgery to make it understandable, I need on the other side to counter the view that poetry is intended to sound like ordinary, everyday discourse. In claiming earlier that in ancient cultures poetry was a *familiar* and *accessible* form of discourse, I did not mean to imply that it was the *natural* mode of discourse for everyday life. For the ancients, poetry was like turkey on Thanksgiving Day is for Americans—familiar, expected, and ritualistic, but not ordinary, everyday fare.

The distinction between poetry and prose is a universal principle. Poetry is a *special* use of language. We can even view it as a *specialized* use of language. But in saying that, I need immediately to add that life is filled with specialized uses of language. The weather expert on the television news speaks a very specialized language, and we do not complain about it. We expect it and learn to understand it.

When the NIV appeared, I was asked to assess its literary merits in a review published by *Christianity Today*. When I gave the new translation a largely negative review, the chairman of the translation committee responded with a point-by-point rebuttal of everything that I had written. In regard to biblical poetry, he theorized that the right language for biblical poetry is always the most "natural" language, meaning most like everyday oral discourse. This is incorrect for literature generally and doubly and triply incorrect for poetry. Thomas Gray, famous for his poem "Elegy Written in a Country Churchyard," correctly claimed that "the language of the age is never the language of poetry," by which he meant that poetry always has an element of strangeness to it, including a higher-than-ordinary incidence of archaism.[5]

Poetry advertises its distinctiveness. It speaks a language of images. It prefers the figurative to the literal and is, in fact, a form of fiction and often fantasy, as we signal by our phrase "poetic license." In real life, people do not go around apostrophizing the trees and rocks, nor do they naturally arrange their utterances in such a way as to state every idea at least twice in parallel grammatical form. Poetry also uses a special diction, as designated by our customary epithet "poetic diction," and this diction is far more conventionalized, stylized, and unchanging than prose is. I would note in passing that the language of biblical poetry shows less linguistic change over a comparable period of time than biblical prose does.[6] Finally, poetry uses a far tighter syntax than prose does, using the line rather than the sentence as its basic unit. Inverted word order is common.

In sum, poetry is not our everyday way of speaking. It possesses, to use a formula of J. R. R. Tolkien, "arresting strangeness." It aims to overcome the cliché effect of language. The poet is a wordsmith, always on the lookout for freshness of expression, ready to unlock what the Old English poets quaintly called "the word hoard" in ever new ways.

Summary. I have taken this excursion into common fallacies regarding poetry in general in an attempt to gain a fair hearing for biblical poetry and the principles that should govern its translation. Let me return to my point of departure: The fact that the Bible, as God's word to people, has so much poetry in it obligates us to believe that people *can* understand poetry and do not need to be protected from it when they read the Bible.

THE PRIMACY OF THE IMAGE IN POETRY

The first principle of poetry is the primacy of the image. An image is any word that names a concrete object or action. Poets think in images and speak a language of images. Modern poet Stephen Spender, in a famous essay entitled "The Making of a Poem," claimed that the "terrifying challenge of poetry" is, "Can I think out the logic of images?"[7] Correspondingly, a good English translation of biblical poetry is one that preserves the imagery of the original, while a translation that turns the concreteness of the original into an abstraction has not respected the principles of biblical poetry. To use a now-common distinction bequeathed by modern brain research, poetry is predominantly right-brain discourse.

This is where translators who think that translating an image into an abstraction gives readers the real meaning of an image or metaphor take a wrong turn. Poets speak a language of images because they want readers to *experience* the content of their utterance *as image and concretion*, not simply as an idea. The meaning that literature conveys is affective, imaginative, and experiential as well as ideational. Literary critic Cleanth Brooks rightly claimed that a poem transacts its business of discourse "by *being* an experience rather than any mere statement about experience or any mere abstraction from experience."[8] In a similar vein, Flannery O'Connor once wrote that "the whole story is the meaning, because it is an experience, not an abstraction."[9]

Some translations—in fact, some prefaces—say in effect that the real meaning of a metaphor like "God is my fortress" is the idea that "God protects me," and they then proceed to translate the Bible's poetry by bypassing the imagery. But imagery and metaphor offer us *an experience*, not simply an abstraction. Poetry is right-brain discourse. To bypass the concretion and go only for the abstract meaning is to miss the power and multiple meanings of the utterance. If a poet had meant only that God is a protector, presumably he would have said that instead of saying that God is a fortress. Biblical scholar Ray Van Leeuwen got it right when he wrote that "biblical metaphors drop into our hearts like a seed in soil and make us think, precisely because they are not obvious at first. . . . It is the foreignness of metaphors that is their virtue. Metaphors make us stop and think, *Now what does* that *mean?*"[10]

MULTIPLE MEANINGS

Additionally, an image, metaphor, or simile usually embodies multiple meanings. Cleanth Brooks called the poetic image "a nexus or cluster of meanings."[11] In Gerard Manley Hopkins's line "The world is charged with the grandeur of God," the word *charged* has three simultaneous meanings: The world is *energized* by the grandeur of God, it has been entrusted with the task of declaring the grandeur of God as a *charge* or responsibility, and the grandeur of God presses itself upon the world like the forward thrust or *charge* of an army. It is the glory of the poetic image to compress multiple meanings in such small compass. I know of no literary scholar who would not reject out of hand an edition of Hopkins's poem in which the opening line reads, "The world is energized with the grandeur of God," thereby eliminating the other legitimate meanings of the word *charged*.

For an example of the inviolability of the poetic image and its multiplicity of meanings, we can look at contemporary renditions of Ecclesiastes 1:2. "Vapor of vapors," the original reads. The poet expects us to let that image sink in. He wants us to recall our own experiences of vapor or mist. *Then* we transfer the meaning over to the subject of life, and when we do so, the meanings are multiple. Vapor is transient and fleeting; it is insubstantial; it is elusive. All of those meanings are important to the book of Ecclesiastes. How do translations that distrust imagery handle the statement? "Meaningless, meaningless." "Futility, utter futility." That is *one* of the meanings of image, but not the *only* one. And it is not necessarily the main meaning, since a good case can be made for the theme of Ecclesiastes being the fleetingness or brevity of life under the sun.

ADDITIONAL POETIC DEVICES

Before adducing more examples of how some translations shortchange poetry by turning images into abstractions, I need to add the related point that poets use *figurative language* as their staple. Poets are always playing the game of make-believe, expressing things in a way that we know to be, at the literal level, a lie (God, for example, is not literally a tower). Metaphor is the chief example, and from the time of Aristotle the literary world has generally agreed that for a poet "the greatest thing by far is to have a command of metaphor."[12] Such figurative forms as simile, personification, apostrophe, and paradox round out the repertoire of most frequently used poetic devices.

How BIBLICAL POETRY FARES IN MODERN TRANSLATIONS

Translations show a wide range in regard to the retention or dissipation of figurative language. Psalm 78:33 makes the statement that God "made their days vanish like a breath" (RSV, NRSV, ESV). Modern translations prefer to dissipate the image in an abstraction: "So he ended their days in futility" (NIV); "So he made their days end in emptiness" (REB); "So He brought their days to an end in futility" (NASB); "So he ended their lives in failure" (NLT).

Not surprisingly, the very poetic book of Job provides many test cases for translations. A master image of the Old Testament is "the hand of God" (e.g., Job 27:11, RSV, NRSV, ESV). Translators who are wary of poetic imagery render it as the abstract "power of God" (NIV) or "in God's power" (NEB, REB; similar in Jerusalem and NLT). Job 32:2 states that Elihu "burned with anger" (ESV), which is more concrete than "became angry" (RSV, REB, NLT) or "became very angry" (NIV) or "grew angry" (NEB). Modern translations generally prefer the more abstract "in my hearing" (RSV, NIV, NKJV, REB) to the more literal and concrete "in my ears" (ESV) as a rendition of Job 33:8.

Excising metaphor and simile in the process of translation is not the only way to violate the integrity of poetry. Reducing multiple meanings to a single meaning will also do the trick. The male speaker in Song of Solomon claims metaphorically and extravagantly that his beloved's eyes are doves (1:15). Out of a rich multiplicity of meanings here (doves are beautiful and peaceful in aspect; they come in pairs; they flutter their wings as a woman flutters her eyelashes), one translation narrows it down to one meaning—a meaning as elusive as the uninterpreted metaphor: "your eyes are soft like doves" (NLT). But that at least preserves a skeleton of the metaphor, as the following does not: "how your eyes shine with love" (GNB), with the doves having flown out of sight.

And then there is the activity known as Spelling It Out. Poetry has a subtlety about it, but translations that begin with the premise of a readership with low abilities eliminate such subtlety. "Your hair is like a flock of goats / leaping down the slopes of Gilead," says the poet in Song of Solomon 4:1 (ESV). How is the beloved's hair like a flock of goats moving down a hillside? Perhaps in its movement as it is blown in the wind. Perhaps in its luxuriant cascading appearance. Perhaps in the association of being soft to the touch. The comparisons in the Song of Solomon, though, are not primarily sensory but instead ask us to make a transfer of *value*. Goats' hair was prized for its value. It was used in making the curtains of the tabernacle (Exod. 26:7) and was among the valuables that the Israelites brought to the Lord on that occasion (Exod. 35:23). To this day it is used in the making of cashmere. So maybe the point of the comparison is that the beloved is the best of her kind, the one of greatest value.

In sum, the straightforward comparison of the woman's hair to a flock of goats teases us into considering multiple possibilities. The poet could have made his meaning explicit, but he did not do so. Translations that have an itch to Spell It Out do what the poet refused to do. One of them reads, "Your hair falls in waves" (NLT). Another reads, "Your hair dances like a flock of goats" (GNB). A good translation trusts poets to say what they want to say and resists the impulse to make explicit what the poet left the reader to discover.

Dynamic equivalent translators expend their energies strenuously (and sometimes ingeniously) to make explicit what the original poets of the Bible left implicit and subtle. The portrait of the physiological symptoms of advancing age in Ecclesiastes 12 is one of the set pieces of poetry in the Bible. The passage is masterful in its indirectness, as various unpleasant features of old age are rendered memorable in a string of subtle metaphors. The appearance of white hair is metaphorically rendered without accompanying explanation: "the almond tree blossoms" (Ecclesiastes 12:5, ESV). Dynamic equivalence dictates that the indirectness and subtlety of the metaphor needs to be dissipated: "your hair will turn white" (GNB); "your hair will turn as white as almond blossoms" (CEV); "white-haired and withered" (NLT).

Psalm 1:1

For a more extended analysis of what it means to retain or dispense with the poetic idiom, we can compare translations of Psalm 1:1. Here is a literal translation of the verse:

> *Blessed is the man*
> *who walks not in the counsel of the wicked,*
> *nor stands in the way of sinners,*
> *nor sits in the seat of scoffers. (RSV, ESV)*

This is a highly metaphoric statement. Wicked people do not literally take walks down a path called "the counsel of the wicked," nor do they literally publish handbooks of advice entitled *The Counsel of the Wicked*. Sinful people do not literally stand together in a field or room called "the way of sinners," and people in a scoffing mood do not take turns sitting in a chair with a sign over it that reads "The Seat of Scoffers." These lines convey their meaning through metaphor, and any adequate translation needs to begin with a grasp of the metaphors.

There is also a subtle and important progression going on in the three parallel lines. For one thing, we note a progressive paralysis as we move from walking to standing to sitting. More importantly, there is a progressive identification with evil. To walk in the way implies individual compliance with evil. To stand in the way implies participation as a member of a group, with the implied picture of a group that has gathered on a path or road. And to "sit in the seat" means, in the Old Testament milieu, to be a member of the policy-making body of a community.

Another translation gives us this version of Psalm 1:1:

> *Happy is the one*
> *who does not take the counsel of*
>   *the wicked for a guide,*
> *or follow the path that sinners tread,*
> *or take his seat in the company of scoffers. (REB)*

A lot has been lost here, beginning with the loss of the evocative power of the opening beatitude, which is meant to be an awe-inspiring *conferring of blessing* on a person. In line 2 we have nearly lost the imagery of the path or way, except for the image of a guide, which is not in the original. The path does make a belated appearance in line 3, but we have lost the specificity of standing on a path. The fourth line partly gets the metaphor correct, but the line is rather wordy and prose-like, lacking the punch of the previous translation. Furthermore, to speak of "sitting in the company" of scoffers obscures the political nuance that the phrase "sitting in the seat" or "sitting in the gate" carries in the Old Testament. Overall this translation wants to preserve the metaphors of the original but is also anxious to Spell It Out, thereby losing some of the vigor and precision of the previous translation.

As we move down the dynamic equivalent continuum, we come upon this translation of Psalm 1:1:

> *God blesses those people*
> *who refuse evil advice*
> *and won't follow sinners*
> *or join in sneering at God. (CEV)*

The vigor of the short lines is admirable, but nothing else commends this translation's handling of the very poetic Psalm 1:1. We have lost the oracular ring that a beatitude provides so well, and there seems to be a bit of an impulse to Spell It Out by making sure that the reader realizes that God is the one who blesses. Except for the possible exception of the word "follow," we have lost the evocative image of the path and the subtly nuanced progressive identification with evil. The idiom is the idiom of the dormitory, not that of poetry.

Here is yet another rendition of Psalm 1:1 that will round out the picture of what happens to biblical poetry in modern translations:

> *Oh, the joys of those*
> *who do not follow the advice of the wicked,*

or stand around with sinners,
or join in with scoffers. (NLT)

The same strictures apply here, too. We have lost most of the images and metaphors, and we have moved even more fully into the colloquial mainstream with the exclamatory "Oh" and the informal constructions "stand around" and "join in."

It should be obvious by now that dynamic equivalent translations, with their unease over anything that makes a reader pause to figure out a statement in the Bible, are the translations that compromise the poetry of the Bible. As Van Leeuwen correctly notes, "The abandonment of basic biblical metaphors in many translations follows naturally from [functional equivalence] theory."[13]

Psalm 73:4-7

Various renditions of the portrait of the prosperous wicked in Psalm 73 yield a similar range of fidelity to the original text or departure from it. Here is one version of the famous portrait:

For they have no pangs until death;
  their bodies are fat and sleek.
They are not in trouble as others are;
  they are not stricken like the rest of mankind.
Therefore pride is their necklace;
  violence covers them as a garment.
Their eyes swell out through fatness,
  their hearts overflow with follies. (ESV)

This is the very touchstone of vivid poetry. The genre is the character sketch. As is customary, we see this character type in terms of both external appearance and inner attitude and behavior. Almost nothing is left abstract in the portrait. Physical robustness is portrayed in the first two lines in imagery that can be interpreted as animal imagery. These healthy specimens have no hunger pangs or pangs of disease. They are so well fed that their bodies are nicely filled out with flesh, and their fur glistens (alternately, *sleek* paints a picture of a muscular body). The next two lines are mainly abstract, though the verb *stricken* is nicely vivid.

Simile takes over in the third couplet, and it is up to the reader to

discover the rich multiplicity of ways in which pride can be a necklace
and violence a garment. With the bulging eyes we return to the visual
mode. In the background is the cultural situation of fatness being a positive quality because it is a sign of sufficient affluence to be able to eat
enough to be fat. The portrait actually sends a double message: Along
with external prosperity that anyone would find appealing, we find a
subtext in which the prosperous wicked are not attractive at all. The
image of bulging eyes is an example: It may signal prosperity, but it is
also grotesque. Similarly, the imagery of overflowing connotes lack of
containment and control.

Here is how another translation committee decided to render the
portrait of the arrogant prosperous:

> They have no struggles;
>   their bodies are healthy and strong.
> They are free from the burdens common to man;
>   they are not plagued by human ills.
> Therefore pride is their necklace;
> they clothe themselves with violence.
> From their callous hearts comes iniquity;
>   the evil conceits of their minds know no limits. (NIV)

Half of the poetic vigor present in the previous translation has been
drained from the passage. The vividness of *pangs* has become the
abstract *struggles*. The bodies that are *sound and sleek* have been
abstracted as *healthy and strong*. The next two lines, with the imagery
of burdens and plagues, are nicely imagistic, and happily the similes of
pride as a necklace and violence as clothing have been retained. But the
final two lines lose the imagistic vigor of the previous translation, as
bulging eyes and overflowing hearts become abstracted into *iniquity, evil
conceits*, and *minds*.

As we traverse the continuum of translations, we find this version
of the portrait of the villains of Psalm 73:

> They seem to live such a painless life;
>   their bodies are so healthy and strong.
> They aren't troubled like other people
>   or plagued with problems like everyone else.
> They wear pride like a jeweled necklace,
>   and their clothing is woven of cruelty.

These fat cats have everything
their hearts could ever wish for! (NLT)

Here we can find illustration of many of my points about how poetry gets lost in many modern translations—the preference for abstraction over image, the impulse to Spell It Out ("plagued with problems," "jeweled necklace," "woven of cruelty"), and in the case of the "fat cats" an instance of overshooting the biblical text and adding something that is not even there.

SUMMARY

Poetry has not fared well with modern dynamic equivalent translations. The reason is simple: The principles that underlie poetry are on a collision course with dynamic equivalence theory. Poetry is *not* immediately understandable. It achieves its effects by deviating from everyday discourse. By its very nature, poetry requires a reader to ponder an utterance. Furthermore, poetry by its very nature delights in multiple meanings, and dynamic equivalent translations want to pare statements down to a single meaning.

Why is it pernicious to drain poetic language from biblical poetry? The aesthetic objection is that it destroys the beauty and power that poetry possesses. The hermeneutical objection is that eliminating the poetic nature of an utterance disregards an author's intention. But quite apart from what some might consider these academic objections, the very nature of the Bible is at stake, both in terms of power of expression and God's inspiration of the words. Ray Van Leeuwen expresses it thus: "The translator who removes biblical metaphors to make the text 'easier' for readers may defeat the purpose of the Holy Spirit, who chose a metaphor in the first place. Metaphors grab us and work on us and in us. They have the spiritual power to transform our minds."[14]

NOTES

1 Northrop Frye, *The Well-Tempered Critic* (Bloomington, IN: Indiana University Press, 1963), 18.
2 Ibid., 25.
3 Michael Holcomb, "The Use of Metaphor in Preaching," dissertation, Bethel Theological Seminary, 1982. Raymond C. Van Leeuwen similarly offers the opinion that "it is not clear to me that replacing metaphors with abstractions makes it easier for readers" ("We Really Do Need Another Bible Translation," *Christianity Today*, October 22, 2001, 32).

4   M. L. Rosenthal, *Poetry and the Common Life* (New York: Oxford University Press, 1974), 10.

5   The best source on the element of strangeness in poetry is Owen Barfield, *Poetic Diction: A Study in Meaning* (New York: McGraw-Hill, 1964).

6   English poetry, too, is linguistically conservative, partly because of such staples as archaism, conventionalized diction, allusiveness to past poetry, and the formative influence of the past history of poetic genres. P. Jouon and T. Muraoka, *A Grammar of Biblical Hebrew* (Rome: Pontifical Biblical Institute Press, 1993), states, "Although our Biblical texts span a good many centuries, the language in which they are written presents an astonishing degree of uniformity" (9).

7   Stephen Spender, "The Making of a Poem," in *Critiques and Essays in Criticism 1920-1948*, ed. Robert W. Stallman (New York: Ronald Press, 1949), 23.

8   Cleanth Brooks, *The Well-Wrought Urn: Studies in the Structure of Poetry* (New York: Harcourt, Brace and World, 1947), 213.

9   Flannery O'Connor, *Mystery and Manners* (New York: Farrar, Straus, and Giroux, 1961), 73. O'Connor is here talking about stories, but the principle applies equally to poetry.

10 Van Leeuwen, "We Really Do Need Another Bible Translation," 31-32.

11 Brooks, *The Well-Wrought Urn*, 211.

12 Aristotle, *The Poetics*, in *Criticism: The Major Statements*, ed. Charles Kaplan (New York: St. Martin's Press, 1975), 46.

13 Van Leeuwen, "We Really Do Need Another Bible Translation," 32.

14 Ibid., 31.

16

EFFECTIVE RHYTHM

I NEED TO CORRECT a possible misimpression right at the start of this chapter. Rhythm is not an inconsequential matter that is of interest only to a handful of persnickety literary folk. On the contrary, it is one of the most important criteria for a book that is read aloud. Good rhythm for a Bible is like a qualifying exam: If a translation cannot measure up on this matter, it is not in the running to be a superior Bible for public use and oral reading in more private situations. Stated another way, the point at which many modern translations most obviously advertise their deficiencies is at the level of rhythm.

UNDERSTANDING RHYTHM

Rhythm is the regular *recurrence* of a pattern of sound. When the medium is language (as distinct from music, for example), rhythm refers to the flow of words and phrases. The *goal* of rhythm is *smoothness*— not monotonously regular, but predominantly so. The very word *rhythm* implies a back-and-forth recurrence, the rise and fall of language. Anything that impedes the smoothness of the flow is detrimental to rhythm. Rhythm in the flow of language consists of multiple elements, which for the English language are these:

• The most important element is the alternation between stressed and unstressed syllables of words.

• The next larger unit of sound is words rather than syllables, so that the length or brevity of a word can become a factor in rhythm.

• In addition to the length or brevity of a word are the opening and closing sounds of a word. For example, some words require a complete break between them when they are pronounced in sequence ("blank look" or "dead corpse," as distinct from "blue sky" or "new car").

• The next unit of sound and meaning is the phrase, and phraseology is an important and often ignored contributor to rhythm.

• The largest unit that contributes to rhythm is syntax—the length of clauses and sentences and their relationship to each other.

The *goal* of rhythm, let me say again, is smoothness of flow and avoidance of staccato effect (except where it is an intended effect).

The best *test* of rhythm is simply to read passages aloud. No formal analysis is needed to distinguish good rhythm from bad, though I have come to suspect that people can become so accustomed to bad rhythm that they lose their ear for good rhythm. If in oral reading a passage ebbs and flows smoothly, avoids abrupt stops between words and phrases where possible, and provides a sense of continuity, it is rhythmically excellent. If a translation clutters the flow of language and is consistently staccato in effect, it is rhythmically inferior.

THINGS WORTH KNOWING ABOUT RHYTHM

Several dimensions of rhythm will provide a helpful context for understanding why rhythm is important in an English Bible translation. The first is that impassioned speech of any type tends toward regular rhythm. One of my graduate school professors claimed in class one day that there are whole pages of Charles Dickens that fall into regular iambic rhythm.

Literary scholars have rightly applied this to the Bible. In his classic essay entitled "The Noblest Monument of English Prose" (a reference specifically to the King James Version of the Bible), John Livingston Lowes wrote:

> The language of elevated thought or feeling is always rhythmic. Strong feeling of whatever sort . . . imposes upon speech a rhythmic beat. . . .
> Now the Biblical literature, to an almost unrivalled degree, is profoundly tinged with feeling. . . . No literature, I think, is so pervaded with profound and passionate emotion as the writings of the Old and the New Testaments.[1]

Again, it is the King James Version of which Lowes speaks, and the passion of which he speaks has been largely drained from the colloquial, matter-of-fact, newspaper-like translations of the modern era.

Secondly, whenever skilled speakers are aware of an audience, their speech tends to take on more formal qualities, including the presence of smooth rhythm. As Northrop Frye expressed it, "Full awareness of an audience makes speech rhetorical, and rhetoric means a conventionalized rhythm."[2] To the degree to which we picture the writers of the Bible as conscious of an audience—and surely that consciousness must be regarded as very high—the more likely it is that rhythm was important to them. Surely such biblical authors as Old Testament kings David and Solomon, Jesus (the *oral* author of much of the Gospels), and Paul were at some level orators. Similarly, to the degree to which Bible translators picture their translation as being read publicly to an audience, the more consciously they might pay attention to the rhythm of what they are producing.

Thirdly, rhythm is essentially an *oral* effect. It enters silent reading at a subterranean level only (though it is probably wrong to regard it as being completely absent). But the moment a statement is uttered orally, its rhythmic goodness or badness at once advertises itself. The applications of this principle to the Bible are multiple. It is generally agreed that most of the Bible arose from an oral culture and that its parts circulated orally both before and after they were written down. Through the centuries, moreover, the Bible has been a book that was read publicly.

All of these considerations make rhythm an essential translation issue, not a peripheral one. For a book that is read aloud as often as the Bible is, and for a book whose utterances are so frequently charged with strong feeling and sublime ideas, excellent rhythm should be regarded as a given. Translators who ignore it pay the inevitable price: The absence of smooth rhythm makes itself felt at once whenever the Bible is read orally.

RHYTHM IN THE KING JAMES BIBLE: GIVING CREDIT WHERE CREDIT IS DUE

While I do not propose a return to the King James translation as our regular English Bible, we have every reason to study and relish what the King James translators managed to achieve in the area of rhythm. The King James Bible is incomparably the best English translation in its rhythm. While we have lost some of the resources that the King James translators had at their disposal (as I will note in a moment), their translation can continue to serve as an inspiration and a model.

Several things worked to the advantage of the King James committee. The Renaissance era was in important ways still an oral culture. Although the printing press had been around for more than a century, resulting in an avalanche of printed material, much more of the daily business of life was still conducted orally than it is today. The Prayer Book (for Anglicans) and the sermon (for Puritans) were central in public worship. For most Bible readers of the era, the Bible was read aloud in family devotions. The result of this oral milieu was that, in the words of one scholar, "The King James men had ears. As Jacobeans they were more sensitive to speech rhythms and more practiced in them, far better trained in rhetoric and respectful of it, than their modern successors."[3]

In addition, the English language was still a heavily inflected language in the seventeenth century. What this supplied was a wealth of unaccented syllables that turn out to be extremely functional in keeping the alternation of stressed and unstressed syllables alive. Here is an example: "beareth all things, believeth all things, hopeth all things, endureth all things" (1 Corinthians 13:7). The unaccented "eth" syllable supplies a very helpful element in the cadence of the sentence. Here are two more examples in which now-obsolete grammatical forms help produce a smooth-flowing rise and fall of language: "I laid me down and slept" (Psalm 3:5); "the heart of her husband doth safely trust in her, so that he shall have no need of spoil" (Proverbs 31:11).

I do not propose that we turn back the clock of time. The inflected elements of Renaissance English clunk in archaic fashion on the modern ear. But it is entirely possible for a modern translation to be closer to rather than farther from the standard of excellence set by the King James Version.

THE GROUND RULES FOR THE REST OF THIS CHAPTER

My format for the rest of this chapter is to compare English translations in regard to their rhythm in selected Bible passages. In all of the specimens I have collected for comparison, I will begin with the King James Version because it almost invariably sets the standard for excellence. I have chosen specimens that cover a range of biblical genres, but they are otherwise randomly selected. As printed below, the syllables in capitals are accented syllables. The vertical lines divide the material into rhythmic feet (the foot being the individual rhythmic unit in a poetic line). To demonstrate what flows well and what is disjointed and staccato, one needs to read the following passages aloud, which I encourage my readers to do.

Psalm 24:1

The King James rendering of Psalm 24:1 is this:

> *The EARTH | is the LORD'S | and the FULness | thereOF;*
> *the WORLD, | and THEY | that DWELL | thereIN.*

The meter flows regularly and smoothly, with six iambic feet and two anapestic feet (iambic rhythm consisting of an unaccented syllable followed by an accented syllable, and anapestic rhythm consisting of two unaccented syllables followed by an accented syllable). The RSV and ESV give us the rhythmic equivalent of the KJV, showing that a translation can update vocabulary without abandoning the KJV rhythm:

> *The EARTH | is the LORD'S | and the FULLness | thereOF;*
> *The WORLD | and THOSE | who DWELL | thereIN.*

The NEB likewise fares well with this verse:

> *The EARTH | is the LORD'S | and ALL | that is | IN IT,*
> *the WORLD | and THOSE | who DWELL | thereIN.*

The first line ends with a jolting, staccato effect, but otherwise the two lines flow well.

The tune changes when we come to most dynamic equivalent translations of the verse. Here is the NRSV rendition:

> *The EARTH | is the LORD'S | and ALL | that is | IN IT,*
> *the WORLD, | and THOSE | who LIVE | IN IT.*

The concluding feet of both lines breaks the rhythm, ending both lines with a staccato effect. The NIV has the same jolting effect at the ends of the lines:

> *The EARTH | is the LORD'S, | and EVerything | IN IT,*
> *the WORLD, | and ALL | who DWELL | IN IT.*

The ends of the lines break the back of the rhythm.

Other translations produce other rhythmic deficiencies with Psalm 24:1. The NASB yields this infelicity:

The EARTH | is the LORD'S, | and ALL | IT | conTAINS,
The WORLD, | and THOSE | who DWELL | IN IT.

Again the lines begin well and end with broken rhythm in the second half. The REB is similar in its difficulties:

To the LORD | beLONG | the EARTH | and EVerything | IN IT,
The WORLD | and ALL | ITS | inHABitants.

Here the rhythm breaks down into staccato effect at various points in both lines.

Psalm 48:1

The KJV, RSV, NASB, and ESV are in agreement with the opening verse of Psalm 48. They translate it thus:

GREAT | is the LORD | and GREATly | to be PRAISED.

The rhythm flows smoothly, beginning with a customary accented syllable and then maintaining the momentum with a nice intermixture of unaccented syllables followed by accented ones. There is a nice balance between the two halves of the line, with each ending with an anapestic foot (two unaccented syllables followed by an accented syllable). Furthermore, both halves begin by accentuating the key word *great/greatly.*

The NEB rearranges the elements of the sentence from the previous translations, but it flows beautifully:

The LORD | is GREAT | and WORTHy | of our PRAISE.

This is the rhythmic equivalent of the previous rendition, except for the opening two iambic feet.

The story is otherwise in the NIV and REB version:

GREAT | is the LORD | and MOST | WORTHy| of PRAISE.

The flow breaks down halfway through the line with the juxtaposition of two accented syllables at the end and beginning of a poetic foot, though the line recovers at the end. (The word *most* needs to be emphasized because its denotative function is to emphasize the adjective ["worthy"] that it modifies; if we do not emphasize it, it is a mere filler word, something that its meaning and intensive function do not allow.)

Psalm 1:3

Here are five versions of Psalm 1:3, printed consecutively to allow for a closer comparison of them:

And WHATsoEVer | he DOeth | shall PROSper. (KJV)

In ALL | that he DOES, | he PROSpers. (RSV, NEB, ESV)

WhatEVer | he DOES | PROSpers. (NIV)

And in | whatEVer | he DOES, | he PROSpers. (NASB)

THOSE PEOple | sucCEED |in EVerything | they DO. (CEV)

The second specimen flows best, with the wavelike effect achieved by a smooth alternation between unaccented and accented syllables. The third specimen is moderately good, but one notices the juxtaposition of accented syllables late in the line that requires a complete break between them in pronunciation. The first specimen (KJV) is cluttered with too many syllables. The fourth specimen begins with too many unaccented syllables to be completely fluent, though the line ends well. The final specimen is staccato in effect.

Psalm 104:33

Here is another cluster of specimens put in sequence:

I will SING | unto the LORD | as LONG | as I [unaccented] LIVE. (KJV)

I will SING | to the LORD | as LONG | as I [unaccented] LIVE. (RSV, NLT, ESV)

I will SING | to the LORD | ALL MY LIFE. (NIV)

The second specimen, consisting predominantly of anapestic feet, flows beautifully. The KJV is not quite as good, with the *unto* resulting in just a little too many consecutive unaccented syllables. In the third specimen, the four consecutive accented syllables at the end of the line bog down the flow.

Psalm 23:1

The KJV, RSV, and ESV knew a good thing when they found it in regard to the opening line of the world's most famous poem:

> *The LORD | is my SHEPherd; | I | shall not WANT.*

Both halves begin with an emphasis on the respective actor for what follows, and the main phraseology of the second unit in each statement results in a mellifluous anapestic construction.

None of the following three specimens is as felicitous as the King James tradition:

> *The LORD | is my SHEPherd; | I shall NOT | BE in WANT.(NIV)*

> *The LORD | is my SHEPherd; | I have EVerything | I NEED.(NLT)*

> *YOU, LORD, | are my SHEPherd. | I will NEVer | BE in NEED.*
> *(CEV)*

The first specimen here stumbles in the third foot with its forced pause between the juxtaposed "not be," both of which, moreover, are stressed. The second specimen becomes suspect with the clutter of syllables in the third foot. An alternative reading of this foot—"I HAVE EVerything"—breaks the rhythm with two consecutive accented syllables with a pause breaking between them. The third specimen suffers from too many accented syllables.

For those of my readers who find this discussion rather technical, let me say again that the test of rhythm is one that anyone can perform without using technical analysis. That test is simply to read the passages aloud. My analysis simply explains *why* we respond to each rendition as we do.

WHAT ABOUT PROSE RHYTHM?

Prose rhythm is different from poetic rhythm because here the recurrent unit is the sentence instead of the line. Poetic feet give way to larger syntactic units, and phraseology (the arrangement of material into phrases as opposed to poetic feet) counts for more than with poetry as the unit that provides the flow of the utterance. Having noted these differences, though, we need to look for the same thing in prose as in poetry—a smooth, wavelike recurrence, the rise and fall of the movement of language. The technical term for this is *cadence*.

1 Corinthians 13:4, 7, 8

Here is what the King James Version gives us in one of its most famous prose passages:

> *Charity suffereth long, and is kind; charity envieth not; charity vaunteth not itself, is not puffed up. . . . Beareth all things, believeth all things, hopeth all things, endureth all things. Charity never faileth.*

What is immediately evident is the wavelike rhythm, the rising and falling of phrases. There is a nice plenitude of unaccented syllables. In fact, iambic feet, the most natural rhythm of the English language, are actually in the minority, being overshadowed by either anapestic feet or dactylic feet (the latter consisting of an accented syllable followed by two unaccented syllables).

The ESV rides the literary coattails of the KJV, which is much to its credit and is something that more translations should aspire to do:

> *Love is patient and kind; love does not envy or boast. . . . Love bears all things, believes all things, hopes all things, endures all things. Love never ends.*

This is more succinct and businesslike than the King James, but it retains the wavelike rising and falling cadence of its predecessor. The key to this is the retention of parallel phrases and clauses, including the doublets early in the sentence ("patient and kind," "does not envy or boast").

With colloquial translations, we leave the realm of accomplished prose rhythm. Here is the NIV rendition:

> *Love is patient, love is kind. It does not envy, it does not boast, it is not proud. . . . It always protects, always trusts, always hopes, always perseveres.*

Upon reading this, I feel as though I have been thoroughly shaken by the shoulders. The movement is graceless, far too abrupt, and lacking in coordinates. There is no rise and fall of movement. Instead we experience a hammerlike grinding out of information. The voice is barking and makes no winsome appeal to the reader. It rushes the reader along as though one is riding a horse at a trot, while the previous two translations invite a leisurely and meditative pace.

Other modern colloquial translations are similar in effect. Here is the CEV:

> *Love is kind and patient, never jealous, boastful, proud, or rude. . . .*
> *Love is always supportive, loyal, hopeful, and trusting. Love never fails!*

There is no rhythm here in the ordinary sense. Instead we are given a mere catalog of descriptors. The touchstone of good prose rhythm—a rise and fall of phrases—is absent. It is as though the text hopes to rush the reader through a tedious task as quickly as possible.

Ephesians 5:19-21

In the original, this passage consists of four participial clauses, flowing in stately parallelism to a climax of eloquence. Here is a modern English translation that does a good job of retaining the rhythm of clauses:

> *. . . addressing one another in psalms and hymns and spiritual songs, singing and making melody to the Lord with all your heart, giving thanks always and for everything to God the Father in the name of our Lord Jesus Christ, submitting to one another out of reverence for Christ.* (ESV)

A succession of participial clauses like this constitutes a rhetorically embellished and sophisticated prose style, and the quoted translation captures it. The passage as here translated is in the best tradition of stately and eloquent English prose.

Journalistic prose dispenses with such stateliness and rhetorical formality. It gets rid of the ongoing momentum of the discourse and chops the grand statement into short, declarative sentences, even introducing a paragraph break into the sequence of participial clauses:

Speak to one another with the words of psalms, hymns, and sacred songs; sing hymns and psalms to the Lord with praise in your hearts. In the name of our Lord Jesus Christ, always give thanks for everything to God the Father.

Submit yourselves to one another because of your reverence for Christ. (GNB)

While the following is not a bad rhythmic performance, it loses the stately eloquence of the successive subordinate participial phrases of the original by chopping the utterance into smaller sentences, and it, too, introduces a new paragraph into a passage that in the original is a series of cumulative participial clauses:

... speak to one another in psalms, hymns, and songs; sing and make music in your hearts to the Lord; and in the name of our Lord Jesus Christ give thanks every day for everything to our God and Father.

Be subject to one another out of reverence for Christ. (NEB; REB similar)

WHY DOES EXCELLENCE OF RHYTHM MATTER?

Why is excellence of rhythm important? One answer is aesthetic: Good rhythm is beautiful, and bad rhythm is grating and ugly. Beauty matters to God, who is its source. If beauty matters to God, it should matter to those who produce and read Bible translations. Literary critic H. L. Mencken, an outspoken non-Christian, called the King James Bible "unquestionably the most beautiful book in the world."[4] It should be more but not less than the most beautiful book in the world for Christians as well, and rhythm is one factor among several that can make it such.

Secondly, good rhythm is essential to any text that is uttered orally. The Bible is preeminently an oral book, read aloud in public worship, on ceremonial occasions, and around the table. Dwight Macdonald has written about modern translations, "The most damaging effect of modernizing the usage is the alteration of rhythm, which is all-important in a book so often read aloud; quite aside from literary grace, the ceremonial effect of the Bible is enhanced by the interesting, varied, and suitable rhythms of K.J.V."[5]

Thirdly, rhythm is an aid to memory as well as to oral performance. A line that flows smoothly is easier to memorize than a line that bumps along and impedes the flow of thought. Good rhythm is often aphoristic in effect. Literary critic F. L. Lucas, in lamenting what modern translations have done with the King James rendition, "Come unto me, all ye that labour and are heavy laden, and I will give you rest," comments that modernization "ruins the beauty of rhythm which has helped the memories of generations, and *kept the Bible running in their heads*" (italics added to call attention to what is often overlooked).[6]

Finally, rhythm is the natural concomitant of impassioned and heightened speech and writing. Earlier I quoted John Livingston Lowes on how "the language of elevated thought and feeling is always rhythmic," and how the Bible "is profoundly tinged with feeling." The decline in rhythmic excellence and the decline in elevated feeling have gone hand in hand in most modern translations, and it is hard to know what is cause and what is effect. Dorothy Thompson has written, "Apart from musical accompaniment, this matter of beat, cadence, the rise and fall of sentences, is part of the magic of poetry and prose, contributing to its evocative character, its overtones and undertones, its symphonic style, which greatly distinguishes the familiar Bible [the KJV]."[7]

Recent translations are quick to claim that they are ideally suited to public reading, but most of the claims are demonstrably false. The loss to Bible readers and Christian worship has been immense.

NOTES

1   John Livingston Lowes, "The Noblest Monument of English Prose," in *Literary Style of the Old Bible and the New*, ed. D. G. Kehl (Indianapolis: Bobbs-Merrill, 1970), 15.

2   Northrop Frye, *The Well-Tempered Critic* (Bloomington, IN: Indiana University Press, 1963), 21.

3   Craig Thompson, *The Bible in English, 1525-1611* (Ithaca, NY: Cornell University Press, 1958), 17.

4   H. L. Mencken, *Treatise on the Gods* (New York: Alfred A. Knopf, 1946), 286.

5   Dwight Macdonald, "The Bible in Modern Undress," in *Literary Style of the Old Bible and the New*, 38.

6   F. L. Lucas, "The Greek 'Word' Was Different," in *Literary Style of the Old Bible and the New*, 51.

7   Dorothy Thompson, "The Old Bible and the New," in *Literary Style of the Old Bible and the New*, 46.

17

EXALTATION AND BEAUTY

THE TOPICS THAT I take up in this final chapter of the book are in some ways a summing up of my main arguments. Individual topics that I have discussed along the way—diction, poetry, rhythm, syntax, and literary qualities more generally—are important not only in themselves but in terms of the final *effect* that they produce. This chapter deals with *effects*.

These effects cover a cluster of interrelated topics—some of them aesthetic, but others simply dealing with how people *experience* the Bible in general. My concern is to delineate the qualities and effects that we have a right to expect in an English Bible translation. When these qualities are missing, it is a symptom that something has gone wrong in the translation process. I also believe that the Bible is hampered in its purposes when these qualities are absent from a translation.

Since I will cover a range of topics, it will be useful simply to list them as a road map to what will follow:

- exaltation
- affective power
- beauty
- dignity
- grandeur (where the original possesses it)
- aphoristic quality
- mystery
- memorability

These are the *qualities and effects* that will occupy this chapter. Here are the specific *ingredients* that either produce or thwart the desired effects that I have listed:

- language
- syntax

- rhythm
- style
- tone

THE KING JAMES VERSION

A good entry point is to begin with the English translation that everyone agrees possesses in the highest degree the qualities I have outlined. The King James Version is the very touchstone of exaltation and affective power. As I did the research for this book, this dimension of the King James Bible kept surfacing. Here are representative statements:

- "To make the Bible readable in the modern sense means to flatten out, tone down and convert into tepid expository prose what in K.J.V. is wild, full of awe, poetic, and passionate. It means stepping down the voltage of K.J.V. so it won't blow any fuses."[1]
- "The supremacy of the King James is one of style, not of scholarship. The men who made it did not set out to manufacture a literary classic—classics are seldom made to order. Yet they did produce one: perhaps the only classic ever turned in by a committee."[2]
- "We are in real danger of losing, in an age of flat prose, an essential and invaluable capacity of the language, fully realized once in the English Bible, but realizable again—the capacity to express by tone and overtone, by rhythm, and by beauty and force of vocabulary, the religious, the spiritual, the ethical cravings of man."[3]
- "Everyone knows that the Authorized Version came at the end of a great period of rich development in Tudor biblical prose and that in literary quality . . . it stands unique."[4]
- "The beauty of this translation . . . has made it peerless among literary masterpieces."[5]

People who prefer a colloquial Bible in the contemporary idiom might complain that the King James Bible is more exalted than the original. In some places this is doubtless true, but not on balance. The real issue is that modern colloquial translations, because of their a priori preference for colloquialism, have given us a Bible that is *less exalted* than the original.

Here is how the KJV typically treats historical narrative:

And it came to pass after these things, that God did tempt Abraham, and said unto him, Abraham: and he said, Behold, here

I am. And he said, Take now thy son, thine only son Isaac, whom
thou lovest, and get thee into the land of Moriah; and offer him
there for a burnt offering upon one of the mountains which I will
tell thee of. (Genesis 22:1-2)

This is awe-inspiring, and not primarily because of the formality that we now attach to archaic language. It was awe-inspiring already when the KJV was published in 1611. The gravity and affective power of the account are inherent in the King James style. Before I argue the point that exaltation is appropriate and colloquialism inappropriate to the content of the passage, let me simply make the preliminary point that colloquial translations lack the quality of exaltation: "Some years later God decided to test Abraham, so he spoke to him. . . . The Lord said, "Go get Isaac . . ." (CEV).

Why is exaltation a desirable feature of style with such a passage? Because of the momentousness of the situation. God is one of the speakers, and God is exalted. Abraham, the human protagonist of the story, is highly conscious of the exalted nature of the One who is speaking, as evidenced by his prompt and obedient response. How does a patriarch speak to God? In the best language that he has at his disposal.

If much of the Bible's prose thus requires an exalted style, poetry requires it even more because of its very nature—heightened speech for heightened feeling and insight. I am grateful for having memorized the following verse in the King James Version as a third grader:

And Samuel said, Hath the Lord as great delight in burnt offerings
and sacrifices, as in obeying the voice of the Lord? Behold, to
obey is better than sacrifice, and to hearken than the fat of rams.
(1 Samuel 15:22)

This is the kind of utterance on which to build a life, rendered memorable by the very language and syntax in which it is expressed. This aphoristic memorability and exalted effect are lost when the passage is rendered in a colloquial translation: "'Tell me,' Samuel said. 'Does the LORD really want sacrifices and offerings? No! He doesn't want your sacrifices. He wants you to obey him" (CEV).

To anyone who values the dignity of the King James Bible and the successors that have perpetuated its tradition, reading a modern translation is, in the words of one literary scholar, like walking through a city that has been bombed: "One looks about anxiously. Is this gone? Does that still survive? Surely they might have spared *that*!"[6]

LOVE POETRY THAT SOUNDS LIKE LOVE POETRY

Love poetry through the centuries has been the very touchstone of exalted speech. It therefore provides a good test case for whether or not a translation has retained the exaltation of the original text of the Bible. Here is a specimen passage from the Song of Solomon (1:15-16):

> *Behold, thou art fair, my love;*
> *behold, thou art fair. . . .*
> *Behold, thou art fair, my beloved,*
> *yea, pleasant. (KJV)*

What is the effect? We are transported to a world of heightened love and exalted rhetoric, far transcending ordinary lovers' ardor and powers of expression. It is always this way with love poetry. In the quoted passage, though, the transport carries the price tag of archaic language. In the same tradition we read this updated version:

> *Behold, you are beautiful, my love;*
> *behold, you are beautiful. . . .*
> *Behold, you are beautiful, my beloved,*
> *truly delightful. (ESV)*

Something has been lost, but the passage retains a quality of exaltation. We know that we are not overhearing the couple next door. And if we have lost a little of the affective power of the King James, we have gained in accuracy and clarity. We lose virtually everything in the following version:

> *How beautiful you are, my darling!*
> *Oh, how beautiful! . . .*
> *How handsome you are, my lover,*
> *Oh, how charming! (NIV)*

Put beside the exaltation and eloquence of the King James tradition, it is hard not to read these lines without a touch of sarcasm and mockery. The rhetoric is that of everyday compliment. There is nothing wrong with everyday compliment, but love poetry trades in *extraordinary* compliment. Bad as the foregoing translation is, it does not bottom out on the scale. The following probably does:

> My darling, you are lovely,
>> so very lovely. . . . *(CEV)*

Is that how love poets speak? No; it is how ordinary people speak in prose.

PROVERBS THAT SOUND LIKE PROVERBS

With the proverb or saying, the ground rules change. A proverb is not exalted in style but instead represents the simple as a form of beauty. We need to remember that there is a simplicity that diminishes but also a simplicity that enlarges. A proverb has an aphoristic quality that is the opposite of the prosaic. It announces upon its very appearance that it is an extraordinary use of language. Its resources include tightness of syntax, occasional inversion of normal word order, conciseness, occasional archaism, and relatively frequent use of imagery and figurative language. Proverbs have arresting strangeness and do not sound like everyday conversation.

Like rhythm, this aphoristic quality is discernible at once to any ear trained for it. As with rhythm, I entertain the possibility that many contemporary Americans have grown so accustomed to the prosaic that they have lost the ability to recognize the aphoristic sparkle when they hear it. Of course, modern Bible translations have often helped dull the perception. One of my classroom assignments is to assign students to find and then share in class a biblical proverb that expresses a key insight of a work like Homer's *Odyssey* or Dickens's *Great Expectations*. I remember how shell-shocked I was the first time a generation raised on contemporary translations started reading their selections. Things simply did not sound right. I could hardly believe that people were reading proverbs.

To illustrate, just compare alternate versions of the same biblical proverb (Ecclesiastes 10:18):

> Through sloth the roof sinks in,
>> and through indolence the house leaks. *(RSV, ESV, NRSV)*

> If a man is lazy, the rafters sag;
>> if his hands are idle, the house leaks. *(NIV)*

If the owner is negligent the rafters collapse, and if his hands are idle the house leaks. (REB)

Some people are too lazy to fix a leaky roof—
  then the house falls in. (CEV)

Owing to neglect the rooftree gives way;
  for want of care the house lets in the rain. (Jerusalem)

A shiftless man lives in a tumbledown shack;
  A lazy woman ends up with a leaky roof. (The Message)

It does not take the proverbial rocket scientist to differentiate the aphoristic from the prosaic.

Here are variants of Proverbs 27:6, on the subject of whose words one can trust:

Faithful are the wounds of a friend;
  profuse are the kisses of an enemy. (RSV, ESV; NASB similar)

Wounds from a friend can be trusted,
  but an enemy multiplies kisses. (NIV)

The blows a friend gives are well meant,
  but the kisses of an enemy are perfidious. (REB)

Wounds from a friend are better than many kisses
  from an enemy. (NLT)

A friend means well, even when he hurts you.
But when an enemy puts his arm around
  your shoulder—watch out! (GNB)

When the Victorian poet Francis Thompson, writing about "books that have influenced me," praised the Bible's aphoristic quality as the thing that took the "firmest hold" on him,[7] he was fortunate that the King James Bible was *the* Bible of the English-speaking world of his day. If Thompson were living today, his contact with the Bible might be in the prosaic tradition that has replaced the aphoristic flair of the King James tradition with tepid expository prose.

The aphoristic bent of the Bible is not limited to the wisdom books but is sprinkled even through the narrative parts. Jesus' resolve to go to Jerusalem to face his passion and execution is memorably captured in Luke's formulation, "His face was set toward Jerusalem" (ESV). The sense of resolve is lost in translations that tell us simply that Jesus "was heading for Jerusalem" (NIV) or that "he was on his way to Jerusalem" (GNB, CEV).

A Pauline aphorism will yield a final example. The KJV rendition of 1 Timothy 6:6 is matchless: "But godliness with contentment is great gain" (NIV identical). Modern translations would have done well to stay with this great proverb, but generally they did not: "but godliness *actually* is a means of great gain, when accompanied by contentment" (NASB); "well, religion does make a person very rich, if he is satisfied with what he has" (GNB); "now there is great gain in godliness with contentment" (ESV); "yet true religion with contentment is great wealth" (NLT); "and of course religion does yield high dividends, but only to those who are content with what they have" (REB).

WORDS OF THE MASTER

The typical discourse of Jesus was highly aphoristic. For an example, we can turn to Jesus' famous aphorism about not forbidding the children to come to him: "Suffer the little children to come unto me, and forbid them not" (Mark 10:14, KJV). It is archaic, but it is powerful and affective. "Let the little children come to me," read other translations (NIV, NRSV). For me that rendition was permanently doomed by a reviewer who remarked that it sounds like a mother at a picnic. Even worse is the following, which sounds like a mother scolding an older sibling: "Let the children come to me; do not try to stop them" (REB). I do not deny that in context the statement has the quality of a scolding, but it is also announcing a kingdom principle, and I believe that Jesus pronounced it with a corresponding dignity. Even more strident is this: "Let the children come to me. Don't stop them!" (NLT).

Someone has written an excellent book on the sayings of Jesus, which according to the book's subtitle depend on "forceful and imaginative language."[8] At one point the author writes, "We can now understand what is lost when we reduce the sayings of Jesus to 'plain speech.' Plain speech . . . has little power to change men."[9] The range of translations proves the point. The following translation preserves the gripping and imaginative force of Jesus' discourse by keeping the text at the oratorical level that we know it possessed in its original context (that context being the Sermon on the Mount):

> *"Therefore I tell you, do not be anxious about your life, what you will eat or what you will drink, nor about your body, what you will put on. Is not life more than food, and the body more than clothing?"* (Matthew 6:25, ESV)

This stirs the soul, and it gains its effects by being exalted and beautiful. The diction, the balance of the clauses, and the formality of the concluding rhetorical question all contribute to the affective power of the utterance.

Here are five translations that reduce the passage to colloquial prose, with the aphoristic quality of the discourse vanishing in the process:

> *"Therefore I tell you, do not worry about your life, what you will eat or drink; or about your body, what you will wear. Is not life more important than food, and the body more important than clothes?"* (TNIV)
>
> *"This is why I tell you not to be anxious about food and drink to keep you alive and about clothes to cover your body. Surely life is more than food, the body more than clothes."* (REB)
>
> *"This is why I tell you: do not be worried about the food and drink you need in order to stay alive, or about clothes for your body. After all, isn't life worth more than food? And isn't the body worth more than clothes?"* (GNB)
>
> *"So I tell you, don't worry about everyday life—whether you have enough food, drink, and clothes. Doesn't life consist of more than food and clothing?"* (NLT)
>
> *"If you decide for God, living a life of God-worship, it follows that you don't fuss about what's on the table at mealtimes or whether the clothes in your closet are in fashion. There is far more to your life than the food you put in your stomach, more to your outer appearance than the clothes you hang on your body."* (The Message)

One of Jesus' most evocative and compressed aphorisms is the command, "Consider the lilies of the field, how they grow" (Matthew 6:28, KJV, ESV). When I probe this great saying with my literature classes, the list of things to which Jesus calls us when he tells us to "consider" keeps expanding. It is a call to contemplation, to observation, to thinking about what we observe, to introspection, to a wise passiveness as we let our observation of nature sink in and affect us. Reduced to a prosaic statement, many of these meanings, as well as the evocativeness of the statement itself, are dissipated: "see how the lilies of the field grow" (NIV); "look how the wild flowers grow" (CEV); "look at the lilies and how they grow" (NLT).

HERE A LITTLE, THERE A LITTLE: HOW TO LOWER THE BIBLE'S VOLTAGE

The qualities of exaltation and affective power consist not so much in big effects as in individual phrases and words. These qualities seep out of an utterance almost syllable by syllable. We can compare the following renditions of Psalm 34:3: "O magnify the LORD with me, / And let us exalt his name together," says the King James tradition (KJV, RSV, NASB, ESV). "Glorify the Lord with me; / let us exalt his name together," reads a modern translation (NIV). To my ear, dropping the "O" and the "and" to produce a brisker statement depletes the statement of much of its grandeur, and the reduction of the statement to two short sentences separated by a semicolon is typical of the staccato and disjointed effect of many modern translations. The stately flow of the two sentences in the first translation, building triumphantly to a climax, has its back broken in the second translation.

How much difference can a single word make when it comes to affective power? A lot. "Truly the light is sweet," says the King James aphoristically (Ecclesiastes 11:7). "Light is sweet," we hear prosaically and curtly (RSV, NIV, NLT, ESV). How much difference can it make to change verbs into adjectives? Quite a lot, according to the late James M. Boice, himself a defender of the NIV. Boice complained about what the NIV did with 1 Peter 5:10, which in the original contains "four powerful verbs, each in the future tense," while the NIV "breaks them up, saying that God 'will himself restore you and make you strong, firm and steadfast.'"[10] Retaining the verbs preserves the vigor: "will himself restore, confirm, strengthen, and establish you" (ESV; NASB similar).

"Behold, I stand at the door and knock," says the King James tradition (Revelation 3:20, KJV, RSV, NASB, ESV). "Here I am! I stand at the door and knock," reads the NIV. It reminds one of the neighborhood brat spoiling a Sunday afternoon nap. "Here I stand knocking at the door" (REB) makes one think that Jesus is wondering why he is doing it. We get the impression of a persistent knocker at the door saying, in effect, "I *know* somebody is at home" when we read, "Listen! I am standing and knocking at your door" (CEV). A note of irritation enters with the rendition, "Look, I am standing at the door, knocking" (Jerusalem).

Luke 24:49 offers another test case. In the rendition "and behold, I send the promise of my Father upon you" (KJV, RSV; ESV is similar), the rhythm is beautiful and the tone consoling. "I am going to send you what my Father has promised" (NIV) sounds curt and matter-of-fact, almost as if to put an end to someone's asking for something.

Again, we can compare versions of Psalm 45:1. In the grand style, the pen of the heart of the ready scribe "overflows with a goodly theme" (RSV, NRSV; similar in NASB and ESV). In the prosaic tradition, the scribe's heart is merely "stirred" (NIV, NEB, Jerusalem). The first tradition retains the poetic effect of grandeur, exuberance, and the quality of being extraordinary (as captured even by the quaintly archaic *goodly*). The prosaic tradition steps down the voltage.

If I seem disparaging, let me say simply that the committees that gave us prosaic Bibles had other options that they refused to accept. In fact, given the prominence of the King James Bible and its historic influence, modern translations chose a *more* difficult path rather than a *less* difficult path in giving us a colloquial Bible. A model existed that could have spared these translators from what they did.

THE IMPORTANCE OF GETTING THE TONE RIGHT

Tone is the literary term that refers to such things as the writer's attitude toward his or her subject matter, the suitability of style for the content, and the correctness of effect on a reader. Much of what I cover in this chapter relates to this question of tone.

John 2:4, from the narrative on the marriage in Cana, offers an example on a small scale. Because Jesus felt a need to assert that his own messianic time plan now took precedence over family ties, he replied to his mother's information that the wine had run out with the statement, "Woman, what does this have to do with me? My hour has not yet come" (ESV; KJV and NASB similar). The epithet "woman" is a neutral address in this context—not rude, but with an edge to it, drawing a boundary around normal familial ties in deference to Jesus' messianic task. The TNIV is so worried about readers' inability to negotiate the meanings of *woman* that they change it to "Mother," which loses the distancing between Jesus and Mary that the original expresses.

To translate the appellative "dear woman" (NIV), besides adding a word that is not in the original, introduces an uncertainty of tone. Is the intention of the "dear" to soften the address by introducing a dimension of endearment into the equation, or (opposite to that) to make the tone even more distant and formal, as when we address a letter in such a way as to say "to whom it may concern," or condescending, as when we say, "Dear woman, how did you think of that?" The NEB translation—"your concern, mother, is not mine"—makes Jesus "merely an Eton boy being snippy."[11]

Or compare these lead-ins to a statement by Jesus: "Verily, verily, I say unto you" (John 5:19, KJV). That is awe-inspiring. "Truly, truly, I say to you" (RSV, NASB, ESV) is also awe-inspiring. "I tell you the truth" (NIV) sounds prosaic and, depending on intonation, either badgering or plaintive. "I tell you for certain" (CEV) is bland and prosaic. "Very truly I tell you" (TNIV) does not conform either to the original or any modern idiom; it is simply odd. The right tone is one that captures the sense of gravity of what Jesus is about to say. In modern colloquial translations, someone has written, it is as though a priest "were officiating in Westminster Abbey in shirtsleeves."[12] What one critic says of the NIV is even truer of dynamic equivalent translations generally— they are "not solemn where solemnity was intended."[13]

When Jesus arrives at the house of the deceased daughter of Jairus, he dismisses the mourners with the words, "Go away" (Matthew 9:24, ESV and others), which is terse but not in such a way as to be inappropriate to the grief of the occasion. A colloquial translation has Jesus say, "Get out of here!" (CEV). Another renders it, "Clear out!" (*The Message*). And another has, "Be off!" (NEB). A critic of the latter translation comments, "It sounds like my cat-loving maiden aunt shooing dogs away from the garden."[14]

These instances of localized tone are almost inconsequential compared to the global issue of the tone of the Bible as a whole. From time to time I encounter the sentiment from dynamic equivalence advocates that the Bible "should not sound like the Bible." Billy Graham endorsed *The Living Letters* by saying that "it is thrilling to read the Word . . . [in] a style that reads much like today's newspaper."[15] I disagree with these verdicts. A sacred book should sound like a sacred book, not like the daily newspaper. It should command attention and respect, and to do so it cannot be expressed in the idiom of the truck stop. The failure of modern colloquial translations is frequently a failure of tone.

The following specimen is entirely representative of the prevailing tone that modern colloquial translations regularly produce. It is the account of Peter's rescue from prison: "Suddenly an angel from the Lord appeared, and light flashed around in the cell. The angel poked Peter in the side and woke him up. Then he said, 'Quick! Get up!'" (CEV). The flashing light making circular motions evokes a picture of either an emergency vehicle arriving on the scene or a Star Wars type of laser weapon. The tone is wrong. Furthermore, angels do not "poke," nor do they speak like a roommate.

The tone of modern translations is not simply inadequate for the dignity of the Bible; it often transposes the Bible into various contemporary contexts. Commenting on the NEB rendition of Jesus' statement "and there are many other points on which they have a traditional rule to maintain" (Mark 7:4), a literary scholar comments, "It is the language of administrators, and even drops to that of politicians."[16]

MYSTERY

A literary scholar has rightly said that "another quality that can fairly be demanded of a Bible is mystery, much of which evaporates in the prosiness" of modern translations.[17] C. L. Wrenn wrote similarly that he "would wish for a kind of language that might retain if possible those sacramental and numinous elements needed naturally for the expression of sacred and mysterious religious truths."[18] Here are two versions of the rescue of Peter from his prison cell—one that evokes a sense of the mystery of what literary scholars call "the marvelous," the other in a style that by my taste reduces the event to something prosaic and matter-of-fact:

> *"And behold, an angel of the Lord stood next to him, and a light shone in the cell. He struck Peter on the side and woke him, saying, 'Get up quickly.' And the chains fell off his hands. . . . He did not know that what was being done by the angel was real." (Acts 12:7, 9, ESV)*
>
> *"All at once an angel of the Lord stood there, and the cell was ablaze with light. He tapped Peter on the shoulder and woke him. 'Quick! Get up,' he said, and the chains fell away from his wrists. . . . He followed him out, with no idea that the angel's intervention was real." (NEB)*

A reviewer of the latter translation complains that "the cell ablaze with light hasn't . . . any mystery: someone must have switched on the supply [of electricity] at the mains."[19]

What I have already said about the dilution and removal of poetry in some modern translations usually involves a loss of mystery as well. We read in the Christ hymn that opens the Gospel of John that all who believed in Christ "were born, not of blood nor of the will of the flesh nor of the will of man, but of God" (John 1:13, KJV, NASB, ESV). This is mysterious, prompting us to wonder what all is involved. Not so in most modern translations: "children born not of natural descent, nor of human decision or a husband's will, but born of God" (NIV); "born not of human stock, by the physical desire of a human father, but of God" (REB).

From childhood, my imagination has been sparked by the magical image of "ivory palaces" (Psalm 45:8, KJV, NASB, RSV, ESV). What are these *ivory palaces*? The image teases us into imagining the splendor of it all. Fortunately for me, I was raised on a translation that retained the mystery of the reference. If I had been raised on modern translations, I would have been deprived of the mystery: "palaces adorned with ivory" (NIV); "palaces panelled with ivory" (REB); "palaces decorated with ivory" (GNB, NLT).

In the King James tradition, when Jesus calmed the tempest on the Sea of Galilee, we read that there was "a great calm" (Matthew 8:26, KJV, GNB, ESV). Modern translations conspire by various means to kill the wonder: "a dead calm" (REB); "everything was calm" (CEV); "suddenly all was calm" (NLT); "it was completely calm" (NIV, TNIV). The mysterious command to "seek the things that are above" (Colossians 3:1, ESV) or "set your hearts on things above" (NIV) becomes the idiom of a commencement address when we are advised to "aspire to the realm above" (REB). As a literary scholar has said, "If passages of the Scriptures are to suggest things of supra-phenomenal reality, it cannot well be done in the natural vocabulary of our current speech."[20]

LANGUAGE THAT ELEVATES

In an earlier chapter I took up the subject of the diminishment of language in modern translations. The antidote to such diminishment is to maintain the elevation of the King James tradition. Literary scholars have made the case repeatedly:

- "The religious passion of Jesus and Paul, transcending modern experience, needs an exalted idiom to be adequately conveyed. . . . Poetic intensity or prophetic exaltation interferes with . . . easy, rapid assimilation partly because such language is idiosyncratic and partly because it strikes down to depths of response which it takes time and effort to reach. Literature, and especially religious literature, is not primarily concerned with being clear and reasonable; it is connotative rather than direct, suggestive rather than explicit . . . incantatory rather than functional."[21]

• "In all languages I know of it has been the universal tendency to express the central ideas of religion in a language more dignified, more archaic even, and with more implicit levels of meaning than that used for the doings of ordinary life."[22]

• "There are . . . many things that modern readers expect of a Bible besides clarity. One is majesty."[23]

• "Every morning before breakfast we assembled in the sitting room and my father read a passage from the [King James] Bible, followed by a prayer. . . . Somewhere, as my father read, I became excitedly aware of something more than the story: of the beauty and glory of the words; of the images they can evoke and the thoughts they can enkindle."[24]

Do we want a Bible that elevates or reduces? The question is as simple as that. The King James tradition consistently calls us to something higher than the everyday:

> So if there is any encouragement in Christ, any comfort from love, any participation in the Spirit, any affection and sympathy, complete my joy by being of the same mind, having the same love, being in full accord and of one mind. (Philippians 2:1-2, ESV)

Everything in the passage lifts us up—the grandeur of the words, of the syntax, and of the sentiments. Dynamic equivalent translations make no attempt at such grandeur, preferring an everyday idiom. Henry Swidel Canby, in an essay entitled "A Sermon on Style," said that "modern English is lacking in eloquence, in its root sense of speaking out, and its acquired meaning of speaking out from the heart."[25]

One way to lose the sublimity of the passage from Philippians is to do a chop job on it:

> Christ encourages you, and his love comforts you. God's Spirit unites you, and you are concerned for others. Now make me completely

*happy! Live in harmony by showing love for each other. Be united in
what you think, as if you were only one person. (CEV)*

But it is also possible for a translation to reduce the effect by talking
something to death with excessive verbiage and by using lifeless buzz-
words from contemporary usage:

> *If our life in Christ means anything to you, if love can persuade at all,
> or the Spirit that we have in common, or any tenderness and sympa-
> thy, then be united in your convictions and united in your love, with
> a common purpose and a common mind. That is the one thing which
> would make me completely happy. (Jerusalem)*

That sounds like a political writer working on an acceptance speech.

THE BEAUTY OF HOLINESS

A final strand in the cluster of qualities that I have discussed in this chapter is beauty. This is an aesthetic quality that is elusive to define but recognizable when we experience it. It can consist of either beautiful words
or beautiful arrangement of words, and its effect is one of pleasure and
exaltation. Beauty of expression ordinarily involves doing something
special with language, so that we sense it as the product of conscious
artistry. Poetry is nearly always beautiful in these ways.

> *Bless the LORD, O my soul,*
> *and all that is within me,*
> *bless his holy name! (Psalm 103:1, ESV)*

Prose can also be beautiful:

> *"But will God indeed dwell with man on the earth? Behold, heaven
> and the highest heaven cannot contain you, how much less this house
> that I have built! Yet have regard to the prayer of your servant and
> to his plea, O LORD my God." (2 Chronicles 6:18-19, ESV)*

But not all translations retain the beauty and dignity of expression:

> *"There's not enough room in all of heaven for you, LORD God. How
> could you possibly live on earth in this temple I have built? But I ask
> you to answer my prayer." (2 Chronicles 6:18-19, CEV)*

There was a time when the English Bible itself set a standard for something that we can rightly call the beauty of holiness. That phrase no longer appears in modern translations (it occurred four times in the KJV), and as a result the very phrase by which to name the quality is increasingly unavailable to us.

SUMMARY: MEMORABILITY AS A TOUCHSTONE

The qualities that I have covered in this chapter can be summed up in a single touchstone. That touchstone is memorability. What a literary scholar said of one modern translation is generally true of all dynamic equivalent and colloquial translations: it "does slip more smoothly into the modern ear, but it also slides out more easily; the very strangeness and antique ceremony of the old forms make them linger in the mind."[26]

It is not only the proliferation of translations that has made Bible memorization difficult, if not actually a lost cause. And not only memorization, we might add, but the practice, once common, of remembering huge numbers of verses and phrases from the Bible without consciously setting out to memorize them, and having them rise naturally to one's consciousness and lips. The loss of a common Bible is part of the problem, but even if all of Christendom chose one of the translations based on modern criteria, the problem would remain. These translations are inherently deficient in the qualities that make for memorability.

IN THE GREAT TRADITION

The accuracy of the King James Version is now considered suspect (as not being based on the best manuscripts), and the English language has moved out from under it. This does not mean, however, that modern translations need to abandon the excellence of the King James translation in the areas of beauty, dignity, and affective power. It is entirely possible for a modern translation to be accurate by the current estimates of accuracy and also to assimilate the legacy of stylistic excellence bequeathed by the King James Bible.

Passages such as the following (taken from the ESV) have the authentic King James ring, showing that a modern translation can be fully accurate and up-to-date in language without stooping to the flat, prosaic quality of everyday conversation:

Therefore take up the whole armor of God, that you may be able to withstand in the evil day, and having done all, to stand firm.
(Ephesians 6:13)

"Immediately after the tribulation of those days the sun will be darkened, and the moon will not give its light, and the stars will fall from heaven, and the powers of the heavens will be shaken."
(Matthew 24:29)

Search me, O God, and know my heart!
  Try me and know my thoughts!
And see if there be any grievous way in me,
  and lead me in the way everlasting!
(Psalm 139:23-24).

NOTES

1   Dwight Macdonald, "The Bible in Modern Undress," in *Literary Style of the Old Bible and the New*, ed. D. G. Kehl (Indianapolis: Bobbs-Merrill, 1970), 40.

2   Craig Thompson, *The Bible in English, 1525-1611* (Ithaca, NY: Cornell University Press, 1958), 27.

3   Henry Seidel Canby, "A Sermon on Style," in *Literary Style of the Old Bible and the New*, 27.

4   David Daiches, as quoted by D. G. Kehl, "Introduction: Logos and Logmachy," in *Literary Style of the Old Bible and the New*, 6.

5   Charles Gulston, *Our English Bible: No Greater Heritage* (Grand Rapids, MI: William B. Eerdmans, 1960), 218.

6   Macdonald, "The Bible in Modern Undress," 37.

7   Francis Thompson, "Books That Have Influenced Me," in *Literary Criticisms*, ed. Terence L. Connolly (New York: E. P. Dutton, 1948), 544.

8   Robert C. Tannehill, *The Sword of His Mouth: Forceful and Imaginative Language in Synoptic Sayings* (Philadelphia: Fortress), 1975.

9   Ibid., 27.

10 James Montgomery Boice and Philip Graham Ryken, *The Doctrines of Grace* (Wheaton, IL: Crossway Books, 2002), 166.

11 The quoted phrase comes from Stanley Edgar Hyman, "'Understanded of the People,'" in *Literary Style of the Old Bible and the New*, 59.

12 F. L. Lucas, "The Greek 'Word' Was Different," in *Literary Style of the Old Bible and the New*, 52.

13 Jakob Van Bruggen, *The Future of the Bible* (Nashville: Thomas Nelson, 1978), 177.

14 Martin Jarrett-Kerr, "Old Wine: New Bottles," in *The New English Bible Reviewed*, ed. Dennis Nineham (London: Epworth, 1965), 126. This anthology of reviews of the NEB is an excellent source on the material that I cover in this chapter.

15 Billy Graham, "Preface" to *The Living Letters* (Wheaton, IL: Tyndale House, 1967).

16 V. S. Pritchett, "The Finalized Version," in *Literary Style of the Old Bible and the New*, 62.

17 Hyman, "Understanded of the People," 59.

18 C. L. Wrenn, review of NEB reprinted in *The New English Bible Reviewed*, 138.

19   Henry Gifford, review of NEB reprinted in *The New English Bible Reviewed*, 110.
20   Wrenn, in *The New English Bible Reviewed*, 136.
21   Macdonald, "The Bible in Modern Undress," 38-40.
22   Wrenn, in *The New English Bible Reviewed*, 138.
23   Hyman, "Understanded of the People," 59.
24   Dorothy Thompson, "The Old Bible and the New," in *Literary Style of the Old Bible and the New*, 44.
25   Canby, "A Sermon on Style," 26.
26   Macdonald, "The Bible in Modern Undress," 38.

CONCLUSION:
WHAT MAKES THE BEST
BIBLE TRANSLATION?

THIS BOOK HAS explored the principles that govern Bible translation theory and practice. While my project began as a quest to find the right principles of translation and to compare how well various translations lived up to those principles, my inquiry rather quickly became a defense of one kind of translation and a criticism of the other. The mingling of positive and negative assessments, combined with the sheer number of principles I have covered, has run the risk of obscuring the principles that characterize a good English Bible translation. In this conclusion, therefore, I will highlight what I believe should characterize an English Bible translation. It is the principles that matter here at the end, not specific Bible translations. This conclusion is a summary of what I have argued in the book; I make no attempt to prove my points here.

ACCURACY

I have not belabored the fact that a translation needs to be accurate, partly because that is a given among virtually all translators, and partly because the rival translation theories do not agree on the criteria for accuracy. But particularly because I have championed literary qualities in an English Bible translation, I want to set the record straight that at no point do I prefer a translation *simply* because it has literary beauty. Accuracy is like a qualifying exam: A translation has to measure up to this criterion before it is entitled to any further consideration.

FIDELITY TO THE WORDS OF THE ORIGINAL

A good English translation preserves the words of the original insofar as the process of translation allows it. Translation of ideas or thoughts *rather than words* is a logical fallacy and a linguistic fantasy. Furthermore, before readers can know what the Bible *means*, they need to know what it *says*. Translators have no right to assume the role of priests, doling out the "right" interpretation to the masses. Readers who do not know the original languages of the Bible deserve to be given the materials with which to do the interpretive work that they do in other verbal situations in life.

Here, too, I need to guard against possible misunderstanding. I do not want an English rendition of a passage that makes no sense. There are, in fact, occasions where translators need to salvage expressions that when translated literally mean nothing to an English reader; but the number of such passages in the Bible is statistically insignificant. Nor do I subscribe to a rigid word for word translation, or one that preserves unnatural syntax from the original. What is at stake is whether or not the first loyalty of a translation committee is to the language of the Bible as opposed to freely and consistently departing from it.

EFFECTIVE DICTION

Clarity is the first quality of diction that an English Bible translation needs to achieve. I am at one with dynamic equivalent devotees in wanting clarity, though I obviously have a higher expectation from Bible readers than dynamic equivalent translations presuppose. Clarity begins with words, however, not simply with ideas. The biblical writers did not write down ideas; they wrote down words. As for the meanings that the words of the Bible declare, some of the meanings are clear and simple, while others are difficult and require not only meditation on the part of a reader but also teaching from Bible scholars.

The second quality that makes for effective diction is accuracy of connotations for words. The two sides of this are (a) conveying the right connotations and (b) avoiding the wrong connotations for the English words that are chosen. As language changes, so do the connotations of some words. English Bible translations therefore need to be up to date with current usage in regard to connotations of words.

A third trait of effective diction is vividness of expression. In particular, it involves preserving the concreteness of the original text and resisting the impulse to turn concrete images into abstractions. While there *are* grand theological abstractions in the Bible, and although there are theological treatises in Scripture, these are in a minority.

THEOLOGICAL ORTHODOXY

One's theological position should not continuously dictate how individual words are translated. Theology derives *from* the Bible and should not manipulate the Bible. But anyone who takes the Bible seriously needs to have confidence that in those rare passages where translators need to choose between theological options, their translation reflects what they have come to accept as theological truth. This is not a requirement that only evangelical Christians make; theological liberals also have their preferred translations based partly on theological considerations.

PRESERVING MULTIPLE MEANINGS

I can imagine that some of my readers have been uneasy with the emphasis on ambiguity that has surfaced at several places in this book. As a literary scholar, I deal regularly with that quality of literary discourse. But I also found while doing the research for this book that the word *ambiguity* has been entrenched in discussions of translation for a long time. That the original text possesses the quality of multiple meanings, multiple interpretive options, and an open-ended or mysterious quality is widely recognized by Bible translators. The question is whether an English translation should preserve these qualities of the original.

On this matter, as on many other translation issues, the crucial question is whether priority should be assigned to what the original text says or to the assumed needs of modern readers. When translation committees assign priority to their audience, they have in that very act decided that certain qualities of the original text are expendable. They may not subscribe to this position consciously or out of principle; it is simply something that happens. I believe that a good English translation passes on the qualities of multiple meanings and mystery that the original text possesses. Another way of saying this is that a good translation resists the impulse to spell everything out.

THE FULL EXEGETICAL POTENTIAL OF THE ORIGINAL TEXT

It is an easy step from what I have just said to claim that a good translation preserves the full interpretive potential of the original text of the Bible. It does not short-circuit the interpretive process. It does not make preemptive interpretive strikes and then hide them from the view of the reader.

We need to remember that ordinary readers are not the only ones who use the Bible. Preachers and teachers also work from the biblical text. They are the ones to whom God and the church have especially entrusted the task of interpretation. When preachers stand before their congregations, they should have before them a translation that allows them to explore the full range of meanings. They should not need to re-translate the text, and they should not have their hands tied by a translation that has reduced the range of meanings that they need to access. When teachers and preachers come to impart theology to their charges, they should not be deprived of the theological precision that the Bible in its original possesses.

A good translation resists the forms of reductionism that characterize many modern translations. It does not reduce the language, the dignity, the theology, or the affective power of the Bible. And while an English translation should not be *more* literary than the original Bible is, it should not be *less* literary either. In the light of modern scholarship, there can be no doubt that the Bible is a continuously literary book.

Expecting the Best from Readers

A good Bible translation does not patronize its readers. It expects the best from them. It does not slant itself to a grade-school level for the simple reason that most Bible readers are *not* grade-schoolers. The Bible deserves the quality of attention and comprehension that we devote to other kinds of reading.

My concern here is not the exact level of reading that is required. In fact, I am suspicious of translations that allow a grade level to set the ground rules for a translation. My concern is the question of what we expect from readers. Some modern translations indulge and insult their readers. They expect less from readers when they read the Bible than when they read other things. A good translation elevates both the Bible and its readers instead of diminishing them.

Transparency to the Original World of the Bible

A good translation is transparent to the original text. It removes all possible barriers to a reader's ability to see and hear what the original text actually said. Of course, this at once rules out the practice of translating in such a way as to change the details that comprise both the text and the world from which it arose and that it evokes. A good translation does not substitute terms and images from the reader's world in the place of what the biblical text contains.

I need to prevent a possible confusion between this kind of transparency and the transparency of which some modern translations speak. By "transparency" they mean that everything is immediately comprehensible to a modern reader. Such transparency is often achieved by changing what is in the original text. The transparency of which I speak is the opposite of that. But we need to note a paradox in this regard: In making the English Bible immediately transparent to a modern reader, some translations *obscure* what the Bible actually says.

One of the things that a reader should be led to see is the nuances of style and theme of the various biblical writers and books. Diversity is present in the original text. It should be there in an English translation as well. But of course if the assumed abilities of a target audience are calling the shots, the result will be a relatively uniform book.

"What You See Is What You Get"

It is difficult to raise ethical objections to dynamic equivalence, but honesty demands that we consider the matter. I believe that it is dishonest to pass off as an accurate version of what the Bible says something that one knows is *not* what the Bible says. I realize that dynamic equivalent translators have a different understanding of the concept of "what the Bible says," and I record my disagreement with their definition.

Most readers of Bible translations do not read with an understanding of the difference between translations that strive to remain faithful to the actual words of the original and those that are casual about the actual words, feeling free to give an interpretation of what the translators think a passage means.

And even sophisticated readers who do know the difference are in the same position, for the simple reason that modern translations do not signal what is in the original and what has been changed or amplified in the translation process. Readers of English translations operate on the premise that they are reading what the original text says. With some translations, they are frequently misled and in some cases virtually deceived.

An English Bible translation should be *reliable*. Readers should not be left to guess what the original says and what has been added or changed by the translators. They should have confidence that what they have been given is close to what the original author wrote. When they compare versions, their heads should not be left whirling by the sheer deviation that the translations show from each other. Essentially literal translations are not wildly divergent, but dynamic equivalent translations *are*.

RESPECT FOR THE PRINCIPLES OF POETRY

As much as a third of the Bible is poetic in form. This extends both to the verse form known as parallelism and to the very idiom in which poets express themselves. The poetic idiom consists of such staples as image, metaphor, simile, personification, allusion, apostrophe, and paradox. These are not limited to the poetic books of the Bible but appear plentifully in nearly all of the Bible.

There are several reasons why an English translation should be true to the poetic parts of the original. To begin, poetry and figures of speech are what the authors who penned them intended. To change what they wrote is to ignore authorial intention. Secondly, for anyone who holds an evangelical view of Scripture, the poetry of the Bible is also what God through the agency of the Holy Spirit moved the writers to write. And thirdly, the power of a poetic utterance resides in its poetic form. To dissipate the poetry is to flatten the effect.

EXCELLENCE OF RHYTHM

A good English Bible translation is rhythmically accomplished. The words and phrases flow smoothly (except where the opposite effect is intended) instead of in a staccato manner. A good translation sounds good when it is read and heard orally. For people who have an ear for rhythm (and since it is mainly intuitive, most people *do* have the ability to recognize good rhythm), judging a good translation from a bad one is like biting into an apple—one knows immediately and instinctively whether it is good or bad.

It is not only pleasing effect that is at stake here, though we should want a Bible that is beautiful rather than aesthetically impoverished. Good rhythm is an enabling quality in situations where the Bible is read and heard orally. One can simply do things in public and around a table with a rhythmically excellent Bible that are impaired with a rhythmically weak translation. Beyond that, good rhythm is part of the affective power of a piece of writing.

DIGNITY AND BEAUTY

A good translation possesses the dignity and beauty that the Bible possesses and deserves. It retains the aphoristic sparkle that is one of the Bible's most distinctive features. It preserves the exaltation that characterizes much of the Bible. When the beauty of the Bible is the beauty of the simple, it will embody that form of beauty too. I myself make no prejudgment of the specific *type* of beauty and dignity that a given passage in the Bible possesses.

A large part of the dignity that an English Bible reader deserves revolves around its language. The language of colloquial, everyday discourse does not command the attention and respect that language on its best behavior does. There *are* colloquial passages in the Bible, but they do not predominate in the original, as they do in colloquial translations. Reading the Bible should be an elevating experience at all levels—affectively, aesthetically, and theologically.

SUMMARY

English Bible translation has lost its way in the past half century. We are farther from having a reliable and stable text than ever before. The only Bible reader who is not perplexed is the one who sticks with just one version and does not inquire any more broadly into what is going on. English Bible readers deserve a translation that they can trust and admire because it represents standards of excellence and dignity.

Appendix
Without Form,
You Lose Meaning

C. John Collins

I AM A PROFESSOR OF Biblical Studies, a pastor, and a father. I teach the Bible, preach from it, and want my children to love it and read it. My purpose in this essay is to show why, from these perspectives, the principles that Professor Ryken advocates are so important in Bible translation.

My Own Background

I went to seminary in 1981, after a career in high-tech engineering. While there, I began to think that insights from the field of linguistics would add a great deal to my work as a student of the Bible. I studied some linguistics and did my Ph.D. research in Hebrew lexicography (the study of word meanings). Among the most valuable mediators of linguistic knowledge were people involved in Bible translation; so I read books and journals from the United Bible Societies and the Summer Institute of Linguistics.[1] This means that along with the insights from linguistic study came an acceptance of the most common theory of Bible translation, dynamic equivalence.

After I finished my Ph.D., I began work planting a church for my denomination. In such a work, which was geared toward reaching people without a church home, I was keenly concerned with "translating" the truths of Christian faith to the level of understanding I assumed these people had.[2]

But the more I preached, the more troubled I became. I was studying the Bible in the original and using a dynamic equivalence translation in church. I found, though, that in order to convey what I wanted peo-

ple to understand, I had to "correct" their version. I found myself saying, "A more literal translation of the original would be . . ." and then
giving something like the NASB. This troubled me because I sensed that
sooner or later the people would neither trust their translation nor read
it to listen to God's voice; but I didn't know how to be true to my conscience. (A "literal" version just didn't seem to be an option.)

Things didn't get any better when I traded my pulpit for a lectern,
but at least I could use a "clunky" literal version in class without worrying how it sounded.

But what would my children read? They loudly rejected a modern
version of the Christmas story that had the shepherds looking for someone "dressed in baby clothes," and they were riveted on the "stuffy" narrative style of the RSV (a version I had once used but now knew to be
"liberal").

I came to feel that what I wanted was a translation that was both literal and readable and that carried something of the charm of the originals. I didn't know then that what I wanted was the kind of version that
Ryken has called "essentially literal." My consistent response on reading
Ryken's manuscript was, "He's nailed it! He's put into words the things
that have been brewing just below the surface of my consciousness."

I never had any desire to bash the translators of these other versions—I honored their motivation to get people into the Bible in an
increasingly Bible-dumb culture. I still honor their motivation and their
scholarship, but I now see that the deficiencies of these versions were a
natural outcome of the translation philosophy behind them.

WHAT IS "ESSENTIALLY LITERAL"?

I think a great deal of my difficulty came from thinking that the options
were just the way the Introduction to the New Living Translation
describes it:[3]

> There are two general theories or methods of Bible translation. The
> first has been called "formal equivalence." According to this theory,
> the translator attempts to render each word of the original language
> into the receptor language and seeks to preserve the original word
> order and sentence structure as much as possible. The second has been
> called "dynamic equivalence" or "functional equivalence." The goal
> of this translation theory is to produce in the receptor language the
> closest natural equivalent of the message expressed by the original-

language text—both in meaning and in style. Such a translation attempts to have the same impact on modern readers as the original had on its own audience.

A dynamic equivalence translation can be called a thought-for-thought translation, as contrasted with a formal-equivalence or word-for-word translation.

This way of describing the situation puts all Bible translations on a continuum from "literal and unreadable" to "dynamic, racy, and intelligible." The showcase example of the "literal" version is the RV/ASV, while the NLT, TEV, or Phillips translation exemplify the "dynamic" side. The NIV would be "mildly dynamic."

But does this actually exhaust the possibilities? I think not. There is what Ryken calls an "essentially literal" and what Van Leeuwen calls a "transparent" translation:

> A transparent translation conveys as much as possible of what was said, and how it was said, in as near word-for-word form as the target language allows, though inevitably with some difference and imperfectly.[4]

In other words, the translation is subject to the constraints of the target language—in our case, the translation must be genuine English. English imposes some limitations on how much we can exploit word order, for example, but those constraints depend on the level of the English. The more complex levels of the language—whether in oratory or poetry, and sometimes even in storytelling—allow for more word order variation than do the simpler, more everyday levels. The King James Version, as both Ryken and Van Leeuwen show, was this kind of translation in its own day.

To be an English translation, the result must of course be English, but the translation philosophies will differ in how the English corresponds to the original. For example, the Tenth Commandment (Exodus 20:17) forbids coveting a variety of things, finishing with "or anything that is your neighbor's" (ESV; compare KJV). In a "wooden" translation—which seems to be what the NLT Introduction means by "literal"—we would represent the Hebrew with "and all which to your neighbor." This is not English, and the KJV/ESV follows the requirements of being essentially literal.[5]

The NIV, "or anything that belongs to your neighbor," is only a small adjustment, though by using "belongs" it runs the risk of suggesting that the man "owns" his wife.[6] Similarly, the NLT points in this direction: "or anything else your neighbor owns" (see also TEV).[7]

This means that we really do not have only two poles between which we must choose a location; instead we have another node altogether. Perhaps we might say that what distinguishes translations is their "level of clarification," as the Tenth Commandment example shows. By that I mean not whether the translation uses clear English, but how far beyond the strict linguistic requirements of the original does the clarification go.

"FORM" AND "MEANING"

As Ryken has shown, the theory of dynamic equivalence is based on a distinction between form and meaning. As John Beekman and John Callow (advocates of dynamic equivalence) put it, "The forms are simply a 'vehicle' with which to get the message across to the recipients."[8]

There is a sense in which this is a no-brainer: The grammatical form by which the Hebrew of Exodus 20:17 expresses its meaning cannot be made English except by some kind of reworking. Were this all that anyone ever meant by the form-meaning distinction, there would be no argument.

This, however, is not what people mean by this distinction. We find recommendations to change parts of speech in the interests of naturalness—say, to change "God is love" (1 John 4:8) to "God loves";[9] or we find recommendations to decide whether phrases like "the love of Christ" that compelled Paul (2 Corinthians 5:14) describe "Christ's love for man" (as in NIV, NLT, CEV) or "Paul's love for Christ."[10]

We will find recommendations that go even further. For example, some translations make figures explicit;[11] compare Proverbs 5:15 in an essentially literal version:

> Drink water from your own cistern,
> flowing water from your own well. (ESV; NIV similar)

The more dynamic the translation, the greater the impulse to clarify for the reader what is the point of the image. Hence we get:

You should be faithful to your wife,
   just as you take water from your own well. (CEV)

Drink water from your own well—
   share your love only with your wife. (NLT)

These two at least keep some of the imagery; but we might dispense with it altogether in the interests of clarification:

Be faithful to your own wife and
   give your love to her alone. (TEV)

Another kind of recommendation is in the literary form: We may collapse parallel lines in Hebrew poetry into one,[12] or perhaps render poetical passages into prose (as Proverbs in TEV, NLT).

We might need, some think, to replace the features of the Mediterranean world of the Bible with things more culturally intelligible. Consider, for example, Psalm 1:3-4 (with the ESV giving an "essentially literal" rendering):

3 He is like a tree
   planted by streams of water
that yields its fruit in its season,
   and its leaf does not wither.
In all that he does, he prospers.
4 The wicked are not so,
   but are like chaff that the wind drives away.

A handbook for translators discusses the problem of translating verse 3:

The picture of fruit trees growing beside a water course in the dry Middle East is quite different from that of trees growing along low-lying or swampy stream beds in the tropics. In the tropics fruit trees are often grown away from streams, since they require better drainage. Accordingly they depend on the rains for their water, and a desirable rendering may be "They are like trees that grow where there is plenty of water" or "They are like trees that grow well because they are well watered."[13]

Similarly, the chaff of verse 4 may pose a difficulty:

> The translation of *chaff* presents no problems in cultures where grains are grown. Elsewhere it is often necessary to use a descriptive phrase which indicates something light and of little value that can be blown by the wind; for example, "dry grass" or "dry leaves."

By this reasoning, the resulting translation will lose the Palestinian flavor of the psalm. It is likely that the translation will substitute new associations, based on the target culture, for those of the imagery in the original. A good reader needs to know that the Bible was written a long time ago for a people far away, at the same time as he knows that it is God's own word for him.

I think these illustrate that one way of distinguishing translations is by the degree to which they have aimed to clarify for the sake of the reader things that otherwise he or she would have to figure out.[14]

Ryken has raised questions about whether we really can separate form from meaning. I think that on any level higher than the grammatical forms that are allowable within the target language, his case must stand. To separate meaning from form in, say, Proverbs 5:15 is to locate the meaning in the cognitive content alone. How do we know that some of the "meaning" does not lie in the exercise of our imaginations needed to process the image—or even that once we have "decoded" it, we have exhausted its possibilities?

WAYS THAT DYNAMIC EQUIVALENCE LOSES MEANING

In this section I want to respond to the following claim, made in the NLT Introduction:

> A thought-for-thought translation prepared by a group of capable scholars has the potential to represent the intended meaning of the original text even more accurately than a word-for-word translation.

My thesis is that, however capable the scholars—and that, mind you, is not under dispute—dynamic equivalence will almost certainly not represent the meaning more accurately than an essentially literal rendering. The very translation philosophy pushes the product away from accuracy.

There are four specific ways that I, as a Bible specialist, find dynamic equivalence to be opposed to accuracy: (1) such translations make interpretive decisions for the reader, and run the risk of deciding wrongly; (2) such a philosophy requires the translator to resolve ambiguities for the reader; (3) this philosophy urges the translator to interpret images and figures for the reader; and (4) this philosophy generally leads to the loss of important repetitions. The feature these defects have in common is that the reader is limited to what the translator allows him to see.

I have selected only a sampling of passages and issues; it would be easy to multiply examples. But what the longer list would add would not justify the tedium, nor do I wish to take over a book whose principal author is someone else!

In some of the cases I will examine, I think the inaccuracies come as a logical consequence of dynamic equivalence; in others, I can't say that dynamic equivalence requires the inaccuracy, only that it fosters it (hence it will be possible to appeal to a potential that was not fulfilled). But at least we can say that it promotes a way of thinking that ignores the concerns I will raise.

Making Interpretive Decisions for the Reader

The first way that the translation philosophy of dynamic equivalence loses meaning is that it requires the translator to make interpretive decisions for the reader. For example, consider the first part of Psalm 1:6 in several versions:

> [F]or the LORD knows the way of the righteous. (ESV)

> For the LORD watches over the way of the righteous. (NIV)

> For the LORD watches over the path of the godly. (NLT)

> The righteous are guided and protected by the LORD. (TEV)

> The LORD protects everyone who follows him. (CEV)

It is easy for the Hebraist to see what has happened here: The translators—or their style consultants—felt that the literal "knows" is too difficult. What does it mean that the Lord "knows" the way of righteous people? Does he *know about* their way? (Doesn't he know about everything?) So they asked the translators to choose a better sense for the Hebrew word.[15] Dynamic equivalent translations have therefore aimed to clarify for the reader what is involved in God's "knowing" the way of the righteous.

Several things are wrong with this approach, however. First, and most seriously, there is no reason to believe that the Hebrew reader could see which sense of the word was present without some thought. I suspect that he too wondered, "What does it mean that the Lord 'knows' the way of the righteous?"

Second, the choice of sense was almost certainly wrong: It is far more likely that the psalmist meant that God "knows with affection" the way of the righteous. "The way" is a figure for the moral orientation of someone's life (as in verse 1), and the attested sense for this verb where God's attitude is in view is "to know with affection or love" or even "to choose" (see Genesis 18:19; Amos 3:2).[16]

Third, it is not clear to me that the Hebrew verb "know" can even have the nuance "watch over" at all. At least I think that every instance in which it has been alleged can be better explained in another way.[17]

If I'm a preacher using one of the more dynamic translations, I'm in a bind—there isn't even a footnote that I can refer the congregation to, giving them an alternative. If I want to make any point about Psalm 1:6, I have to say, "I know what the translation in your lap says, but I think a better rendering would be . . ." We all know how effervescent the spoken word is; so our hearers are mostly left with a vague sense of distrust.

Let me give another example, which illustrates how, even when we must clarify a phrase, we should do so in a way that does not foreclose the readers' and preachers' interpretive options beyond necessity. A literalistic rendering of 1 Corinthians 7:1 is: "Now concerning the things whereof ye wrote: It is good for a man not to touch a woman" (RV).

There is general agreement among modern commentaries on this text that Paul is quoting back to the Corinthians a slogan that some in this church were using. Perhaps those who wrote to Paul wanted him to pass judgment on the slogan. The RV allows this by using the colon (:) to introduce the last clause.

There is also general agreement that the word "touch" is used as a euphemism for "have sexual relations with."[18] (If you read what follows, with its talk of "conjugal rights" and not "depriving one another," this is inescapable.) Therefore, if translators fear that literalistic readers will not see the euphemism, they have not gone very far in interpretation if they render the verse:

> *Now concerning the matters about which you wrote: "It is good for*
> *a man not to have sexual relations with a woman." (ESV)*

There is room for disagreement, however, about what kind of relations the Corinthian party thought it good to forego: Were they against married people having relations, or against marrying to begin with, or something else? That is an interpretive decision, not a linguistic one, and is better left for the reader to puzzle out and for the preacher to explain. Dynamic equivalent versions, however, are committed to clarifying such things; hence we get:

> *Now for the matters you wrote about: It is good for a man not to*
> *marry. (NIV; TEV and CEV similar)[19]*

> *Now about the questions you asked in your letter. Yes, it is good to*
> *live a celibate life. (NLT)*

For myself, I think it's pretty clear that Paul was dealing with the proposal that married couples refrain from embracing and that he goes on to disagree. In verses 3-5 he tells couples to give each other their conjugal rights and to be sure only to call a halt to sexual relations for a limited time, for specific purposes. He's applying principles such as Proverbs 5:15-20 ("rejoice in the wife of your youth" [ESV]) to a delicate situation in Corinth. This also implies that "have" in verse 2, "each man should *have* his own wife and each woman her own husband" (ESV), means "have sexually."[20]

The trouble with the dynamic translations, though, is that they have followed the logic of their translation philosophy and sought to clarify—and their clarification is in the less likely direction. Why couldn't they leave the reader something to figure out? Granted, the NIV, TEV, and CEV all offer my option in the margin; but it would have been better as the text. The NLT is even worse, since it has Paul agreeing with the Corinthians and endorsing celibacy—a controversial subject among Christians—and without so much as a footnote.

This shows why Professor Ryken is right on target when he rejects the motto "all translation is interpretation"—we have to distinguish between different kinds of "interpretation."[21]

Here is another kind of clarification that, in my judgment, leads to inaccuracy. The Old Testament has a proper name, Sheol, that designates the place where people go when they die—or is it *some* people, but not others? Deciding whether Sheol is the common lot of all or only the place for the wicked is an issue in Old Testament studies. It is also possible that the word is not used the same way in every place.[22]

The right thing to do in such a case would be to use the proper name in the translation and leave it to the interpreters to sort it out (perhaps with a glossary or note to help readers). The impulse to clarify, however, cannot allow this: It insists that the translator decide what it is and give that to the reader. Hence the NIV goes with "grave" as its normal rendering (typically with a footnote indicating the presence of the proper name).[23] Other dynamic equivalent translations, such as the TEV, CEV, and NLT, do something similar.

Now, I am convinced that in many cases Sheol is a poetic name for the grave (we might call it "the Grave"); but in cases where there is a distinction between the godly and the wicked, it is only the wicked who go to Sheol. This, I think, is clear in Psalm 49:14-15 in the ESV:

> [14] *Like sheep they are appointed for Sheol;*
>   *Death shall be their shepherd,*
>   *and the upright shall rule over them*
>   *in the morning.*
>   *Their form shall be consumed in Sheol,*
>   *with no place to dwell.*
> [15] *But God will ransom my soul from the power of Sheol,*
>   *for he will receive me.*

"They" in verse 14 are the careless rich of verse 13—that is, they are ungodly, and they are headed to Sheol (a grim place indeed). The pious sing with the psalmist the words of verse 15 and do not expect to go there at all (see also Psalm 73:24 for the hope of glory that the godly have). That is, according to this psalm, everyone dies (verse 10); but not everyone goes to the same place.

An essentially literal translation makes this clear—but it also allows those who think Sheol is always a fancy name for the grave to live with the English text. That is, it leaves the decision to the reader. The dynamic equivalent versions, however, make up the readers' minds for them (and hamstring the expository preacher). For example, consider the NIV of these verses:[24]

14 Like sheep they are destined for the grave,
    and death will feed on them.
  The upright will rule over them in the morning;
    their forms will decay in the grave,
    far from their princely mansions.
15 But God will redeem my life from the grave;
    he will surely take me to himself.

I may wish to dispute the sense of this translation—does verse 15 mean that I don't expect to be buried?—but the point I am making here is that this translation cloaks the interpretive issue altogether.[25]

The final example of how the impulse to clarify leads to mistranslation is the case of gender language. Now I am fully in favor of changing "if *any man* would come after me" (Luke 9:23, RSV) to "if *anyone* would come after me" (ESV)—this is a more accurate version of the Greek. However, there are words in Hebrew and Greek that specifically mean "man" or "son," and a reliable translation will express that.

The problem comes when the passage clearly applies to women and girls as well as to men and boys. The impulse to clarify pushes the translators to remove the gender specificity of the original. For example, consider Psalm 1:1

> Blessed is the man
>   who walks not in the counsel of the wicked.
>   *(ESV; NIV is similar).*

The Hebrew term means "man," as in "adult male human being." A similar case is Proverbs 2:1, which begins:

> *My son, if you receive my words . . . (ESV; NIV similar).*

The Hebrew term certainly means "son," as in "male descendant."

Old Testament wisdom works by giving you a concrete example and asking you to make the necessary changes in order to apply it to yourself. So in Psalm 1 we have a specific man who is an example for all the godly to follow—whether they be men, women, boys, or girls. Similarly, Proverbs 2:1 offers us the example of a particular father speaking to his son—not in order to exclude mother speaking to sons (after all, compare 1:8), nor fathers and mothers to daughters, but in order for us to envision something concrete.

Dynamic translations completed after the mid-1980s are more sensitive to gender language. Hence, for example, we find that the CEV and NLT try to make the applicability clear:

Psalm 1:1:

God *blesses* those people *who refuse evil advice. (CEV)*

Oh, the joys of those who do not follow the advice of the wicked. (NLT)

Proverbs 2:1:

My child, *you must follow and treasure my teachings. (CEV)*

My child, *listen to me. (NLT)*

We do not have to guess why the NLT did what it did; in the preview to the NLT, we read (regarding Proverbs 6:1):

> The Hebrew term *my son* (or *my sons*) is used twenty-seven times in the book of Proverbs. In most instances, as in this verse, the message applies equally to sons or daughters, so the NLT translates it "my child."[26]

We may assume that the same reasoning lies behind their Psalm 1:1.

The problem with this is that it crosses the line between interpreting what a text means in its context and applying that text in our own experience. I think the translation has overstepped a boundary: It is the job of readers and preachers to learn the rules for biblical interpretation and application, while translations should give us an accurate idea of what the text says. Didn't a daughter in the original audience have to do the same?

This overstepping is the logical consequence of the requirement to clarify, combined with the discarding of the form of the original. That very form is the only thing that provided any constraints to clarification.

These examples all share a common problem: They result from a translation philosophy that emphasizes "clarification" on behalf of the modern reader. The irony is that following this impulse has so often resulted in *less* accuracy in the end product.

Resolving Ambiguities

Psalm 63:11 has a grammatical ambiguity in the Hebrew:

> *But the king shall rejoice in God;*
>   *all who swear* by him *shall exult,*
>   *for the mouths of liars will be stopped. (ESV)*

By whom do the people in the second line swear—God or the king? I think we can make a good case for it being God, but the Hebrew reader had to resolve the ambiguity.

The impulse to clarify, however, requires that the dynamic versions settle it for the reader:

> *But the king will rejoice in God;*
>   *all who swear* by God's name *will praise him,*
>   *while the mouths of liars will be stopped. (NIV)*

> *Because God gives him victory,*
>   *the king will rejoice.*
> *Those who make promises in God's name will praise him,*[27]
>   *but the mouths of liars will be shut. (TEV)*

> *Because of you, our God,*
>   *the king will celebrate*
>   *with your faithful followers,*
> *but liars will be silent (CEV).*

The NLT, whose second line is "All who trust in him will praise him," keeps the ambiguity but joins other versions in losing the imagery of the last line: "while liars will be silenced," losing the picture of their mouths being plugged. The most dynamic, the CEV, loses the notion of taking oaths in God's name and reduces it to "faithful followers."

These versions may be right in their choice, but they have done work for the English reader that the Hebrew reader would have had to do.

Interpreting Images and Figures

As Ryken observes, the Bible is full of images and figures; part of the way the Bible works is by these images possessing our imagination and fostering new connections. Therefore for the translator to interpret these images is to short-circuit the imaginative process.

In Psalm 2:12, the psalmist invites the Gentile kings who have rebelled against the Lord and his anointed king to submit to the "Son" (the Davidic king, see verse 7). The exact language of the Hebrew is "Kiss the Son" (ESV, NIV). The kiss here expresses religious homage, which is suited to the king who is God's Son.[28] The impulse to clarify changes the concrete action into an abstract: "show respect to his son" (CEV), "submit to God's royal son" (NLT).[29]

In doing this, we have lost some of the flavor of the ancient Near-Eastern world of the Bible. We have also lost a theological point. In the Psalms, the attitudes of the heart need to be consummated in actions of the body (such as kneeling), because the body and soul are intricately tangled together. In other words, something that the translators discarded as just the form (kissing) actually carries some of the meaning; so the result is less accurate.

Loss of Important Repetitions

Biblical authors will sometimes repeat a word or phrase in order to emphasize it, or to make it clear that they are still talking about the same subject. Recent advances in biblical studies have highlighted the ways that authors use thematic words. The name for this is concordance (agreement).

I will discuss three areas of concordance here. The first is repetition within a particular text—a chapter or a whole book. The second is the way one text uses the words of an earlier text, showing that its principles are in effect. The third is the way New Testament authors use the Old Testament.

Such concordance is part of the communicative effect, and the reader should be allowed to see it. Dynamic equivalent versions, however, apparently consider it to be part of the form and therefore do not bring it to the reader. I suspect that the reason this happens is the way that dynamic equivalence aims at immediate intelligibility for the translated text. This aim produces a focus on the immediate context at the expense of the larger context. In other words, it aims to optimize at the local level and therefore loses optimization at the global level.

An example of concordance within a book is the "seed" theme in Genesis. The Hebrew word translated "seed" can either mean "seed from a plant" or "offspring." Like the English words *seed* and *offspring*, it can either be collective (offspring in general) or singular (some particular offspring). Hence the English word *offspring* is a good choice to represent this Hebrew word (now that KJV "seed" is outdated).

This is an important term in Genesis: God makes promises to Abraham and his "offspring"; he promises to make Abraham's "offspring" numerous. The genealogies of Genesis tie in to this interest in offspring. And at times we have to decide whether the "offspring" is a specific descendant or the general run of descendants. For example, in Genesis 3:15, is the woman's offspring, who will bruise the serpent's head, a specific individual or all her descendants? This decision lies behind Paul's comment in Galatians 3:16 that the promise came not to "offsprings" but to an "offspring."

Desmond Alexander, who has studied Genesis and its genealogies extensively, laments what English versions since the RV have done with this repetition:

> Closely linked to the genealogical structure of Genesis is the frequent use of the Hebrew word *zera'* which is perhaps best translated as 'seed'. Unfortunately, the NIV translates *zera'* using a variety of terms—the most common being 'descendants', 'offspring', 'seed', 'children', 'family', 'grain', 'semen', 'line', 'people'. For this reason the importance of the concept of 'seed' in Genesis is easily missed. *zera'* is a keyword, however, occurring 59 times in Genesis compared to 172 times in the rest of the Old Testament.[30]

Other dynamic versions (TEV, CEV, NLT) are similar in their range of translation for this Hebrew word. This variation has three defects: It obscures the importance of this theme; it deprives the reader of the task of deciding whether the offspring is singular or plural; and it makes Paul's argument in Galatians 3:16 unintelligible (see below for more on this).

A New Testament example of a key word is the Greek word translated "abide" or "remain" in John 15 and the letters of John (see Table 1). In John 15, this Greek word appears in verses 4 (3 times), 5, 6, 7 (twice), 9, 10 (twice), and 16. In each case the RSV and ESV have "abide" for the verb; had they chosen "remain" it would be just as good—the key thing is that they captured the repetition. Jesus' disciples must abide in him as a branch abides in the vine; Jesus wants his word to abide in his disciples (which seems to be another way of describing their abiding in him); the disciples are to abide in Jesus' love just as he abides in the Father's love; and Jesus appointed them that they should bear fruit and that the fruit should abide. This is a way of describing their continued Christian life and how they are to continue in their faith and loyalty. And there is the assurance that, just as they continue, the fruits of their lives will continue.

The RSV and ESV are accurate translations because they show the repetition to the English reader. The NIV is almost as good; it has "remain" everywhere, except in verse 16. There instead of "that your fruit should abide," it has "fruit that will last" and thus loses the connection between the disciples' abiding and their fruit's abiding. The TEV does something quite similar, using "remain" and "fruit that endures."

The NLT has dropped concordance in a major way. Of the eleven uses of the Greek verb, seven are rendered "remain," while the other four are paraphrased. "Unless it remains in the vine" (verse 4) becomes "if it is severed from the vine"; "if anyone does not remain in me" (verse 6) becomes "anyone who parts from me"; "if you remain in me and my words remain in you" (verse 7) becomes "if you stay joined to me and my words remain in you"; and in verse 16 we have "fruit that will last." The CEV has done something similar. "Remain in" becomes "stay joined to" in verses 4-7a; but then we find other paraphrases in the rest of the passage. Instead of the words "remaining in" (or "staying joined to") in verse 7, we have "let my teachings become part of you." "Remain in my love" (verse 9) becomes "remain faithful to my love for you"; the same expression in verse 10 is "keep loving." (And in verse 16 the fruit will last.)

The image of a branch remaining in the vine and drawing its life from it is crucial to understanding how the disciples are to relate to Jesus, and seeing the parallel is crucial to perceiving the analogy. By failing to represent concordance, the NLT and CEV have made it harder to see the analogy, and this means they have *obscured* the message, not clarified it. The NIV and TEV do not fail quite so badly, but they still lose the nexus of verse 16 with the rest of the chapter.

What has happened here? I suspect that someone decided that "remain in" needed clarifying; but once the translators went down that road they hit some bumps. To "stay joined to" someone makes some sense (though I don't see it as much of an improvement over "remain/abide in"), but how can you speak of words "staying joined to" someone, and how can you "stay joined to" someone's love? So they needed a further paraphrase, which took them even further from the original. That is, the attempt to optimize at the local level (the phrase or the verse) led to failure to optimize at the more global level (the discourse). In this case, that global failure means a failure to convey the intended meaning of the discourse. Keeping closer to this aspect of the form of the original would have led to a more accurate communication.

This same word is a key word in 1 John, appearing twenty-three times (and twice in 2 John). The translation "remain" would work in every instance; the RSV/ESV with "abide" in twenty-two instances only has to resort to a synonym in one place (1 John 2:19, "if they had been of us, they would have *continued* with us"). As in John 15, the concern is with believers "abiding in" Christ, in the light, in the Son and the Father, and in the teaching, but not in death. At the same time we read of God, God's Word, God's anointing, and God's love abiding in believers. These are two sides of the same coin, alternate ways of describing genuine spiritual life; and the concordance allows us to see that.

The dynamic equivalent versions fail to convey this message because they focus on optimizing phrases and clauses for immediate clarity. The NIV, the most mildly dynamic of these, renders our word "live," "remain," "continue," and "be" and even drops the word altogether once (1 John 3:15). We get some concordance, as in 1 John 3:24:

> *Those who obey his commands* live *in him, and he in them. And this is how we know that he* lives *in us . . .*

But we also lose a great deal of it. For example, in close proximity we go from "remain" (twice each in 1 John 2:24 and 27) to "continue" (verse 28), and the idea at the end of verse 27 is the same as that at the beginning of verse 28 (they are both commands, "remain in him"). Further, we have lost the connection between remaining (or abiding) in Christ and having his Word remain in us, since the translators used different words for the two expressions.

Other versions, such as the TEV, CEV, and NLT, continue the pattern we find in the NIV, as Table 1 shows.

We have therefore lost an element of these two letters of John that gives them theological cohesion, which means we have lost some of the message. But we have also lost the connection between the letters and the Gospel. We ought not hide verbal parallels from the reader when those verbal parallels have a bearing on the same topic.

An example of the second kind of concordance is the way that the Old Testament reverberates with echoes of Exodus 34:6-7, which proclaims the "name" of the Lord:

> ⁶ *The* LORD *passed before him and proclaimed, "The* LORD, *the* LORD, *a God merciful and gracious, slow to anger, and abounding in steadfast love and faithfulness,* ⁷ *keeping steadfast love for thousands, forgiving iniquity and transgression and sin, but who will by no means clear the guilty, visiting the iniquity of the fathers on the children and the children's children, to the third and the fourth generation." (ESV)*

At the foundation of God's relationship with his people is his benevolence. That is why they can ask him for forgiveness, that is why he helps them in their troubles, that is why he keeps his promises to them. It is small wonder that such a truth should be cited so often. A good translation should allow the reader to see the connection with this foundational text.

In this section I will consider two kinds of allusion to Exodus 34:6-7 in the rest of the Old Testament. First, I will consider places where the two attributes "merciful and gracious" are used together. Second, I will examine how two penitential psalms evoke Exodus 34:7a.

The two adjectives "merciful and gracious" show up in ten passages that look back to Exodus 34:6 (sometimes in reverse order, "gracious and merciful"), as Table 2 shows. The Old Testament authors meant for their readers to be able to perceive the allusion, and a good translation will enable the English reader to do the same.

So how do the English versions do? The ESV, true to its "essentially literal" philosophy, allows the reader to see them all. The NIV, which is only "mildly dynamic," does pretty well, with only Nehemiah 9:31 being the odd man out (but inexplicably, in view of verse 17).

The NLT, which is still fairly conservative, does pretty well, except at Jonah 4:2, Psalm 112:4, and Psalm 145:8. Losing the feel of an allusion leads to losing some of the message (for example, how did Jonah know what God is like?). Actually, the case of Psalm 112:4 is catastrophic, because it loses the connection not only with Exodus 34:6, but also with Psalm 111. Psalm 111 is praise toward God in the light of his character and works; verse 4 says the Lord is "gracious and merciful." Psalm 112 is a Wisdom Psalm, showing the blessedness of the man who fears the Lord. Verse 4 tells us that the good man is "gracious, merciful, and righteous" (ESV)—that is, in him you can see something of what the Lord is like (an Old Testament version of 2 Peter 1:4, as it were). At least, that's how I see it. The NLT, by focusing on the local context, keeps its readers from even considering concordance.

When we get to the TEV, the situation is hopeless. Their wording from Exodus 34:6, "full of compassion and pity," does not show up at all in the allusions. There is no clear pattern behind the renderings in the allusions.

The CEV is a little better. It collapses the two adjectives in Exodus 34:6 into one, "merciful," and "merciful" appears in the allusions. The allusions consistently use "merciful and kind," and this makes us wonder why they did not use both words in Exodus.

Let's look at the second group of allusions to the passage in Exodus. Two of the most poignant psalms of confession and forgiveness, 32 and 51, use the wording of this passage as the reminder that it is God's benevolence to which they appeal. Consider especially the beginning of Exodus 34:7, "keeping steadfast love for thousands, forgiving iniquity and transgression and sin." As you can see from Table 3, the three "sin-words" of Exodus 34:7 appear in the psalms; in my view, this is to allow the Hebrew worshiper to remember the foundation of his covenantal life.

In Psalm 32:1-2, we find all three sin-words from Exodus, together with the verb "forgive." In verse 5, we come full circle with "and you forgave the iniquity of my sin." Similarly, Psalm 51:1-2 has the three sin-words from Exodus.

A good essentially literal version will allow the reader to see this evocation, as the ESV has done. The NIV could have done so, though their three sin-words in Exodus are slightly different; but they did not. The TEV and NLT made it hard for themselves by collapsing three Hebrew words into two English ones in Exodus. The general tendency of the dynamic versions is to reduce the number of different English sin-words in Psalms 32 and 51—I suppose for the sake of making those passages easier for the reader. But in making it easier for the English reader they have actually deprived him or her of the chance to see something that is there. The form—in this case the allusion to Exodus—carries some of the meaning.

The third kind of concordance that I will discuss is that between the

Old Testament and the New Testament passages that use it. The general principles of how a good version should handle New Testament citations of the Old deserve a full-length article of their own, but we can say, at the most basic, that they boil down to this: "Render the Old Testament and New Testament places in a way that shows both their similarities and differences."

My judgment is that, overall, the NIV has made a serious effort to follow this principle. There are places, however, in which their concern for optimizing on the basis of local intelligibility has led them away from it. I cannot tell that the other dynamic versions have made much of an effort in this direction at all; their translation philosophy leaves little room for it.

I will take three verses to illustrate my points: 1 Peter 3:15a (using Isaiah 8:13), Romans 4:8 (using Psalm 32:2), and Galatians 3:16 (using Genesis 13:15 or 22:18?). I have summarized the versions for the first two in Tables 4 and 5 below; the table for the third, Table 6, has a different format.

Let us begin with 1 Peter 3:15a, which borrows language from Isaiah 8:13. Table 4 shows that the literalistic RV and the essentially literal ESV are very close—they differ in replacing "sanctify" with the clearer "regard as holy," and in how they analyze the grammar of "Christ *as* Lord" or "Christ *the* Lord."[31] In both cases, however, the English reader can see that Peter has adapted Isaiah's language about the Lord and applied it to Christ; this is therefore a "deity of Christ" text.

How does this citation fare in the dynamic versions? The NIV of Isaiah 8:13 is close to the ESV, both being under the influence of the RSV. When we look at the other versions of Isaiah 8:13 (NLT, TEV, and CEV) and all four dynamic versions of 1 Peter 3:15a, we should recall what Professor Ryken says about destabilizing the biblical text; but I want to focus my attention elsewhere. The NIV of 1 Peter 3:15a is the easiest to guess at. No doubt the translation committee deemed "sanctify Christ" or "regard Christ as holy" too difficult, and since popular lexicography holds that "to sanctify" means "to set apart," then we can get what the NIV has. But not only has this lost the evocation of Isaiah 8:13—it has also undertranslated "sanctify" by leaving out an element: It should be "set apart *as holy*." A similar process probably lies behind the other versions, and we may make similar critiques of them. Note that the trend of the dynamic versions is to wander away from the notion that Christ is Lord (that is, the incarnate God of the Old Testament) and to head toward honoring him as lord (that is, Master) of one's life.

Now let us turn to Romans 4:8, which uses Psalm 32:2 (actually, Romans 4:7-8 cites Psalm 32:1-2), as presented in Table 5. In the context of Romans 4, Paul is speaking of how things are "counted" or "reckoned" (verses 3, 4, 5, 6, 8, 9, 10, 11, 22, 23, 24—all using the same Greek verb). He started with Genesis 15:6 (cited from the Septuagint), where "Abraham believed God, and it was counted to him as righteousness" (Romans 4:3, ESV). The Hebrew verbs in Genesis 15:6 and Psalm 32:2 are the same, and "count" is a good translation in both places. The RV uses "reckon" throughout Romans 4—which would be all right, except that the translators had used "count" in Genesis 15:6 and "impute" in Psalm 32. (This was a failure of their literalism; the KJV was more careful.) The ESV chose an English verb that works in Genesis 15:6, Psalm 32:2, and throughout Romans 4—and in this way the reader can see the flow of Paul's thought and why he brought these texts together. (Notice as well that the Greek in Romans 4:8 differs a little from the Hebrew of Psalm 32:2, and the ESV reflects this difference.)

The NIV has done the right thing with the citation, but the citation and the source are *too* close—due to the NIV's shrinking the sin-vocabulary of the psalm, as discussed above. However, they sought no concordance with Genesis 15:6 or the rest of Romans 4, using "credited" there (a bad choice for reading out loud, by the way). This means that the English reader cannot see what Paul was doing, bringing these texts together because of their similar wording and theme.

The other dynamic versions have made no effort to show the reader what is happening in the Greek, either of the citation or of the rest of Romans 4. Concordance is lost, again because of local optimization: Romans 4:3 becomes "Abraham believed God, so God declared him to be righteous" (NLT), "Abraham believed God, and because of his faith God accepted him as righteous" (TEV), "God accepted Abraham because Abraham had faith in him" (CEV). Because of this effort to paraphrase the citation of Genesis 15:6,[32] the thematic word of Romans 4 is lost.

Our final example of an Old Testament citation is Galatians 3:16. There Paul is showing why his mission fulfills the Genesis promises made to Abraham. In the ESV it reads,

> Now the promises were made to Abraham and to his offspring. It
> does not say, "And to offsprings," referring to many, but referring to
> one, "And to your offspring," who is Christ.

There is plenty of room for discussion on this verse: Was Paul thinking of the promises of the land to Abraham and his offspring (as in
Genesis 13:15), or the promises that through Abraham's offspring blessing would come to the Gentiles (as in Genesis 22:18)? What did Paul
mean by emphasizing the singular of a noun that could be used collec-
tively? I think I can answer these questions;[33] but my point now is that
a translation does not need to. Instead it should pass on these questions
to the English reader, since they are there for the Greek reader. The literal translation is the only one that is likely to do this, because it will
choose a word like "seed" (KJV, RV) or "offspring" (ESV) for the
Genesis texts and will leave it to the reader to decide whether it is one
or many (just as the Hebrew reader had to). Then all the reader of
Galatians 3:16 has to do is decide which of the Genesis references lies
behind Paul's argument.

The dynamic versions, under the impulse to relieve the reader of
ambiguity, tend to make the decision for him in Genesis (as we saw
above). Table 6 shows the results. The NIV quite properly has "offspring" in the two Genesis passages, but for reasons we can only guess
has "seed" in Galatians 3:16.[34] The English reader has no clue what
point Paul is making. It gets worse with the other dynamic versions. Try
to figure out the structure of Paul's argument from these. And why the
NLT supplies the words "of course" in the last clause of Galatians 3:16,
when they have made it hopelessly obscure, is beyond me to say.

Had these versions started out with the intention of passing on to
the English reader the effects given to readers of Hebrew and Greek, they
would have sought to represent these citations much more closely.

SUMMARY

Let me recap what I think these examples illustrate. My objective has
been to discern whether or not dynamic equivalence (as it claims) does
an equal—or even better—job of conveying meaning in comparison to
the essentially literal approach. I find that it fails, and fails consistently,
and the more dynamic the translation, the worse the failure.[35] I think
that the explanation for this lies in two main impulses that undergird the

dynamic equivalence philosophy: the separation of form and meaning, and the desire to clarify the meaning of the text beyond what is actually present in the linguistic details of the text.

Someone may wish to defend dynamic equivalence as a principle by saying that all the examples I have discussed are cases of the misuse of the theory, and not necessary consequences from it. I will grant that this may be true in some cases, but the defense would be much more credible if the problems were not so pervasive and the examples so easy to find. I think this shows that, at the very least, the theory promotes a way of thinking that will result in these problems.

I began this essay with a word of testimony, and I will end with one. Before I began working with Dr. Ryken, I had no idea how frequently and systematically the two impulses of dynamic equivalence noted above lead translations astray. I suspected that the problem was not with the translation principles so much as with translators' inattention. Now I have become a radical: I think that only an essentially literal translation philosophy has any hope of giving a Bible to the people that merits their regular use.

NOTES

1 Some of the most important books were Eugene A. Nida, *Toward a Science of Translating* (Leiden: E.J. Brill, 1964); Eugene A. Nida and Charles R. Taber, *The Theory and Practice of Translation* (Leiden: E.J. Brill, 1982); John Beekman and John Callow, *Translating the Word of God* (Grand Rapids, MI: Zondervan, 1974). The United Bible Societies also publish the journal *The Bible Translator* and a number of commentaries and monographs to help translators.

2 My inspiration was C. S. Lewis; see his essays in *God in the Dock* (Grand Rapids, MI: Eerdmans, 1970), which urges that candidates for ordination show that they can translate traditional theology into ordinary language: "Christian Apologetics," 89-103 (especially 98-99); "God in the Dock," 240-244 (especially 243); "Before We Can Communicate," 254-257 (especially 256).

3 Of course, this translation came out in 1996; but this Introduction expresses the view that has been common for many years.

4 Raymond C. Van Leeuwen, "We Really Do Need Another Bible Translation," *Christianity Today*, October 22, 2001, 28-35, at 30.

5 The Hebrew word for "all" here has the nuance "any," the verbless clause requires the adding of "is," and the dative "to your neighbor" expresses possession (which has a range of nuances: "my God" is not the same as "my rake"). Even the literalistic RV is the same here.

6 He doesn't; see Christopher Wright, *God's People in God's Land* (Carlisle, UK: Paternoster, 1997), 181-221, on the wife's status in Old Testament law.

7 This adds a further level of interpretation: The phrase might refer to "anything else"—that is, anything that is not in this list—or it might be a summary of the things we should not covet. But these versions leave no allowances for the second option.

8 Beekman and Callow, *Translating the Word of God*, 25.

9 Ibid., 26: "The natural way of expressing the truth of this part of the verse is to say,

'God loves.'" It is unclear from the context whether they think that the two *English* sentences are equivalent; I hope that they do not.

10 Some changes of parts of speech are not included in this principle: for example, we can render the Hebrew "the name of his holiness" as "his holy name" without departing from the essentially literal pattern.

11 See for example, Beekman and Callow, *Translating the Word of God*, chapter 9, "Translating Metaphor and Simile" for some recommendations. Granted, these authors were writing for people who would translate the Bible (and especially the New Testament) for tribal peoples who had no scriptural background whatever; hence their goals were understandable for the very first Bible for an unreached people. We might question whether this is the best thing in the long run for a people's Bible; but in any case, in this chapter I am addressing the issue of Bible translation *into English*.

12 See, for example, Jan de Waard and William A. Smalley, *A Translator's Handbook on the Book of Amos* (London: United Bible Societies, 1979), 11: "However, the important point to remember here is that such parallelism should come into a translation where it contributes to effective communication in the language of the translation and should not be carried over only because it is in the Hebrew or an English translation of the Hebrew. This means that quite often when something is said twice in the Hebrew in this way, it will be said only once in good translation."

13 Robert Bratcher and William Reyburn, *A Translator's Handbook on the Book of Psalms* (New York: United Bible Societies, 1991), 19-20.

14 As I will argue below, in many cases the reader of the original had to figure these things out; so the translator is interposing himself between the text and the reader in the receptor language.

15 No one disputes whether words have more than one sense, nor whether translators must at times choose among the possible senses. The question is how thoroughgoing we should be in such choosing.

16 See the Hebrew commentary of Amos Hakham, *Sefer Tᵉhillim* (Jerusalem: Mossad Harav Kook, 1979), 5.

17 In this respect I think the classic dictionary by F. Brown, S. R. Driver, and C. A. Briggs, *A Hebrew and English Lexicon of the Old Testament* (Oxford: Clarendon Press, 1906), 393a-395a, is sound and reliable. They list Psalm 1:6 under the sense, "take notice of, regard" (394a).

18 See, for example, Henry George Liddell and Robert Scott (revised by Henry Stuart Jones and Roderick McKenzie), *A Greek-English Lexicon* (Oxford: Clarendon Press, 1996), 231a-b; they list our verse under sense 5 and give examples from other Greek sources. (See also Genesis 20:4, 6 in the Septuagint.)

19 All three offer an alternative in the margin that is closer to the ESV.

20 For a good discussion, see Bruce Winter, *After Paul Left Corinth: The Influence of Secular Ethics and Social Change* (Grand Rapids, MI: Eerdmans, 2001), 215-240.

21 See Chapter 5, fallacy number 2.

22 For a good discussion, see D. Alexander, "The OT View of Life After Death," *Themelios* 11:2 (1986): 41-46, which also contains a bibliography.

23 They do so under the influence of an argument from R. Laird Harris, "The Meaning of the Word Sheol as Shown by Parallels in Poetic Texts," *Bulletin of the Evangelical Theological Society* 4 (1961): 129-135.

24 For the difference between the second line of verse 14 in the ESV and NIV, see C. J. Collins, "Psalm 49:15 [ET v 14] *mawet yir'em*: 'Death Will Feed on Them' or 'Death Will Be Their Shepherd'?" *Bible Translator* 46:3 (Fall 1995): 320-326.

25 The NLT and CEV are even worse. They render the two instances of Sheol in verse 14 as "grave," and the one in verse 15 as "death."

26 *Holy Bible: New Living Translation*, Text and Product Preview (Wheaton, IL: Tyndale House Publishers, 1996), 18.

27 This introduces an ambiguity not present in the Hebrew: Whom will they praise?

28 See C. John Collins, "*n-sh-q*," in Willem A. VanGemeren, ed., *New International Dictionary of Old Testament Theology and Exegesis*, Vol. 3 (Grand Rapids, MI: Zondervan, 1997), 196-197 for a discussion of this.

29 Strangely enough, even the literalistic NASB succumbed in this verse with "do homage to the Son."

30 T. Desmond Alexander, *From Paradise to Promised Land: An Introduction to the Main Themes of the Pentateuch* (Grand Rapids, MI: Baker, 1995), 8.

31 For more detail on text and grammar, see Charles Kuykendall and C. John Collins, "1 Peter 3:15a—A Critical Review of English Versions," forthcoming in *Presbyterion: The Covenant Theological Seminary Review*.

32 Neither the TEV nor the CEV coordinated their Genesis 15:6 with Romans 4:3. The NLT, to its credit, did so.

33 See my forthcoming article, "Galatians 3:16: What Kind of Exegete was Paul?" in *Tyndale Bulletin* 54:1 (2003): 75-86.

34 My edition of the NIV lists Genesis 12:7; 13:15; and 24:7 as the Old Testament texts being cited in Galatians 3:16, and all of them have "offspring."

35 This explains why the mildly dynamic NIV is not so far off in many cases. The TNIV, a new revision of the NIV, seems to have followed a more dynamic approach and thus introduces many more problems.

TABLE 1: OCCURRENCES OF GREEK *menô*, "REMAIN, ABIDE" IN
JOHN 15, 1 JOHN, AND 2 JOHN

Ref.	ESV	NIV	NLT	TEV	CEV
J 15:4	Abide . . . abides . . . abide	Remain . . . remain . . . remain	Remain . . . Remain . . . A branch cannot produce fruit if it is severed from the vine	Remain . . . Remain . . . remains	Stay joined . . . stay joined . . . stay joined
J 15:5	abides	remains	remain	remains	stay joined
J 15:6	abide	remain	parts	remain	stay joined
J 15:7	abide . . . abide	remain . . . remain	stay joined	remain . . . remain	Stay joined to me and let my teachings become part of you
J 15:9	Abide	remain	remain	remain	remain faithful
J 15:10	abide . . . abide	remain' . . . remain	remain . . . remain	remain . . . remain	I will keep loving you, just as my Father keeps loving me
J 15:16	that your fruit should abide	fruit that will last	fruit that will last	fruit that endures	fruit that will last
1J 2:6	abides	live	live	remains	If we say we are his
1J 2:10	abides	lives	walking	lives	we are in the light
1J 2:14	abides	lives	living	lives	God's message is firm in your hearts
1J 2:17	abides	lives	live	lives	live
1J 2:19	continued	remained	stayed	stayed	stayed
1J 2:24	abide . . . abides . . . abide	remains . . . remain	remain faithful . . . continue to live in fellowship	keep in your hearts . . . keep that message . . . live in union	Keep thinking about . . . be one in your heart
1J 2:27	abides . . . abide	remains . . . remain	lives . . . live	remains . . . remain	stays . . . stay one
1J 2:28	abide	continue	continue to live	remain	stay one
1J 3:6	abides	lives	continue to live	lives	stay one
1J 3:9	abides	remains	God's live is in them	God's very nature in in him	lives

TABLE 1: CONTINUTED

Ref.	ESV	NIV	NLT	TEV	CEV
1J 3:14	abides	remains	But the person who does not love them is still dead	still under the power of death	still
1J 3:15	abiding	has eternal life in him	And you know that murderers don't have eternal life within them	a murderer does not have eternal life in him	murderers do not have eternal life
1J 3:17	abide	be	be	how can he claim that he loves God	we cannot say we love God
1J 3:24	abides . . . abides	live . . . lives	live . . . lives	lives . . . lives	stay one
1J 4:12	abides	lives	lives	lives	lives
1J 4:13	abide	live	live	live	we are one
1J 4:15	abides	lives	lives	lives	stays one
1J 4:16	abides . . . abides . . . abides	lives . . . lives	live . . . live . . . lives	lives . . . lives . . . lives	keep on . . . stay one . . . stay one
2J 2	abides	lives	lives	remains	the truth is now in our hearts
2J 9	abide . . . abides	continue . . . continues	For if you wander beyond the teaching of Christ . . . But if you continue in the teaching . . .	stay . . . stay	Don't keep changing what you were taught about Christ . . . But if you hold firmly to what you were taught . . .

TABLE 2: EXODUX 34:6 ("MERCIFUL AND GRACIOUS")
IN THE OLD TESTAMENT

Ref.	ESV	NIV	NLT	TEV	CEV
Ex 34:6	merciful and gracious	compassionate and gracious	merciful and gracious	full of compassion and pity	merciful
Jo 2:13	gracious and merciful	gracious and compassionate	gracious and merciful	kind and full of mercy	merciful, kind
Jon 4:2	"	"	gracious and compassionate	loving and merciful	kind and merciful
Ps 86:15	merciful and gracious	compassionate and gracious	merciful and gracious	merciful and loving	"
Ps 103:8	"	"	"	"	merciful, kind
Ps 111:4	gracious and merciful	gracious and compassionate	gracious and merciful	kind and merciful	kind and merciful
Ps 112:4	gracious and merciful	" "	generous, compassionate	merciful, kind	"
Ps 145:8	gracious and merciful	"	kind and merciful	loving and merciful	merciful, kind
Ne 9:17	"	"	gracious and merciful	gracious and loving	merciful, kind (jumbled order)
Ne 9:31	"	gracious and merciful	"	gracious and merciful	merciful and kind
2Ch 30:9	"	gracious and compassionate	"	kind and merciful	kind and merciful

Table 3: Exodus 34:7a

Ref.	ESV	NIV	NLT	TEV	CEV
Ex 34:7	forgiving iniquity and transgression and sin	forgiving wickedness, rebellion, and sin	Forgiving every kind of sin and rebellion	forgive evil and sin	(not translated)
Ps 32:1-2	transgression . . . forgiven . . . sin . . . iniquity	transgressions . . . forgiven . . . sins . . . sin	rebellion . . . forgiven . . . sin . . . sin	sins . . . forgiven . . . wrongs . . . doing wrong	sins . . . forgive . . . sins
Ps 32:5	forgave the iniquity of my sin	forgave the guilt of my sin	And you forgave me! All my guilt is gone	forgave all my sins	Then you forgave me and took away my guilt
Ps 51:1-2	transgressions . . . iniquity . . . sin	transgressions . . . iniquity . . . sin	sins . . . guilt . . . sin	sins . . . evil . . . sin	sins . . . sin . . . guilt

TABLE 4: 1 PETER 3:15 USING ISAIAH 8:13

Version	Isaiah 8:13	1 Peter 3:15a
RV	The LORD of Hosts, him shall ye sanctify; and let him be your fear, and let him be your dread.	But sanctify in your heats Christ as Lord . . .
ESV	But the LORD of Hosts, him you shall regard as holy. Let him be your fear, let him be your dread.	but in your hearts regard Christ the Lord as holy . . .
NIV	The LORD Almighty is the one you are to regard as holy, he is the one you are to fear, he is the one you are to dread.	But in your hearts set apart Christ as Lord . . .
NLT	Do not fear anything except the LORD Almighty. He alone is the Holy One. If you fear him, you need fear nothing else.	Instead, you must worship Christ as Lord of your life.
TEV	Remember that I, the LORD Almighty, am holy; I am the one you must fear.	But have reverence for Christ in your hearts, and honor him as Lord.
CEV	I am the one you should fear and respect. I am the Holy God, the LORD All-powerful.	Honor Christ and let him be the Lord of your life.

TABLE 5: ROMANS 4:8 USING PSALM 32:2

Version	Psalm 32:2a	Romans 4:8
RV	Blessed is the man unto whom the LORD imputeth not iniquity	Blessed is the man to whom the Lord will not reckon sin
ESV	Blessed is the man against whom the LORD counts no iniquity	blessed is the man against whom the Lord will not count his sin
NIV	Blessed is the man whose sin the LORD does not count against him	Blessed is the man whose sin the Lord will never count against him
NLT	Yes, what joy for those whose record the LORD has cleared of sin	Yes, what joy for those whose sin is no longer counted against them by the Lord
TEV	Happy is the man whom the LORD does not accuse of doing wrong	Happy is the person whose sins the Lord will not keep account of
CEV	Our God, you bless everyone whose sins you [combining two lines into one] forgive and wipe away	The Lord blesses people whose sins are erased from his book

TABLE 6: GALATIANS 3:16 AND BACKGROUND

Version	Galatians 3:16	Genesis 13:15	Genesis 22:18
RV	Now to Abraham were the promises spoken, and to his seed. He saith not, And to seeds, as of many; but as of one, And to thy seed, which is Christ.	For all the land which thou seest, to thee will I give it, and to thy seed for ever	And in thy seed shall all the nations of the earth be blessed. Because thou hast obeyed my voice.
ESV	Now the promises were made to Abraham and to his offspring. It does not say, "And to offsprings," referring to many, but referring to one, "And to your offspring," who is Christ.	for all the land that you see I will give to you and to your offspring forever.	and in your offspring shall all the nations of the earth be blessed, because you have obeyed my voice
NIV	The promises were spoken to Abraham and to his seed. The Scripture does not say "and to seeds," meaning many people, but "and to your seed," meaning one person, who is Christ.	All the land that you see I will give to you and your offspring forever.	and through your offspring all nations on earth will be blessed, because you have obeyed me
NLT	God gave the promise to Abraham and his child. And notice that it doesn't say the promise was to his children, as if it meant many descendants. But the promise was to his child—and that, of course, means Christ.	I am going to give all this land to you and your offspring as a permanent possession	and through your descendants, all the nations of the earth will be blessed—all because you have obeyed me.

TABLE 6: CONTINUED

Version	Galatians 3:16	Genesis 13:15	Genesis 22:18
TEV	Now God made his promises to Abraham and to his descendant. The Scripture does not use the plural "descendants," meaning many people, but the singular "descendant," meaning one person only, namely, Christ.	I am going to give you and your descendants all the land that you see, and it will be yours forever.	All the nations will ask me to bless them as I have blessed your descendants—all because you have obeyed my command.
CEV	That is how it is with the promises God made to Abraham and his descendant. The promises were not made to many descendants, but only to one, and that one is Christ.	I will give you and your family all the land you can see. It will be theirs forever!	You have obeyed me, and so you and your descendants will be a blessing to all nations on earth.

INDEX